T0305257

Moving People and Knowledge

This book is dedicated to Dr Brian Harry Ackers and in loving memory of Helen Margaret Wright Ackers

Moving People and Knowledge

Scientific Mobility in an Enlarging European Union

Louise Ackers

Professor of Socio-Legal Studies and Founding Director, European Law and Policy Research Group, Liverpool Law School, University of Liverpool, UK

and

Bryony Gill

Research Fellow, European Law and Policy Research Group, Liverpool Law School, University of Liverpool, UK

Edward Elgar
Cheltenham, UK • Northampton, MA, USA

Published by
Edward Elgar Publishing Limited
The Lypiatts
15 Lansdown Road
Cheltenham
Glos GL50 2JA
UK

Edward Elgar Publishing, Inc.
William Pratt House
9 Dewey Court
Northampton
Massachusetts 01060
USA

A catalogue record for this book
is available from the British Library

Library of Congress Control Number: 2008935922

Mixed Sources
Product group from well-managed
forests and other controlled sources
www.fsc.org Cert no. SA-COC-1565
© 1996 Forest Stewardship Council

ISBN 978 1 84376 985 9

Printed and bound in Great Britain by MPG Books Ltd, Bodmin, Cornwall

Contents

Figures

Tables

Acronyms and abbreviations

APRE	Agency for the Promotion of European Research (Agenzia per la Promozione della Ricerca Europea)
BAS	Bulgarian Academy of Science
BBSRC	Biotechnology and Biological Sciences Research Council
BMBF	German Federal Ministry of Education and Research (Bundesministerium für Bildung und Forschung)
CaSE	UK Campaign for Science and Engineering
COO	Country of origin
CSLPE	Centre for the Study of Law & Policy in Europe (Leeds University UK)
DAAD	German Academic Exchange Service (Deutscher Akademischer Austauschdienst)
DfES	Department for Education and Skills (UK)
DFG	German Research Foundation (Deutsche Forschungs Gemeinschaft)
DTI	Department of Trade and Industry (UK)
ECJ	European Court of Justice
EMBO	European Molecular Biology Organization
E-MeP	European Membrane Protein Consortium
EPSRC	Engineering and Physical Sciences Research Council
ERA	European Research Area
ESRC	Economic and Social Research Council
EU	European Union
GDP	Gross domestic product
HEFCE	Higher Education Funding Council for England
HEIs	Higher education institutions
HEPI	Higher Education Policy Institute (UK)
HESA	Higher Education Statistics Agency
HHMI	Howard Hughes Medical Institute (USA)
HSM	Highly skilled migration
IMPAFEL	Impact Assessment of the Marie Curie Fellowship Scheme
IOM	International Organization for Migration
ISRF	Wellcome Trust's International Senior Research Fellowship
LAT	Living apart together

MOBEX2   Mobility and Excellence in the European Research Area:
          Promoting Growth in an Enlarged Europe
MOBISC   Mobility and Progression in Science Careers: Equal Pay,
          Career Progression and the Socio-Legal Valuation of
          Care programme
PAN   Polish Academy of Sciences (Polska Akademia Nauk)
R&D   Research and Development
RCUK   Research Councils of the United Kingdom
TMR   Training and Mobility in Research programme

Foreword

Recent decades have seen an unremitting interest on the part of researchers, policy makers and the general public in the mobility of people of Eastern Europe (EE). After nearly fifty years of administratively suppressed outbound migration and delimited migration potential, the population of that part of Europe has finally become free to move. What was largely expected around 1990 was not only a shift from a low to high incidence of East-to-West mobility but also a profound change in its forms and types: from a predominance of outflows for humanitarian reasons (family reunion, 'repatriation' of ethnic minorities, asylum seeking) to a regular and steady emigration flow. It was believed that migration, by becoming possible for everybody instead of being an option available only to a tiny proportion of the population, would involve great masses of people. Those expectations have only partly been realized. On one hand, the real-life migration-related phenomena turned out to be richer and more complex, and, on the other hand, it appeared to be somehow blurred and more difficult to capture.

Apart from the collapse of the Soviet bloc and Soviet-style socialism – both of which paved the way to the increased international mobility of Eastern Europeans – there was also a wide array of other powerful factors playing significant roles.

The transition to market economies, a process during which each country of the region took its own course, led to a substantial intra-regional differentiation in economic performance, availability of jobs and wage levels. Newly emerging centres of economic dynamism spurred the mobility of people travelling between countries of EE. Various primitive forms of mobility such as the short shuttle movements of petty traders that developed in the early 1990s became a prototype for more long-distance, westward mobility that characterized the end of the decade. Needless to say, the introduction of visa-free travel to the West greatly contributed to that mobility. Lower costs and the increased effectiveness of international transportation and communication greatly facilitated quick, multiple, roundtrip journeys across Europe.

A particularly strong magnet that attracted migrants from EE was the combination of much higher wages and an unsatisfied demand for relatively cheap labour in the West. Access to Western labour markets, however, was considerably restricted. Under these conditions, population move-ments from EE were generally characterized by clandestine motives and forms. While the vast majority of migrants from EE sought employment in foreign countries – which was undoubtedly the main motive behind their migration – they were compelled to declare other purposes to both the administration of their country of origin and host countries simply in order to be allowed to (until 1989) leave or (until at least 2004) enter and remain. This forced them to adapt to an unstable and disadvantageous if not pre-carious situation in the labour market and in social life in general. Even after 1989, when exiting EE countries was permissible and residents could easily enter many countries of their 'traditional' destination, migrants, as a rule, could legally only be tourists in those countries, which was rarely their actual motive for embarking on a journey to a foreign country.

Because of their more or less irregular status, most migrants originating from EE suffered from discriminatory practices pervasive among employ-ers, and, in particular, were significantly underpaid. As a means of coping with that situation, migrants developed a peculiar pattern of mobility that enabled them to revalorize the 'real value' of their foreign earnings: 'incom-plete migration', a circulation of individual household members, often repeated, characterized by short-term employment abroad and a very high rate of earnings remitted or repatriated to the migrant's home country – where the cost of living was substantially lower. By spending most of the 'foreign money' earned in the country of origin, the migrant's real wages became relatively high and afforded migrant households a decent – if not a substantially improved – living standard.

Since 1 May 2004, with the first EU eastward enlargement, this situation has become even more complicated. Some people (in fact, hundreds of thousands) from eight EE countries have moved for work to Britain, Ireland and Sweden, where restrictions to labour market were lifted, whereas many of their compatriots continued to move to other EU or EEA countries to be employed there as seasonal or guest workers – though some-times under the guises of 'tourist' or 'student' or 'self-established entrepre-neur'. At the same time, the citizens of other EE states, notably the highly mobile people from Ukraine, Romania, Moldova and Bulgaria were left behind, still forced to engage in various forms of 'irregularity' in Western labour markets.

All these factors produced quite a new migration reality in Europe char-acterized by, on one hand, the very existence of large numbers of highly mobile people from EE who easily adapt to local administrative rules or loopholes and to specific and variable labour market situations, who are capable of profiting from those situations and exploiting opportunities of living in transnational social spaces, and, on the other hand, by specific partly symbiotic and partly competitive relationships between their countries of origin and, eventually, their destination.

I hasten to admit that the complexity of this new reality and the pace at which it has evolved has left researchers hardly able to cope with it, a bit surprised and maybe even feeling helpless.

The intrinsic value of this book lies in its meticulous analysis of current scientific mobility, using, as an example, Bulgarian and Polish scholars in the West (Britain and Germany). But, it is also much more than this. For it encapsulates most of the above-mentioned characteristics of recent East-to-West European population movements. Focusing on a very specific type of mobility, namely that of natural scientists, it accurately describes the essence of those movements, in all their intricacy and complexity. It departs from a tendency still prevalent in much literature – that is, attempting to understand the present European migration reality by means of traditional concepts and frameworks – and, instead, takes a quite innovative approach to mobility. In this approach, mobility is described as a combination of highly diversified, fluid movements, capable of metamorphosis, which reflect individual trajectories of movements over the span of one's life cycle and professional career. The holistic stance adopted by the authors enables them not only to track individual series of mobility episodes but, in addition, and above all, to link those episodes to migrants' family conditions, to his/her connections to and positions in various networks, and to labour market dynamics both in the home and potential host countries. Furthermore, it effectively incorporates the 'circulationist perspective' into the mainstream of mobility studies, and also accounts for social costs and benefits in both the sending and receiving countries. I have little doubt that this book presents itself as one of the few rare, groundbreaking endeavours in the area of migration studies.

Marek Okólski
Professor and Director, Centre of Migration Research,
University of Warsaw, Poland

Acknowledgements

The research on which this book is based could not have taken place without the funding provided by our two sponsors: the Economic and Social Research Council (ESRC) (project reference L14425004) and the Anglo-German Foundation (project reference 1468). Special thanks go to the Director of the ESRC's Science and Society Programme, Professor Steve Rayner, and the Programme Administrator, Anne-Marie O'Brien, for their continued support and active engagement with the research.

We would also like to thank our project partners – Anna Kicinger and Professor Marek Kupiszewski of the Central European Forum for Migration Research in Warsaw and Nikolina Sretenova of the Bulgarian Academy of Science – for their contributions. Jessica Guth, of Bradford University Law School, led the German component of the research, and co-authored Chapter 3.

The authors and researchers extend their sincere gratitude to the respondents who gave generously of their time, openly shared their experiences and made us feel welcome. The subject is both sensitive and complex, and generalizations, as always, have a tendency to mask complexity and nuance. We hope that our respondents and the wider scientific community in Bulgaria, Poland, the UK and Germany will find our analysis of the situation to be valuable and insightful, even if, at times, they do not agree with it.

Special thanks must also go to Dr Fiona Wood and Professor Marek Okólski for their comments on a draft of the book and to Dr Keleigh Coldron for her invaluable assistance in the production of the final manuscript.

Finally we would like to thank Blackwell Publishing and the Policy Press for allowing us to reproduce some of our previous material in Chapter 1 (Ackers, 2005a, 'Moving people and knowledge: the mobility of scientists within the European Union') and 5 (Ackers and Stalford, 2007, 'Managing multiple life-courses: the influence of children on migration processes in the European Union') respectively.

1. Introduction: moving people and knowledge – defining the research agenda[1]

ABOUT THIS BOOK

This book explores the relationship between highly skilled, scientific migration and the transfer of knowledge within the European Union (EU). It addresses the effects of these forms of mobility on the individuals concerned, in terms of their career progression and well-being, and on the selected countries – both sending and receiving – in terms of sustainable scientific development and capacity. The book is grounded primarily in an empirical study of natural scientists, in the academic sector, moving between two sending countries (Poland and Bulgaria) and two receiving countries (the UK and Germany). It is based on fieldwork undertaken during the A8 countries' accession to the EU, in the lead up to Bulgarian and Romanian EU membership; a timely point to consider the 'human face' (Smith and Favell, 2006) of a new wave of East–West mobility. The study involved a range of methods including literature review, legal and policy analysis and face-to-face interviews with key informants and mobile scientists in the four locations.[2] Although the research was based in four individual countries, the countries concerned were part of an enlarging supranational body: the EU. Regionalization and Europeanization are highlighted as further dynamics shaping the processes of migration, providing different lenses through which to view to understand the significance and effects of mobility.

This book consists of nine chapters. This introductory chapter reviews some of the academic literature and research on highly skilled migration and brain drain. This review, coupled with a pilot study focusing on scientific mobility between Italy and the UK,[3] played an important role in shaping the research agenda for MOBEX2 project (Mobility and Excellence in the European Research Area: Promoting Growth in an Enlarged Europe). It concludes with an outline of key issues raised in the literature that appear to be salient to an understanding of the impact of highly skilled migration. The empirical findings in relation to these issues and themes are then presented in subsequent chapters.

1

Chapter 2 goes on to examine the patterns of mobility exhibited by our respondents, with a focus on the frequency, duration and permanency of flows, including returns. The following three chapters examine migration motivations and triggers in more detail. Chapter 3 focuses on what can loosely be described as professional factors related to the quality of positions and ability to work effectively in science. This is followed by two chapters that look at the influence of more personal factors, including the presence of partners (Chapter 4) and children (Chapter 5) on scientific mobility. Together these chapters support a more grounded understanding of the factors shaping the patterns observed – why scientists move in the way they do – and the characteristics of migrants (that is, who moves). An understanding of these processes helps us to predict the potential for return but also, importantly, to understand the extent to which highly skilled migration is highly selective, as is often assumed.

Chapter 6 examines the role that networks and connections play in shaping both migration flows and the distribution of scientific knowledge and expertise. It details the characteristics of scientific connectedness and the relative importance of different forms of connections to mobility and the knowledge transfer process. Chapters 7 and 8 move on to consider the *impact* of highly skilled, scientific migration on the countries concerned with a focus on the relationship between migration and the sustainability of science. Chapter 7 focuses on the experiences of internationalization in the context of the receiving countries, whilst Chapter 8 examines the impact of mobility on the sending regions of Poland and Bulgaria. Finally, Chapter 9 draws together the key findings and presents some conclusions based firmly in our empirical data and the experiences of the scientists we have spoken to in the course of the research.

This opening chapter now proceeds to map out the overarching themes relevant to highly skilled migration that are addressed in greater detail in the subsequent chapters.

The language of brain drain entered the migration literature in the 1960s and focused primarily on the perceived losses of highly skilled workers from Europe – predominantly the UK – to the US, which Lowell (2003: 1) describes as the 'world's largest skills magnet'. While this concern persists and continues to dominate political debates in the UK, the research and policy agenda has shifted somewhat to encompass flows of highly skilled migrants from developing regions to the West. Despite evidence of significant imbalances in the geography of current intra-EU flows (Ackers, 2003; Williams, Baláž and Wallace, 2004; Van de Sande, Ackers and Gill, 2005; Williams, 2006), relatively little attention has been paid to this issue.

Recent research has begun to criticize the inherently negative connotations of brain drain, reflecting an appreciation of the complexity of the phenomenon and the limitations of attempts to conceptualize highly skilled migration (HSM) as a 'zero-sum game'. Salt (1997: 5) describes brain drain in terms of 'net unidirectional flows of HSM' or the 'reverse transfer of technology'. According to this definition, brain drain occurs in circumstances where a direct relationship exists between the direction of flows and the transfer of knowledge. Presumably the size of these flows – in proportion to the science base of the regions concerned – is also important. Evidence of significant outflows of scientific talent – unmatched by compensatory inflows or returns, such as the case of Italy, for example (Gill, 2005) – may indicate a net loss of knowledge or scientific expertise to the sending country and a potential gain to the recipient(s). The concept of brain circulation supports a broader approach, encouraging us to conceptualize migration in terms of ongoing processes rather than single permanent moves, but also, importantly, to distinguish the issue of knowledge transfer from the physical presence of the individual migrant. It recognizes that forms of knowledge transfer may take place in other ways.

Meyer (2003) supports the circulationist perspective, arguing that mobility is varied: it may be temporary with occasional returns; it may be multidirectional instead of unilateral; and it may affect developed as well as developing countries or regions. Regets (2003: 1) similarly observes the emergence of new locations or 'hub' countries as 'the creation and transfer of knowledge, the emergence of a skilled and educated workforce, and the fostering of commercial ties are shared to some extent by countries on both sides of the "equation"'.

The brain circulation paradigm enables us to consider more carefully the potential consequences of HSM and its impact on regions and individuals. There is some danger that this new paradigm – which characterizes HSM as a 'normal' and even desirable process (Meyer, 2003: 1) – might induce complacency and throw a 'gloss' on these processes. The routine exchange of high-level skills reflects the healthy operation of labour markets and the transfer of knowledge. However, it is important to address the issue of reciprocity, balance and differential opportunity. In earlier work, Meyer, Kaplan and Charum conclude that, notwithstanding the 'polycentric' nature of HSM, 'the flows seem to always go from the less developed "haemophiliac regions" to the more competitive places' (2001: 309). Williams et al. (2004: 38) identify 'near unanimity in the migration literature that international migration flows effect net redistribution of resources and welfare from spaces of origin to spaces of destination . . . sending countries experience human capital losses and social investment embedded in individuals'.

There is also evidence in the literature of an acceleration in current trends. Mahroum (2001), for example, points to increasing levels of specialization at the highly skilled end of labour markets, which, coupled with scarcity and 'imminent demographic decline', will support further the global sourcing of skills. He concludes that as migration is becoming an 'inseparable segment of national technology and economic development policies . . . competition for highly skilled labour will continue to be fierce' (ibid.: 27). Others predict 'enormous changes in the magnitude, composition and direction of international migration' (Iredale and Appleyard, 2001: 3), 'aggressive shifts' in policies to recruit highly skilled workers (Lowell, 2003: 2) and a growing skills war (Iredale, 2001).

The question is whether such numerical imbalances matter and whether existing explanatory paradigms take the debate and our understanding of the impact of HSM forward. According to Iredale (2001: 7) 'the current state of theory in relation to HSM is far from adequate in terms of explaining what is occurring at the high skill end of the migration spectrum'. Capturing the nature and impact of the HSM phenomenon demands new theoretical and methodological approaches capable of going beyond the mapping of flows to begin to explain the processes of migration and career decision-making and the relationship between these and knowledge transfer. King (2002: 89) explains that 'established forms of international migration . . . have for too long now shaped our thinking about how migration is conceptualised and theorised'. In particular, he notes the contribution of skilled and professional people and student mobility to these new and more diverse modalities deriving from 'new motivations, new space-time flexibilities, globalisation forces and migrations of consumption and personal self-realisation' (ibid.). Taken together, these changes in patterns and motivations blur the 'never straightforward boundary between migration and mobility [and] melt away some of the traditional dichotomies' (ibid: 90).

WORKING AND MOVING IN SCIENCE: KNOWLEDGE MIGRANTS?

Rather than discussing the processes shaping HSM in a vacuum, it is important to embed this discussion within the specific context of scientific migration and the nature of science careers. Iredale (2001: 15) points to the 'unique situation that pertains in each professional area and the need to differentiate by profession when examining skilled migration'. Chompalov (2000: 32) similarly refers to the 'specificity of scientific labour markets', which he describes as more internationalized, comparatively smaller and with relatively higher mobility than other labour markets. For Dickson (2003: 1) the 'universality of science has made the problem worse, since it means that those trained in one country can, almost more than in any other profession, easily function in another that offers them better working conditions'. Our own work – which focuses on the natural sciences – has shown important differences both at disciplinary and national level in the relationship between migration and progression in science careers. It also identifies the different kinds of pressures faced by scientists in the academic sector and those in transnational companies (Ackers, 2005b). Recent work on scientific mobility has tended to focus on the latter group, highlighting the importance of industry-driven flows and the lubrication provided by companies and relocation agencies in these circumstances (Iredale, 2001; Baláž and Williams, 2004). Generally, scientists in the academic sector do not enjoy the 'ease of migration' provided via these 'organizational channels' (Peixoto, 2001: 1030). So, while academic science careers place enormous pressure on people to move in order to access the best opportunities and develop their skills, the kinds of structured organizational support associated with relocation policies of large multinational companies do not exist. Typically, academic scientists and their families are moving with little corporate support. Rarely do they receive assistance with accommodation, or support for partners in terms of finding employment or more general integration opportunities for their families. The nature of the process also differs. Scientific migration in the academic sector is not so much driven by industrial recruitment companies but rather takes place through networks, individual motivation and risk. Williams and colleagues (2004: 30) emphasize the role that 'ad hoc networks' play in the migration decisions of academics, arguing that previous studies have 'downplayed the role of other forms of recruitment, including self-recruitment, recruitment through networks of friends and family, recruitment from student mobility and "staying on" practices'.

Given the lack of practical and organized support for mobility in the academic sector, why do scientists move? A recent study of the migration motivations of highly skilled migrants in the UK – which included a sample of biotechnologists – found that 'while prospects for economic improvement in terms of earnings were a significant factor for some from developing countries it was not a dominant factor overall. As such, the surveyed migrants can be considered "knowledge migrants" rather than economic migrants' (DTI, 2002: 12). The report identified a number of 'motivational factors' that included: aspects of employment (that is, career advancement opportunities, the existence of global centres of excellence, wage differentials and quality of research facilities); wider economic and quality of life factors (that is, living conditions); and more esoteric issues such as the personal development associated with travel and experiencing another culture. Another report (Martin-Rovet, 2003: 1) places similar emphasis on occupational-related dynamics and identifies concerns around status and autonomy that are less directly connected to economic rewards: 'researchers want centres of scientific excellence and access to the best and latest scientific equipment. They want increased research funding and better salaries. They look for a society where science is respected and where their social status is esteemed'. Other authors talk more generally of 'the drive of scientific curiosity' (Mahroum, 1998: 18) and the 'dream of self-realization' (King, 2002: 95) to describe some of the non-economic deter-minants shaping HSM.

Our own work with male and female scientists in the EU suggests that a wide range of concerns shape migration decisions and that both the menu and the priority attached to individual factors varies over the life-course. The reference to career advancement opportunities in the DTI report cited above is unsurprising and constitutes a clear motivational factor in most forms of labour migration. Certainly many scientists, particularly from countries with a weaker science base and more limited employment oppor-tunities, move to access improved opportunities. However, experience of international mobility is not only a way of accessing better opportunities abroad: it is also a means of gaining necessary credentials for their subse-quent progression in home labour markets. Career progression in scientific research *demands* a very high level of mobility in order to achieve the level of international experience necessary for progression.

In practice, the specific emphasis placed on what has become known as the 'expectation of mobility' differs significantly between disciplines (Mahroum, 1998) and national contexts (Ackers, 2003). Disciplines such as physics and more highly specialized areas of science – where physical access to key infrastructures is essential to the research or the development of new skills – place an even stronger emphasis on mobility. The premium attached to international experience (and having worked abroad) is generally much higher in most EU Member States than it is in the UK, partly explaining why so many EU researchers come to the UK and so few UK nationals leave (the level of internationalization and language proficiencies being other key factors). The pressure to gain international experience through mobility is particularly associated with those in the early stage of their research career (Van de Sande et al., 2005).

Where a strong 'expectation of mobility' exists and directly shapes the career prospects of scientists, it is difficult to speak of migration as either voluntary or forced in the traditional sense.[4] It is thus perhaps useful to think in terms of a continuum of choices and constraints shifting over time and space and the life-course (King, 2002: 92). In most cases, and certainly in the context of HSM, this distinction between voluntary and forced migration is tenuous and potentially misleading. The extent to which moves in search of economic improvement or career progression constitute a form of voluntary or forced migration depends on context and also the individual's perception of that. While income differentials and the cost of living constitute key variables, they are not exclusive governing factors. The respective weight attached to such considerations may vary between individuals and over the life-course as decisions are under constant appraisal and review. Where employment opportunities are unavailable, then the language of voluntarism is perhaps inappropriate. Similarly, while simple formulaic approaches prioritizing economic determinants might satisfactorily explain the mobility of young, single researchers, they may be less effective in explaining the moves of partnered scientists, particularly when (as is often the case) both partners are scientists and the needs of children or elderly parents come into the equation (Ackers, 2004a; Ackers and Stalford, 2007).

Scientists place considerable emphasis not only on their personal financial situation (and pay), but on the funding of science more generally and the impact of this on their ability to work effectively – that is, 'to do good science'. In his analysis of Italian scientific migration, Dickson (2003: 1) concludes that 'many scientists leave their home countries not so much because of wages but rather to seek an environment in which they can work effectively with enthusiasm and support'.

Working effectively in science often implies access to high-quality infrastructure, facilities and human capital (in the form of top-quality researchers). These kinds of resources are not randomly distributed but increasingly 'clustered' in resource-rich, often highly specialized, centres or institutes. Our previous research corroborates the emphasis in the DTI report mentioned above on the attraction of such global centres of excellence. The growing tendency of scientific opportunities to 'cluster' in this way – encouraged by national and European policy – reinforces the 'expectation of mobility' and the pressure on scientists to tolerate repeated international moves. For Mahroum (2003: 2), such centres have a 'magnetic' and multiplying effect, drawing 'star scientists' who 'though few in number, are critical to the movement of staff. They tend to go where the best facilities are, and their reputation attracts the best young talents'. Linked to the issue of 'clustering' is the progressive internationalization of science, which Mahroum (ibid.: 4) describes as 'a strong pull-driver of talent from overseas . . . a prerequisite for sustained participation in, and access to, the international pool of researchers'. Reinforcing this point, Meyer (2003: 2) refers to the international mobility of the highly skilled as a 'natural extension of the traditional cosmopolitan character of the world's scientific community'. Our own findings underwrite the importance of international environments and research clusters to both the migration and location decisions of migrant scientists. Science clusters in the 'golden triangle' region spanning Oxford, Cambridge and London offer mobile scientists a wider range of opportunities and more cosmopolitan and international environments, which they generally prefer for scientific and social reasons. They also increase the opportunities for scientists in dual science career couples to secure proximate employment (Ackers, 2004a).

In addition to these resource-related considerations linked to the nature of science funding, another dimension of the quality of working environments referred to by scientists concerns the level of autonomy associated with their work and the freedom to work effectively. Migrant scientists talk of the attraction of transparent and fair (meritocratic) recruitment and progression systems with objective approaches to the evaluation and rewarding of excellence (Ackers, 2003; Van de Sande et al., 2005). Pelizon (2002: 3) refers to the 'cumbersome appointments system' in Italy, for example, which makes it 'difficult for Italians to navigate and virtually impenetrable for foreigners', arguing that it is the greater and 'fairer' opportunities abroad that attract scientists.

Even in situations of profound economic hardship, scientists attach great importance to these wider systemic factors. Referring to the Bulgarian context, Sretenova (2003: 8) points to the influence of the 'special personality' and value systems of scientists and the priority they ascribe to working conditions and infrastructures that enable them to do good science:

> [F]aced with the personal choice . . . it is no surprise that the most brilliant and skilful scientists (be they young or established) prefer the mobility option and a nomadic style of life in order to be able to practice their profession in an effective and productive way instead of being frozen at home.

Developing this point about the importance of 'social' factors, she cites a Bulgarian scientist in the Netherlands who refers to the advantages of the 'freedom' associated with working in Western Europe: the informality, transparency and openness of debate associated with science that is absent in Bulgaria.

Of course, economic issues remain highly influential in migration decision-making processes and scientists frequently refer to the salience of income differentials and, more commonly – perhaps reflecting the specific nature of scientific employment – contractual insecurity, as factors shaping both outward moves and potential return (Ackers and Oliver, 2007). However, they rarely see this in narrow terms but within the context of wider costs of living (including travelling), social benefits (especially health care and child care) and access to pensions. As noted earlier, both the menu and significance of the factors identified above might change over time as careers develop and lives evolve. They may also be gendered. The DTI study notes how skill levels, 'life-stage' and country of origin shaped the way individuals responded to the 'motivational factors' identified. Partnering, particularly in the context of dual science career situations, constitutes a serious challenge to migrant scientists, as does parenting and the need to support family members in other countries (Ackers, 1998, 2003; Kofman, 2002).

This section has emphasized the importance of understanding the context within which scientists are moving. Scientists working in different disciplines, sectors and national contexts face very different pressures and opportunities. These shape their migration decisions. Life-course and career trajectories also have an important influence on the priority attached to mobility or international experience and the ability to respond to it. In order to understand the impact of international scientific mobility on the regions concerned, we need to consider the 'quality' of scientific flows.

ASSESSING THE QUALITY OF FLOWS: WHICH SCIENTISTS MOVE?

Understanding the impact of HSM on sending and receiving countries requires more than the measurement of the direction and volume of flows. The processes of knowledge acquisition and expenditure are fluid and evolutionary and extend over time and space. From a research point of view, it is necessary to take into account the level (seniority or experience) of migrants and to capture, as far as is possible, their relationship to 'excellence' and potential. Salt (1997: 5) defines a highly skilled migrant as someone possessing a 'tertiary-level education or its equivalent in experience'. This is the criteria we used in previous studies of intra-EU flows, which have sampled a population of scientists from doctoral level upwards. This is not to imply that the loss of more junior talent is less serious. In the context of the 'old' (EU15) Member States, undergraduate mobility has become a normal and desirable phenomenon underwritten by European Commission (EC) funding. The presumption is that the majority of these undergraduates return home enriched by the experience without any major repercussions in terms of 'balanced growth'.

Arguably, the scope of any new research should curb the existing boundaries between undergraduate and other forms of academic mobility (King, 2002; Ackers, 2003; Baláž and Williams, 2004). Broadening the geographical canvas to encompass accession countries may support this approach. In situations where up to 70 per cent of undergraduates 'seriously consider' moving abroad (as in Bulgaria, for example), these countries might be at risk of losing 'the youngest, most able people with the greatest potential in the most important sectors or disciplines for the future economic development of their countries' (Salt, 1997: 23). A recent report echoes these findings, noting the 'brain and youth drain' facing new Member States (Krieger, 2004). The results of their attitudinal survey suggest that some 10 per cent of younger people in Bulgaria and Romania show a 'firm intention' to leave.[5] The 'typical migrant' in these situations is 'young, well-educated or studying third-level education and living as a single, non-cohabiting person' (ibid.: 3). Krieger argues that these trends may 'erode a country's long-term competitive position [with] negative repercussions on a country's developmental process' (ibid.: 1). Baláž and Williams (2004: 25) note that undergraduate mobility has been neglected in migration theory, yet this 'provides the "seeds" for future international skilled labour migration'. This is echoed by King (2002: 99) who observes that 'the migrational significance of students going to university has scarcely been studied'. Our own work supports this contention. A very high proportion of scientists moving at doctoral and post-doctoral level had experienced some form of undergraduate mobility and often used the networks developed then as the basis for future mobility. Sixty-two per cent of the Fellows interviewed as part of the impact assessment of the EC's Marie Curie Fellowship Scheme had previously lived abroad at some point prior to their application (Hansen, 2003; Van de Sande et al., 2005).

Although evidence suggests a link between undergraduate and subsequent highly skilled mobility, the majority of undergraduates will not seek to progress in research, preferring instead other employment areas. For this reason, it is perhaps more 'efficient' to address some of these issues around undergraduate mobility retrospectively in research terms as part of a biographical or life-history approach. Moreover, while undergraduate flows may be numerically dominant, flows at doctoral and post-doctoral level may be of greater concern because of the significant investment the sending country has made to their education up to that point. Sretenova's (2003: 4) 'methodological frame' for studying the effects of highly skilled migration proposes a focus on post-doctoral scientists (and above) who are 'holders of at least a PhD degree'. According to this approach one could argue that although undergraduate or even doctoral mobility may represent a precursor to HSM, it is not constitutive of it. Considerable disagreement exists over when a science career commences or, put differently, what defines the 'early stage' of research careers. In some countries and disciplines, the doctorate is considered to form part of pre-career entry training (as a 'student'), while in other cases the doctorate is considered to form part of the early career itself (Ackers, 2005c). Perceptions of the most appropriate level to study HSM may reflect these disciplinary and national differences and skills shortages.

Media and policy attention, in the UK at least, has tended to focus predominantly on the movement of the best-known, established researchers. In support of this emphasis, Mahroum (1998: 17) suggests that it is not singularly a question of volume but the *quality* of flows that shapes the impact of HSM, with movements of the 'brightest and best' having the greatest impact. At this level, even small international movements can have very serious negative effects on source countries and institutions: 'the departure of a few top-level specialists in certain sectors of basic research could lead to the collapse of national scientific schools' (Salt, 1997: 22). We have already noted the ability of science clusters to attract 'star scientists' and the multiplier effect of this in terms of subsequent recruitment. The mobility of such established scientists and the consequences of this in terms of the losses of human capital – their own expertise and their research group's – coupled with sources of external funding, represents a serious concern for less developed regions. The notion of 'quality' needs some unpacking also, however, as it conflates two related issues: first, the loss of very senior or experienced scientists; and second, the loss of the most able or with most potential at *whatever level* – a process referred to by Wood (2004) as 'skimming' and 'poaching'. So, while Cismas (2004) agrees that highly skilled emigration from Romania is taking place in a context of labour surpluses and that Romania simply cannot 'absorb' all of its graduates, she expresses fears that a significant number of the *top ones* are leaving. From a research point of view, this issue is difficult to capture, not least because different systems have very different approaches to the conceptualization and measurement of excellence. For example, how do we assess the relative quality of those scientists who remain and those who leave? While there is some logic to the inference that the 'best' are leaving, it is also important to exercise some caution here as it assumes that migration and employment processes are relatively meritocratic and efficient. Both career progression and migration are driven as much by networks and connections than quality per se, potentially subverting the meritocratic principle (Van de Sande et al., 2005).

The issue of 'quality' is important to the evaluation of impact because it tells us something about the contribution a scientist is able to make and the potential consequences of their mobility, and also because it reflects the level and geography of investment in human capital. Put simply, where is 'value-added'? How do we compare (both in terms of economic impact and ethical responsibilities) the situation of a person who moves to the UK for their undergraduate degree and doctoral research and then remains, to someone who has trained in Bulgaria and reached an established position and then leaves? Tomiuc (2003: 2) expresses concern at the outward migration of 'elites' from South Eastern Europe, which he suggests has reached 'alarming proportions' and constitutes a 'huge blow to the economy, because the higher education of one person is something quite expensive and the investment was made by the [home] State'. Meyer (2001: 92) similarly argues that most data on 'brain drain' is retrospective and 'ignores when and where . . . skills have been developed'. Research on HSM needs to capture the diversity of flows and also the geography of investment in human capital that these imply. Closely linked here is the issue of temporality and the significance of return.

MIGRATION OR MOBILITY: THE TEMPORAL QUALITY OF MOVES?

The language of brain drain implies unilateral and essentially long-term or even permanent flows of human capital. Clearly an important factor to take into consideration when assessing the potential impact of scientific migration is the issue of duration or permanency. This is significant for both the sending regions (and the extent to which their emigrants return home furnished with new skills, approaches and expertise) and for receiving regions concerned about safeguarding the investments they have made through retention. On a theoretical level, this raises questions around the very concept of migration. One of the 'binaries' identified in King's (2002) mapping exercise is the traditional distinction in migration research between those researchers who focus on permanent forms of 'migration' and those whose work considers more temporary forms of 'mobility'. The general consensus – at least among HSM theorists – is that this distinction now holds little validity and may constrain our understanding of this phenomenon (Iredale and Appleyard, 2001). Just as internal and international migration may be interwoven, the temporal nature of scientific moves may vary both between individuals and over the life-course and career trajectory. Our research suggests that scientists make at least one international move with subsequent moves often to different locations (Ackers, 2003; Van de Sande et al., 2005). King (2002: 98) characterizes these forms of movement as 'multiple and spatially capricious'.

While any arbitrary distinction between forms of migration based on the length of stay (or the concept of 'settlement') at a theoretical level may be spurious given the fluid quality and unpredictability of these processes, the issue retains its relevance in terms of assessing impact at the regional and individual level. Recent work on HSM in the EU indicates a shift in favour of more temporary moves. Piracha and Vickerman (2002: 1), for example, suggest that 'within Europe, most migration is not permanent, but part of a process of mobility in which both return and serial migration are natural economic responses to a dynamic economy'. Williams et al. (2004: 29) similarly argue that the 'temporality of skilled labour migration is changing . . . longer-term migration has increasingly been replaced by more diverse shorter-term flows, so that it is more apposite to refer to circulation and mobility than to migration'. Writing in the context of accession, Okólski (2001: 329) describes 'settlement migration'[6] as a 'tiny part of all movements' in Europe, a sentiment echoed by Haug and Diehl (2004a: 15) who conclude that 'the desire for temporary migration dominates over that for permanent'.

This work supports the emphasis on fluidity and 'circulation', and potentially allays the fears associated with 'brain drain'. Developments at the legal and policy level and, in particular, the extension of free movement rights post-enlargement, may reinforce this tendency. While the dominant view, at least in political and media circles, reflects concern that EU enlargement may result in a significant out-migration of highly skilled workers, it is likely that these provisions will have a more complex effect. Conceivably, the 'looser' post-transition regime enabling people to move to and fro, will support a higher degree of 'circulation' or 'shuttle migration', yet the net flows may remain unidirectional. Okólski (2000: 338) suggests that the post-enlargement legal regime may lubricate return on the grounds that 'absence from the home country does not prejudice future freedom of migration by the same person or the members of his family'.

In addition to the potential effects of accession on the exercise of mobility, quite dramatic changes in the accessibility and costs of travel and the rapid development of new communications systems might be expected to support greater 'circulation' than in the past. In our previous research, many scientists spoke about the influence of cheap flights on their location decisions and also the benefits of laptops in promoting more flexible approaches to work, enabling them to tolerate extended forms of 'commuting' or 'shuttle migrations'. Speaking in the context of Central and Eastern European countries (CEE) over a decade ago, Biggin and Kouzminov (1993) identified the relatively high costs of air travel as a holding factor, restricting both emigration and return. This situation is changing rapidly with the falling cost of air travel across Europe and improved technology that supports distance working. Salt and Ford (1993) even suggest that modern air travel means that it may no longer be necessary to have a permanent expatriate presence. Meyer (2001: 94) similarly refers to the impact of developments in 'communication, transportation, geopolitics and intercultural relations in fostering these new forms of movement'. The net impact of these developments on the temporal character and geography of migration flows is difficult to predict. For some, they may actually lubricate moves, encouraging people to leave who might otherwise have stayed. For

others, they may support the kind of exchange and knowledge transfer that
obviates the need for migration as such. They might also impact on location decisions. Respondents in the pilot study emphasized the importance
of location in the 'escalator' regions of South East England, for example,
to EU migrant scientists who wish to either retain close contacts with Italy
for personal or professional reasons or who were actively trying to manage
dual career situations (Ackers, 2004a). Haug and Diehl's (2004a) analysis
of the migration intentions of Bulgarians illustrates this relationship
between distance and temporality, distinguishing favoured locations for
those intending to migrate in the long term (when the US assumes first
place) and more temporary moves (where Germany is the prime location).

Williams and colleagues (2004) identify a number of important directions for future research on HSM. Starting from the premise that 'the
changing nature and duration of the fixity of labour mobility flows and circuits in institutionally specific spaces is one of the keys to understanding
uneven regional development in Europe' (ibid.: 27), they chart the inter-
section of three different forms of mobility: human capital, financial
capital and knowledge over time and space. On the one hand, their reference to 'flows' and 'circuits' builds on the circulationist argument emphasizing the fluid and ongoing nature of human mobility. But on the other,
they suggest that human mobility is 'temporally and spatially "stickier"
than most other forms of mobility' and that migrants become 'locked into'
particular places or develop 'place attachments' that restrain movement
(ibid.: 38). The concept of 'stickiness' and the reasons why people become
'locked into' spaces remains undeveloped, but the authors do give some
indication of potential variables. Referring to the role of regulation on
migration flows and uneven development they conclude 'the selective
easing of immigration does not automatically lead to transfers of
significant additions to human capital. Knowledge does not simply trans-
late into action. Rather, the potential for action is dependent on position,
in terms of class, gender and ethnicity' (ibid.: 43). This raises concerns
around two dimensions of 'stickiness': first, whether the structural determinants identified in migration research are uniform or whether different
groups of migrants might perceive and prioritize different structural determinants depending on their personal situation; and second, whether the
'potential for action' reflects differential opportunity and agency.

While the contextual factors outlined above can be expected to shape the
resource framework within which migration decision-making takes place,
it is important to remember that migrants are human beings with person-
alities and families. King (2002: 101) emphasizes the need for new methodological approaches to recognize the 'double embeddedness of migration'.
At the macro scale, he suggests, migration research needs embedding in the

societal and social processes of sending and receiving countries. Then, at the individual scale, 'migration must be embedded in a migrant's life-course' (ibid.: 101). This second dimension of context has a significant impact both on migration processes in general (and the propensity to move) and, on the specific temporal nature of migration. The concept of fluidity needs to be complemented with an understanding of viscosity and the processes contributing to this 'stickiness'.

Some scientists are less 'footloose' than others, reflecting the demands of different stages in the life-course, personal situations and – potentially – gendered responses to these. It is quite common in migration research to link the notion of temporality with more complex and subjective notions of 'settlement' and integration. Salt (1997: 4) thus refers to the reluctance of migration researchers to 'accept that HSM is really migration at all, since there is *no intention to settle* in the destination country' (emphasis added). From a pragmatic point of view an intention to settle is important in the context of the distributional consequences of highly skilled migration, the association between such intentions and the level of engagement of the persons concerned with the host society more generally is questionable. While Okólski (2001: 7) links the perceived trend in favour of more temporary forms of mobility to notions of limited 'settlement', his analysis does not fit very well with what he also identifies as the emergence of 'split living arrangements'[7] associated with 'incomplete migrations'. Okólski suggests that social integration in the host country is not an issue for highly skilled migrants 'whose basic function and main purpose of movement precludes that kind of integration or makes it a matter of relatively low priority . . . [and] are hardly involved in the public life of destination countries' (2000: 334). Forms of 'split living' may arise, as Okólski suggests, in situations in which the family remains 'settled' in the sending region with the worker effectively commuting across international space. Our research has identified numerically significant forms of 'split-living' arrangements reflecting increasing levels of post-migration, cross-nationality, partnering and parenting. In one study, some 47 per cent of respondents were in international partnerships (Ackers and Stalford, 2004). Other studies have also identified the specific challenges faced by the growing number of scientists managing dual science career situations. Here, partners may live in two different locations, neither of which may be their country of birth. Such transnational families often include children who may be born in the host state or elsewhere. In such circumstances the notion of 'settlement' is highly complex. It should certainly not be assumed that there is no intention to 'settle' nor that migrants in these more fluid and complex transnational situations place less priority on integration or involvement.

While arbitrary distinctions between temporary and more permanent moves may hold little value in terms of understanding migration behaviour or settlement, length of stay remains significant in important ways, particularly in terms of accruing citizenship entitlement for migrants and their families. Our research suggests that this is a significant consideration for scientists with partners and/or children who need to reassure themselves that their mobility will not jeopardize their own citizenship status, their partner's right to work and the wider family's social entitlement (Ackers, 2003: Ackers and Stalford, 2007).

The issues raised here in terms of life-course and gender shape both the initial decision to (e)migrate and subsequent moves or returns. In practice, early stage research mobility – of younger scientists moving during doctoral or early post-doctoral appointments – is less likely to be affected by concerns around family. To that extent, these emigrants are generally more footloose (Ackers, 2003). This contention is supported by other work that indicates a high level of feminization of early stage mobility followed by a marked decline (Haug and Diehl, 2004a; Lungescu, 2004).

In addition to more structural concerns around the funding of science, the nature of science labour markets, free movement and employment rights, life-course is an important dimension when studying the temporal character of HSM and its impact on sending and receiving countries. The tendency for mobility to become more 'sticky' over the life-course might thus restrict subsequent mobility (and the propensity to return) for those scientists who establish partnerships and families. Linked in important ways to these concerns around length of stay and permanency of moves – and of great significance to current political debate – are the issues of retention and return.

RETENTION, RETURN AND REINTEGRATION

From the perspective of receiving countries and regions, there is a concern to retain scientific expertise – to 'lock them in' to the system – particularly when the host country has made a major investment in terms of training and development. Iredale (1999) identifies retention and successful labour market integration as a key issue for host countries. The importance of retention becomes clear when we consider the critical reliance in some disciplines and institutions on migrant labour.[8] In this context, the UK government's review of skills shortages in science (Roberts, 2002) predicted that the positive effects of science mobility – from the UK's perspective – may be mitigated by the propensity of foreign scientists to return. However, no evidence is presented to support this contention. Another UK study found that 'a relatively high proportion of the skilled migrant workers interviewed are planning to stay' (DTI, 2002: 64). Clearly, these issues of post-migration retention are highly significant dimensions of the knowledge transfer equation. However, the temporal dimension of this requires careful attention. For example, when can we say someone has left or returned and for how long will they remain? Moreover, as Regets (2003: 2) cautions, if they do leave can we assess that in terms of net loss when 'they still provide much in the way of research and teaching before they depart'? This draws our attention to the issue of 'skills expenditure' (the corollary of 'investment'). We have so far assumed that migrant scientists in the receiving countries are able to use their skills. Sretenova (2003: 4) adds to her list of 'useful conceptual tools' the concept of 'external brain waste' to denote situations in which scientists migrate but are not able to 'use their qualifications' effectively in the host state. In such cases, there may be evidence of 'brain drain' but limited commensurate 'gain' to the receiving region. Sensitivities about the ethical dimensions of HSM have meant that these concerns about retention in receiving countries have remained somewhat implicit and figure less strongly on the political agenda. The interest in return is primarily focused on its significance to the sending regions (Gill, 2004).

One 'binary' that King (2002) does not explicitly identify concerns the tendency of migration research to deal separately, both theoretically and empirically, with the issue of migration (which generally implies outward moves) and return. The issue of return needs to be considered in the light of movement in general. Arguably, from a scientific perspective, it is not so much the issue of out-migration, as such, but the overall balance of flows and whether the country in question is attractive to highly skilled migrants at all. Notwithstanding the importance of personal and family ties to return decisions, our research suggests that the factors shaping the return decisions of Italians may be similar to those restricting the attractiveness of Italy to other scientists. The problems with funding, the nature of recruitment and progression and the very lack of an international presence in Italy deter both Italians and other nationalities. With reference to the Italian context, Cismas (2004) stresses the importance of placing the return issue within the wider context of international flux, arguing that it is important both to encourage return and attract foreign scientists so as to avoid what she calls 'local thinking'. Arguably, an influx of foreign blood might have a bigger impact on cultural attitudes than returnees who are often viewed with some suspicion and jealousy in the 'home' countries. The issue of return, as a specific element of fluidity, must be considered in the wider context of in-migration and circulation and the focus should extend beyond a preoccupation with numbers to take account of the quality of flows and the nature of knowledge transfer processes.

Despite the symbolism attached to return, there is considerable evidence suggesting that return flows may not lead to an equivalent transfer of knowledge. To achieve such transfers, returning scientists need to be able to re-enter local labour markets and work in an environment conducive to the exercise and nurturing of their skills and knowledge. In more general terms, our work supports Balter's (1999: 1524) findings that many 'Europeans who do post-docs abroad face re-entry problems and struggle to reintegrate themselves into their native scientific communities'.

The corollary of international brain drain may not be flourishing national labour markets. Some authors are less pessimistic about the current 'asymmetry' of flows given the problems of over-supply and unemployment in some countries. The concepts of 'internal brain waste' or 'stagnation' have been used to describe situations in which scientists are forced to move intersectorally or combine scientific positions with other employment in order to make a living. Salt (1997: 22) describes this as a form of deskilling, which occurs 'when highly skilled workers migrate into forms of employment not requiring the application of the skills and experience applied in the former job'. The effects of scientific emigration need to be considered alongside the alternative prospects of 'internal brain drain' within countries, which may dwarf the losses through international migration.

Korys (2003: 36) identifies the saturation of the labour market with specialists in some disciplines in Poland as a factor generating an 'in-group drive to work abroad'. Furthermore, this drive to emigrate and realize higher financial returns may, ironically, increase incentives to undertake training in the home country. Lowell and Findlay (2001: 1) thus refers to the extent to which the 'possibility of emigration for higher wages can stimulate individuals to pursue education', encouraging economic growth in the sending region. On this basis, it may be possible to identify an optimal level of skilled migration, in a given context, that serves to augment these incentives without damaging the national science base. This does, of course, beg the question – raised earlier – of how the countries concerned underwrite the costs of, and provide the personnel to educate potential emigrants.

In situations of labour surplus, it may be politically and economically more acceptable for these scientists to work abroad. Indeed, it could even be a form of 'investment', allowing the receiving countries to underwrite the costs of their continued training until they are required back home. By way of illustration, Meyer (2003: 2) refers to China's 'deliberate policy' aimed at 'storing brainpower overseas for subsequent use'. Such situations can, however, change quite rapidly. Referring to the Italian context, Hellemans warns against complacency based on notions of over-supply predicting some serious challenges to the economy. She suggests that the 'exodus of scientists' must be viewed in the context of the demographic ageing of its population of active scientists, about 30 per cent of whom are due to retire by 2005 (2001: 4). The demographic situation in scientific employment in the accession countries is also quite alarming and may indicate significant changes in the labour markets in the next ten years.

In addition to the lack of positions in sending regions, scientists often express concerns about their ability to re-enter domestic labour markets, particularly when these are associated with forms of protectionism and 'position blocking'. Where networks are of particular importance to progression, the dislocation caused by migration opens up 'gaps and discontinuities in the home country's networks [which] . . . often made the outcome of their undertakings unpredictable, sometimes, even frequently, leading to a decision to re-emigrate' (Meyer, 2001: 101). Chompalov (2000) identifies the specific phenomenon of 'position-blocking' in the Bulgarian context, suggesting that representatives of the old elite prefer to cling to well-established positions, especially in view of the instability and tightening of the national labour market. Williams and colleagues' (2004: 41) concept of 'location-specific insider advantages' perhaps describes situations such as these in which social networks 'accumulated through living and working in the same place' lock people into national systems and restrict mobility. Fear of re-entry then may result in stasis in home labour markets, restricting the opportunities available for those who have left and would be interested in returning. These situations may have important demographic consequences and gendered outcomes. Langer (2004) refers to the existence of a 'gerontocracy' or 'mafia of oldies' in the CEEs, blocking the progression, and return, of young researchers.

The volume of return, although symbolically important, is clearly only one dimension of the equation. Understanding the consequence of migration – in terms of the flows of knowledge and the benefits and losses to the regions and individuals concerned – demands a greater focus on the nature of their work and the exercise of skills. Securing a 'position' and the remuneration that goes with it is an important factor to consider, particularly in terms of the personal costs of return. For many scientists, however, concerns about their ability to return to a position in which they are able to exercise their skills and work effectively dampens their propensity to return. Furthermore, from the regions' perspective, failure to offer conditions capable of harnessing the skills of returning scientists as the basis for scientific development raises questions about the potential of return migration. This brings us to the critical issue of the relational nature of skills (see Meyer, 2001; Williams, et al., 2004): while knowledge is clearly embedded in individuals, scientists are not simply passive vessels of knowledge that can be transported and utilized in a similar fashion in different situations.

Skill or knowledge can only be understood in the context of the environment within which it is being used: 'total human capital will be articulated in the context of a different set of localised and distanciated social relationships' (Williams et al., 2004: 32).

Other authors have drawn attention to a range of factors shaping the relationship between human mobility and the transfer of knowledge. Harris (2004), for example, refers to the complexity of the knowledge transfer process and the importance of recognizing the limitations of attempts to directly transpose techniques and approaches developed in resource-rich to resource-constrained conditions. She argues that researchers in these situations may have more to learn from researchers working in similar contexts. Skills and approaches learnt in the host countries may, therefore, not produce equivalent results in a different research environment.

We have already noted the attraction of centres of excellence to potential migrants: the same can be said in relation to return. These not only serve as magnets to potential returnees but also shape the relationship between return and knowledge transfer. Effective knowledge transfer in this context depends on whether the location is a 'critical, institutionalised learning space' (Williams et al., 2004: 34). Such spaces are generally found in more dynamic regions and especially global cities, and do not always exist in the home countries or regions.

Harris (2004: 7) draws our attention to a further set of issues relating to the working context restricting scientists in 'low income countries [where] research is a luxury owing to economic constraints and many scientists hold several other jobs'. This situation is quite common in some Southern European countries and emerged as a major concern in Greece and, to a lesser extent, Italy where scientists either take on more than one full-time position due to the low levels of remuneration, or supplement unpaid work in science with paid work in other areas for long periods of time (Ackers, 2005b). In the Bulgarian context, Sretenova (2003) refers to the phenomenon of 'flying academics' juggling more than one lectureship often in different cities, with implications for their ability to conduct research effectively.

In many situations then, scientists may have difficulty expending their scientific skills and knowledge on return. This issue raises other broader questions about the quality or scope of skills. It is easy, and convenient in research terms, to equate the concept of skill directly with scientific qualifications. Recent work, however, underlines the importance of defining skills more loosely. Korys (2003: 51) notes the impact of highly skilled migration into – and return to – Poland, not only on the diffusion of technology but, more broadly, on approaches to the organization of work and working time, introducing 'new management techniques or the capitalist ethos of work'. Williams et al. (2004: 36) conclude that return is:

more likely to be innovative where there was critical mass in the level of return, geographical concentration of returnees, migration has been of medium-length duration, the migrants were well educated, economic differences between the origin and destination were relatively small, and return was organised in the context of national or regional economic policies.

Understanding the impact of scientific mobility thus demands detailed attention to the specificity of national context in order to capture how knowledge is generated, transferred and used. This is important to the analysis of impact in a regional sense but also in terms of individual opportunity. Those unable to take advantage of mobility may forgo the advantages of higher salaries and working conditions and find it difficult to progress or work effectively in local science labour markets. Our research suggests that the ability to respond to the opportunities – in terms of career but also quality of life – is neither universal nor random, but dependent on family status, life-course and gender dynamics (Ackers, 2003). Research in this field needs to address the question of whether those 'frozen' brains left behind or indeed those 'stored' abroad are gendered. In addition to these concerns around the significance of return, others have drawn attention to some potentially compensatory trends mitigating the effects of highly skilled migration.

SCIENTIFIC DIASPORAS AND THE TRANSFER OF KNOWLEDGE

Recent attention to the potential value of scientific 'diasporas' suggest a complex relationship between human flows and the transfer of knowledge and a potentially more direct compensatory effect. Meyer's (2001: 91) research on 'intellectual diaspora networks' optimistically concludes that 'highly skilled expatriate networks, through a connectionist approach linking diaspora members with their countries of origin, turn the brain drain into a brain gain'. Others support this, arguing that 'international knowledge networks' might constitute a 'powerful means of profiting from skilled emigration' (Lowell, 2003: 2) through the 'exchange of knowledge and useful contacts' (Regets, 2003: 1). While Mahroum (2003) acknowledges the potential of diasporas to contribute to the international transfer of knowledge, he is less positive, suggesting that the focus on diasporic communities might reflect a kind of 'resignation' on the part of sending countries, which have reached the 'irreversible point' and have 'given up on trying to attract the diaspora back' (ibid.: 3). Furthermore, he alludes to the potential of diasporas to augment out-migration: 'the fast growth of scientific diaspora . . . can by itself act as a magnet . . . Local talent seeking maximum career return find now an easier and greater access to international careers through their own diaspora' (ibid.). Such networks may 'facilitate the migration process' and diminish the risks and costs of migration (Meyer, 2001: 93). Korys (2003: 5, 36) would also appear to see the diaspora primarily as a means of promoting out-migration: 'building-up migration networks [facilitates] foreign migration' both through the exercise of networks but also in terms of the 'social memory of migrations [as] routes to success'.

Our previous research provides evidence of the 'channelling' function of diasporas with migrant scientists and especially established senior scientists (Mahroum's 'research stars') acting as bridge-heads for fellow migrants (Van de Sande et al., 2005). Meyer's (2001: 93–4) conclusion that networks are 'making migrants' and 'most positions are acquired via connections', has a strong resonance with our findings, and this may encourage situations in which employment opportunities are allocated on grounds other than individual excellence. Rather than selecting the 'brightest and the best' on the basis of individual merit and competition, HSM may be skewed by the power of networks. As Meyer (2003: 96) proposes, 'this is not a volatile population of separate units in a fluid environment but rather a set of connective entities that are always evolving through networks, along sticky branches'. Earlier we noted the potential of cheaper travel and improved communications technology that may help to maintain these 'umbilical ties' with regions of origin. In addition to the point about travel, Meyer and colleagues (2001) refer to the emergence of a series of trends supporting the rapid emergence of new science diasporas. They call the first of these the dual life setting of many highly skilled expatriates, and underline the importance of understanding the relationship between personal and family ties and scientific careers. Their second point refers to the impact of critical mass or higher densities of expatriates which, they suggest, is conducive to more frequent interactions and collective endeavours.

EXPATRIATE VERSUS SCIENTIFIC DIASPORAS

The current emphasis in the diaspora debate has been on the potential impact of expatriate networks. While this focus might be appropriate in some contexts, it is worth reflecting upon the nature of networks among the highly skilled and the relative importance of expatriate and scientific or professional connections. This raises interesting issues about concepts of community and the relative value and role of different forms of community to scientific migration. Certainly links with the home country will continue to have an important bearing on migration decisions. Focusing on the

African context, Gaillard and Gaillard (2003: 2) conclude that diaspora may constitute 'little more than a friendship network'.

Certainly, one might predict a relationship between HSM and the development of international scientific networks, particularly in the scientific sector where such networks are so important. Earlier we referred to the blurring of boundaries between forms of more permanent migration and ongoing internal or international mobility. The issue of ongoing international mobility via conferences and research collaboration is a particular feature of scientific research that is likely to shape the impact and experience of mobility and potentially temper any direct relationship between migration (or residence) and the transfer of knowledge. A recent study of the relationship between gender, mobility and progression in science careers (Ackers, 2007) provides some indications of the amount of time scientists spend on foreign travel in order to present papers at international conferences, to develop collaborative projects and to visit key research infrastructures and centres of excellence. It is not uncommon for scientists to report spending at least six weeks per year working abroad. Academic careers are perhaps somewhat unique in this respect in fostering such a close relationship between concepts of excellence (and progression) and international activity. Mobility, in the context of scientific careers, could thus be seen as operating on two interlinked continua: the first might 'measure' the physical employment-related moves made by scientists in the course of their careers; the second might capture the degree of ongoing employment-related travel. Meyer et al. (2001) talk of 'scientific nomadism', while Williams et al. (2004: 42) use the concept of 'diverse temporalities' to describe the nature of academic scientific mobility that incorporates short-term visits, fellowships and 'longer-term migration for individual career development'. These forms of mobility do not necessarily occur in a linear fashion but reflect an ongoing spatial manifestation of career and family-related mobility. Williams et al. (ibid.: 43) conclude that 'we simply need to know more about the spatial practices of workers and how these contribute to the spatiality (the concentration and diffusion) of knowledge and capital'.

Whereas the focus on expatriate links has led to a preoccupation with the impact on sending regions, attention to the contribution of scientific or subject networks encompasses the multidirectional nature of flows with important implications for all regions concerned. Can we conclude, for example, that the return of a leading migrant scientist to his or her home country implies a total loss of knowledge or input? Many scientists retain links with host institutions when they return home or move elsewhere, building a web of relationships across time and space, which shape not only their own careers but those of their students and colleagues.

The impact of networks on knowledge flows remains unclear and further research is required to develop our understanding of how these processes operate in different cultural and scientific contexts and how they impact on sending and receiving countries and individuals. The challenge lies in developing research tools capable of capturing the quality of these networks. As Baláž and Williams conclude (2004: 4), existing research gives 'little insight into how human capital transfers are constituted'. Vizi's (1993: 102) inference of a simple and direct correlation between migration and knowledge transfer – 'when the best scientists leave their laboratories, they take with them not only their scientific knowledge, but also their reputations' – clearly fails to grasp the wider contextual issues and the dynamics of knowledge generation and transfer. Meyer (2001: 95) challenges this kind of approach and its implicit conceptualization of skills as 'individual-based properties bounded by human bodies', arguing that skills are relational and that scientists are composite entities whose embedded knowledge can only be understood in the context of its connection with extensive networks at home and abroad.

CONCLUSIONS: A NEW RESEARCH AGENDA

This chapter, through analysis of existing literature and research has tried to identify some of the key 'variables' shaping scientific mobility and its impact. Building on our own research findings from the MOBEX pilot study and the work of others, it has defined the parameters of the current MOBEX2 study indicating the importance of encompassing the following considerations:

- the migration trajectories of scientific migrants including the frequency, permanence and location of moves, the issues of retention (and settlement) and the propensity to return;
- the dimensions and geography of scientific flows;
- the quality or characteristics of flows (who is moving and at what stages in their career trajectories), where investments are made and skills generated (and who underwrites the costs);
- the effect of life-course, partnering and parenting on mobility and the (gendered) effects of this on the demographic and social balance of scientific labour markets in sending and receiving regions;
- the extent to which international migration spawns other forms of knowledge generation and transfer that are not directly related to physical presence, such as diasporic networks and more specific forms of scientific exchange;

- the alternatives to migration and the consequences of these (what would happen if people did not move).

These considerations shape the analysis presented in the remaining chapters. Capturing the complex dynamics of these processes presents important methodological challenges. Baláž and Williams (2004: 23) suggest the need to adopt a 'total human capital' approach, which pays more attention to individual social biographies. They also emphasize the importance of context to understanding how 'structural parameters' relate to 'individual agency' and the 'relational nature of skills' (ibid.: 24). King and Ruiz-Gelices (2003: 24) similarly argue for a biographical approach to support an understanding of how 'individuals enrich their biographies through social and geographical mobility'.

This review of the literature and research played a critical role in the design of the MOBEX2 research strategy. The pilot study made us very aware of the importance of both national and occupational context to an understanding of migration dynamics. For that reason we decided to focus on a limited number of countries and on a specific group of natural scientists. The face-to-face interviews with mobile scientists in the pilot study also supported the emphasis on biographical approaches advocated above. In practical terms this resulted in an online survey followed by in-depth biographical interviews (n = 89) with mobile scientists in all four locations. Both the survey and the interviews were designed to generate information that would enable us to reflect on the questions outlined above. The pilot study involved work with an Italian research partner and a division of labour along national lines. This meant that the UK-based team did the interviews with Italians in the UK but not with returnees in Italy. In retrospect we felt that this approach, whilst efficient, limited our overall understanding of the situation and the different perspectives of these two groups. Furthermore, it restricted the opportunity for a broader ethnographic element to the work. Visiting science labs in the UK for the purpose of the interviews was, in itself, a valuable experience for the researchers. This element was built into the new study, giving the UK team the opportunity to visit and spend time in research institutions in Poland and Bulgaria.[9]

We have referred, above, to the importance of understanding the migration trajectories and the temporal quality of scientific mobility. Gamlen (2005: 15) argues that little research exists 'on actual mobility patterns to support the shuttle migration thesis'. The following chapter considers precisely this issue in the context of our work with Polish and Bulgarian scientists.

NOTES

1. This chapter is an updated version of an earlier article written by Louise Ackers in 2005 and published in the journal *International Migration*. It is used here with kind permission from Blackwell Publishing (Ackers, 2005a).
2. A summary of the approach is contained in Annex 1.
3. The pilot study was funded under the ESRC Science and Society Programme (Project RES-151-25-00).
4. Recent years have witnessed cases of 'forced' migration from Central European countries in response to political oppression or famine. Nevertheless, Okólski (2004: 330) suggests that 'with the exception of the outflow from Bosnia and Kosovo, much of the recent East–West ethnic movement has been taking place without severe tension or pressing need to leave the country of origin'.
5. A similar figure for Bulgaria is cited in Chompalov (2000). Attitudinal surveys are often relied upon as a predictive tool in the absence of 'hard' data on migration trends. The reliability of this approach is, however, questionable and figures often vary significantly, reflecting the wording of the question and the sampling method used. The figures used here illustrate the point rather than lend validity to them.
6. 'Settlement' migration refers to forms of migration where people move with the intention of settling there for a long period or permanently. A very common practice amongst scientists – and others – is to move with the intention of leaving/returning but then to establish a career or family and eventually 'settle' in the host country.
7. This idea resonates strongly with the concept of LAT – living apart together – couples recently identified by Williams (2004) and Roseneil (2006).
8. Further details are provided in Chapter 7.
9. Further details of the research strategy are contained in Annex 1.

PART I

Understanding migration behaviour and patterns

2. Circulators, returners and settlers: migration trajectories and patterns

INTRODUCTION

This chapter is organized in two parts. The first part proceeds with discussion about the scale of out-migration from Poland and Bulgaria; this in combination with discussion about the demographic challenges they face, helps to contextualize the analysis of the impact of such flows for sending regions presented later. The second part of the chapter describes the patterns of mobility exhibited by our respondents in the MOBEX2 study. The object there is not to map the geography or volume of intra-EU scientific flows as such but rather to identify the characteristics of mobility patterns.

I ASSESSING THE VOLUME AND QUALITY OF SCIENTIFIC EMIGRATION FROM POLAND AND BULGARIA

According to Kupiszewski (2002: 643), 'forecasting international migration is the most difficult task that demographers face'. Kupiszewski goes on to list the key problems frustrating accurate statistical analysis of flows, including: lack of uniform definitions and the inability to distinguish long-term settlement from short-term migration and capture 'pendulum migrations'. His overview of current data uncovered massive differences between migration figures sourced in the country of origin and host countries (which in some cases vary by a magnitude of 30-fold). Kupiszewski concludes that 'neither the German nor the Polish migration data present reliable or realistic statistical information' suggesting that estimates are often little better than a 'statistical fiction' (ibid.: 629).

Other experts in the field of highly skilled migration come to similar conclusions. Kicinger (2005: 33), for example, refers to the lack of reliable data on the number of scientists leaving Poland given the fact that figures conflate emigration with intersectoral losses: so we can estimate how many people leave science but not where they go to. For Iglicka (2000), official statistics do not allow for a proper analysis of migration, as much migration is not officially recorded. On that basis, such data can provide the 'starting point for further in-depth analysis' (ibid.: 64). In the Bulgarian context, Haug (2005) points to significant problems with available data. According to her, at the present time 'no information system exists which could be the basis for estimating the character and context of the external migration process in Bulgaria. There is thus a serious lack of information' (ibid.: 2).

Attempts to forecast migration based on surveys of migration potential – which are increasingly used in the post-accession period with important symbolic and political effect – are described by Kupiszewski (2002: 635) as highly misleading on the grounds that there is 'no proven link between migration intentions and actual migration'. Gächter (2002: 10) agrees and points to the dangers of this kind of data: 'surveys of the desire to emigrate have become a fixture of political life. In reality . . . they gauge a current sentiment . . . but leave us completely in the dark about both current and future migration'. For Chompalov (2000), the concept of migration potential is itself highly contested. Gamlen (2005: 15) makes the same point in the context of measuring return rates, arguing that 'brain circulator supporters have frequently confused migrant intentions with migrant behaviors, implying that rates of "intention" or "commitment" to return are an indication of actual return rates'.

Where does this leave us in terms of assessing the volume of flows? The following discussion considers some of the figures that have been presented in relation to migration flows but does so in the context of this scepticism about data quality and reliability. It then analyses some of the perceptions of our respondents and their own experiences of the volume of flows.

A recent OECD report (Katseli, Lucas and Xenogiani, 2006b) on the impact of migration on sending countries, indicates high rates of brain drain in parts of Eastern Europe. The report defines as high situations where between 10 per cent and 20 per cent of a country's tertiary educated adults are absent from the home country (ibid.: 19). While such general trends provide a useful backcloth, it is important to consider the specific situation facing individual countries. Chompalov (2000: 6) alludes to the importance of carefully contextualized studies given the diversity of factors influencing brain drain and the 'difficulties of trying to encompass separate migrant flows under a common theory'. The two sending countries identified in MOBEX2 can be distinguished in many ways, not least by their size, level of economic development, location and political status (in terms of the timing of accession to the EU).

In 2006, Bulgaria had a population of 7.6 million. According to the Bulgarian National Statistical Institute, 'Bulgaria's population is shrinking' as a result both of migration and declining fertility. The Institute suggests that 650 000 people (8 per cent of the population) emigrated in the period

immediately following transition (1989–96) and 180 000 via migration in
the period 1992–2001 (cited in Haug and Diehl, 2004b: 4). However, Haug
and Diehl (ibid.) contend that 'temporary migration is now the dominant
pattern' and half of Bulgarians in Germany remain for less than five years.

The Bulgarian Census (2001) remains a critical source of estimates of
migration potential. On the basis of this data, Haug and Diehl (ibid.: 10)
identify a number of groups including potential long-term migrants with
an intention to settle abroad (8.5 per cent) and a group of labour migrants
who intend to stay abroad for a year or more to work (6.8 per cent).
Together these groups of potential longer-stayers cover about 15 per cent
of the Bulgarian population. The Census also suggests that younger people
(aged 20–29) show a greater interest in longer-term migration, with nearly
a quarter of this group considering moving for work or to settle. Haug and
Diehl also single out academics as a specific category, which shows the
highest overall propensity to mobility: nearly a quarter of this group
expresses an interest in shorter stays abroad (ibid.: 11).

Rangelova and Vladimirova (2004: 8) talk of a 'massive external migration' commencing in 1989 and gradually stabilizing. According to them,
since 1989 the country has lost about 10 per cent of its total population.
The transition to a market economy has precipitated further migrations
mainly of 'young and active people' and also of 'scientists and highly
qualified experts' (ibid.). Rangelova and Vladimirova cite figures to suggest
that some 11.5 per cent of this latter group have left Bulgaria compared
with 15 per cent in Poland. Others present more cautious figures, suggesting that almost all of the initial first wave (post-1989) emigration involved
the return of Turkish-speaking Bulgarian nationals to Turkey (Bobeva,
1997; Gächter, 2002). If we exclude these, Gächter (2002: 18) reports flows
of less than 4000 Bulgarians per year. This rather contradictory and con-
fusing picture gives little real impression of the level of scientific mobility
and emigration.

Figures on the level of employment in science research are a little more
reliable, although it is very difficult to ascertain the nature of an employee's
role and the extent to which they are actively engaged in research (as opposed
to teaching, for example). Eurostat figures reveal that there were 15 853
research and development personnel in Bulgaria in 2005 – 10 172 in the gov-
ernmental sector, 3367 in the higher education sector and 2062 in business
(Gotzfried, 2007: 5). Slantcheva (2003) provides slightly different figures for
the academic sector, which suggest that Bulgarian universities employ about
50 000 members of faculty. This group comprises about 500 professors,
13 000 docents (habilitated lecturing staff) and 24 000 'assistants'.

Poland is a much bigger country than Bulgaria with a population of 38.1
million (making it the sixth largest EU Member State).[1] Okólski (2006: 48)

reports significant post-transition emigration flows and a 'great overrepresentation of emigrants with high quality human capital'. During this period, 'flows of highly skilled migrants were so great that they constituted approximately one fourth of the university graduates of all higher education institutions' (ibid.). However, in the period following the transformation the situation changed and flows included a decreasing proportion of highly skilled people. According to Okólski, the proportion of emigrants with a higher degree fell from 9 per cent in 1989 to 4 per cent in 2003 (ibid.).

More recent migration trends are a direct result of marked increases in undergraduate registrations (the educational breakthrough), coupled with economic crisis and deteriorating Polish labour markets. Okólski (2006) argues that these processes have encouraged increasingly selective out-migration especially to the UK: 25 per cent of flows to the UK since 1997 have been graduates, compared with only 11 per cent of those going to Germany. He nevertheless concludes that this process 'does not have a mass character and its scale and significance are decisively incomparable to the phenomenon faced in the 1980s' (ibid.: 50). A study by Hryniewicz, Jalowiecki and Mync (1997: 45) in the early 1990s reported a loss of about 10 per cent of researchers from the eight largest research centres in Poland. With an eye on future trends, Kupiszewski (2002: 633) suggests that 'educated Poles consider emigration as a much less attractive option than working in Poland'. On this basis, he predicts no significant increase in outflows of highly skilled migrants post-accession, not least because of decreasing differentiation in incomes coupled with the non-pecuniary costs of migration and difficulties in adjusting.

To give an impression of the dimensions of scientific employment, Kicinger (2005: 13) reports that 56 495 researchers were employed in Poland in 2002. This includes 25 577 technical scientists, 17 675 natural scientists and 16 301 medical scientists. The majority (37 275) were employed in the university sector, a further 11 761 in R&D units, 4449 in the Polish Academy of Science and 3010 in business enterprises. She further reports that 32 054 candidates were registered for PhDs in Poland in 2003.

The following section reports on the perceptions and experiences of the MOBEX2 respondents in response to a series of questions about the volume of emigration. In the main, scientists felt unable to report on wider trends or statistics and talked about their own experiences. Although these individual responses cannot be said to be statistically reliable in any respect, they do give a closer impression of the potential impact of losses at the level of discipline, institution and group.

Bulgarian respondents generally reported very high rates of scientific emigration at all levels and disciplines. One of the key informants interviewed, for example, who is the Director of a Bulgarian Academy of Science research centre, reported a loss of 50 per cent of staff in the field of biochemistry and molecular biology during the transitional period (that is, post-1989). Concern about the situation in Bulgaria has led Boyko, a computer scientist working in industry in the UK, to do a little research on the volume of emigration in his field. According to the results of a series of Internet-based searches Boyko concludes: 'There is definite impact. More than 200 000 people with my specialty have left Bulgaria. Yes, it was between 100 and 200 000. I can't remember exactly now but it was a huge number for Bulgaria'.

The following examples are typical of a large number of responses and relate to the scientists' own perceptions and experiences.[2] Dessislava, a senior scientist in Bulgaria, explains how the overwhelming majority of her colleagues have left her institute either to go abroad or leave research:

> There were 60 scientists in the institute and the people of my generation, say 40–45, we are now only three or four. Most of my colleagues simply left: two left science completely, the others went somewhere else in another group in the States, in Canada. Yes, there is a brain drain, a lot of good people are leaving Bulgaria. With numbers I don't know, 98 per cent of the people who went did not come back according to my calculations, so among 400 people I know – four more or less of course, let's say 1 or 2 per cent returned.

Yulian, a senior physical scientist working in Bulgaria, estimates on the basis of his experience that 'eighty per cent of PhD students here go abroad'. Andrey, a post-doc in the UK, talks dramatically of the 'emptying' of Bulgaria: 'A lot of the people working in science with very good qualifications have just left the country. In some fields like molecular biology there are lots of positions in Western countries. Almost all the qualified people left. Bulgaria is empty now of this kind of people'.

Polish respondents also reported very high levels of emigration, although perhaps not quite as dramatic as their Bulgarian peers. Ania, a Polish doctoral researcher in the UK, recalls the situation at the end of her Masters degree: 'When I was doing my MSc I think our supervisor had ten people and I think seven are now abroad, which means only three people stayed in Poland'. Lech, a Polish post-doc in Germany, explains how high levels of circulation at post-doctoral level in his field are quite normal. However, it appears that only two of his peers were currently working in Poland:

> In protein crystallography it's very common that after PhD you go abroad for a post-doc for a few years and all of my friends from my department did it. When I started my PhD something like five PhD students became doctors and only one person is still working with my boss at the university. One guy he went to another department and the rest of the people they left: one of my friends is living in the US and she has no plans to go back. One guy spent four years in New York and went back to Poland and I'm here and my friend came here four years ago and she's not going back to Poland.

Bozena, a Polish doctoral researcher in biological sciences suggests that about 60 per cent of his peers left Poland after their Masters degree: 'In my year of studies there were maybe 25 people and I think 15 for sure went abroad, if not more'. Wanda, another doctoral researcher, describes similar levels of migration with about 75 per cent of his peers who progressed on to doctoral research moving abroad: 'Thirty people were studying biotechnology and 20 of those went on to do a PhD and 15 of those 20 did that abroad'.

Beata's experience encourages us to exercise caution in the interpretation of figures, however. Although many graduates went abroad to do their doctorates she reports that a significant proportion of these were in fact registered for their doctorates in Poland, mitigating the loss and increasing the potential for return: 'People do their PhDs mostly abroad but in cooperation with another university so they are actually going to do their defence in Poland'.

Our respondents generally conveyed a powerful impression of a very high level of outward mobility in their fields. Their ability to place this in the context of the number of people in their peer group or lab does indicate a potentially high local impact. Many of them talk of what seem like very high numbers of students leaving at postgraduate (that is, post-Masters) level. This observation echoes concerns expressed in the literature about what is increasingly referred to as a youth drain. In the Slovakian context, Baláž, Williams and Kollar (2004) combine a range of data sources and methods including intention surveys, expert opinions and a comparison of labour markets and educational statistics to estimate the scale of youth brain drain. On the basis of their findings, they predict 'striking annual average losses of around 14,000' with more conservative estimates amounting to over 7000 graduates per annum (ibid.: 4). According to the authors, this rate of loss in the Slovakian context can generate substantial 'direct production losses' because 'graduate or youthful skilled migration' implies the loss of workers who 'generate considerably higher output than even those who have completed secondary education' (ibid.: 23).

The Demographic Consequences of Migration

On a general level, serious concerns have been expressed about the twin effects of selective out-migration of younger citizens coupled with declining fertility rates in Central and Eastern Europe. Bulgaria has one of the lowest fertility rates and highest proportion of retired people in Europe (Gächter, 2002; Ghodsee, 2002; Haug, 2005). Dimiter Dimitrov, Deputy Minister of Labour and Social Policy in Bulgaria reportedly stated that by 2050 around 38 to 40 per cent of the population would be of non-working age (Social Rights Bulgaria, 2007). Together these processes contribute to concerns about an ageing population and demographic decline. In the Polish context, Kicinger (2005: 45) reports low and declining fertility rates: the fertility rate in 2003 was 1.22, the lowest for 50 years. According to Iglicka (2003: 5) 'all scenarios lead inescapably to . . . an acceleration of population ageing [in the CECs]'.

Rangelova and Vladimirova (2004: 9) argue that 'the most important factor which influences migrant behaviour is age, followed by educational level'. The combination of depopulation through migration with the growing ageing of the population and extremely low fertility rates (exacerbated by selective out-migration) has led to a 'continuing deterioration of the demographic situation in Bulgaria, which now ranks amongst the top ten countries in the world in terms of the proportion of the population aged 60 and over' (ibid.: 27). These broader demographic trends have a specific manifestation in the scientific sector. Chompalov (2000: 2) expresses concern that 'several waves of brain drain have altered the age structure of R&D manpower in Bulgaria'.

In addition to general perceptions of fairly large-scale, ongoing, out-migration, respondents commonly spoke of the relationship between migration and demographic imbalance in scientific labour markets. Dessislava reflects on the absence of scientists in her age group (that is, 40–45 years old). Other respondents referred to the existence of a generation gap or, as Pepka calls it, a 'big hole': 'I think that there is a big hole between the young people and the older people, a hole not only in interests but also in years; there is a group around 30 and a group who are about 60 and between there is a big gap'. Valentina similarly refers to a deficit in the in-between generation: 'Now we have students and professors and the in-between people are somewhere else'.

Roumen, a senior scientist in Bulgaria, suggests that the demographic problems in science are not directly connected to scientific recruitment in the UK but reflect a broader trend affecting many Eastern European countries (and presumably linked to the decline in funding and relative attractiveness of positions in science):

> This is a general problem, it isn't down to the UK. It is a characteristic of Eastern bloc countries. There is a generation gap, a strong older generation, which is now virtually dying out or leaving science or going into retirement. In any case they will vanish and these are the well-known people dedicated to science. Science is strongly decimated now. In five to seven years they will vanish and then there is almost no one. The young generation is pretty unknown, those who were the brightest, the smartest, went abroad.

Svetlana, a Bulgarian lecturer in the UK makes a very similar point to Roumen: both make reference to the quality issue, suggesting that the brightest scientists left. Svetlana, however, indicates that many of those who stayed did so mainly for family reasons:

> A lot of people have left, that is really a problem. The institute where I used to work they have PhD students and the moment they finish their PhDs they're gone and there is a complete gap until you come to the professorial level, which is maybe five years away from retirement and nothing in between. It is devastating. Most of the colleagues from my generation who I worked with have left. Very few stayed. Those I worked with were professionally very successful. For people working there it was absolutely no problem to find a position abroad and they did. The people who stayed there, it was mainly through family considerations.

Andrey, a senior research fellow in the UK, makes the obvious link between demography and seniority, concluding that the only younger people that remain in key disciplines are effectively technicians: 'Initially they practised to keep their positions [when they left] but in such institutions like molecular biology or nuclear physics or chemistry they have only technical assistance and all the scientists are abroad'. Vladimir refers to the losses of the 'middle generation' of scientists and its impact on scientific quality in Bulgaria:

> I'd say today it's very difficult to say Bulgaria is good at something because a lot of people who used to be professors are not there any more. They've left the country . . . now there is a gap in ages, there are very old professors who are unable or unwilling to go abroad and very young students and postgraduates and graduate students who just started now so the middle generation of 30- and 40-year-olds found their way to other countries.

It is perhaps interesting to note that the comments made above by Bulgarian respondents included two returnees – Dessislava and Roumen. Both of these are senior scientists and are aged 41 and 60 respectively. Andrey, Vladimir and Svetlana are UK-based researchers and once again all aged over 41. This would suggest that the same view is held in both locations and that this group is talking very much about their own generation of researchers. There was less concern expressed about a generation gap in the interviews with Polish scientists, although Lech makes a similar observation, linking the generation gap with the paucity and quality of positions:

> It's a big disaster. Already it's maybe not a very big problem but a problem because we have a lot of PhD students and a lot of professors and nothing in-between. At the time when I finished my PhD, 25 people did PhD studies with me and more or less at the same time we finished and the university had only one-year contracts.

Reference to this generation gap draws attention not so much to research stars but to research potential and particularly the mid-career positions held by scientists in their late 30s and 40s.

Respondents' observations are largely supported by available data, which indicate a significant ageing of the Bulgarian scientific population. Bulgaria has one of the largest proportions of ageing scientists in Europe, with nearly half of all scientists and engineers aged between 45 and 64 (Wilén, 2006: 3). Slantcheva (2003: 448) provides a further breakdown: of habilitated (senior) staff, 42 per cent of docents are above 55 years of age. Of professors, 21 per cent are between the ages of 55 and 59 and 69 per cent are aged over 60. Ninety-one per cent of professors are aged 55 and over. Georgieva (2004: 365) reproduces similar figures, arguing that 73 per cent of professors in Bulgaria are aged over 60 and 47 per cent over retirement age. At the other end of the spectrum, Velev (2002: 2) reports that only 14.4 per cent of academic staff are aged 35 and under, reflecting the 'catastrophic' widening of the generation gap in Bulgarian scientific employment. A decision to extend the retirement age by five years has, according to Velev, exacerbated the problem.

Dabrowa-Szefler (2004: 44) makes a similar observation in relation to the Polish context, demonstrating a growth both in the population of researchers aged 50 to 59 and 60 and above, but also in younger, early-career (especially doctoral) researchers. However, it is unclear from Dabrowa-Szefler's analysis that this reflects out-migration as Chompalov (2000) suggests. The demographic ageing of the Polish scientific population would seem to reflect the marked decline in new positions, employment opportunities and career prospects for mid-career researchers and position-blocking by established staff. In that context, emigration needs to be seen as the effect of labour market forces and not the cause of them – a point we return to in Chapter 8.

In addition to this, the concern expressed in much of the literature about a growing youth drain was also echoed in the interviews. Although MOBEX2 focused on mobility at doctoral level upwards, the work with respondents tracked mobility back to their undergraduate experience and demonstrated a close relationship between mobility at undergraduate level – or earlier – and subsequent migration and location decisions. For that reason it is perhaps worth addressing the phenomenon of undergraduate mobility here, not least because mobility at this level is predicted to increase most as a result of accession to the EU.

Youth Drain

Krieger's (2004: 7) analysis of migration intention in the new Member States predicts a 'youth drain of nearly 10% in the next five years for

Bulgaria and Romania as well as a brain drain and an increasing feminization of migration'. Haug and Diehl's (2004a) analysis of figures from the German State Ministry of Education also show a tenfold increase in the number of Bulgarian undergraduates in Germany in the period from 1993–2002 – with 2771 registrations in 2002 alone – suggesting a marked increase in undergraduate mobility. Okólski (2006: 53) argues that 'as far as the mobility of scientific workers is concerned, the key issue is migration of students. The recruitment of students is one of the most obvious ways to "win brains over" '. Okólski bases this conclusion on the evidence of far greater migration potential amongst students, 'due to age, being prone to risk, language and cultural skills' (ibid.) and cites survey findings of migration intentions, which suggest that some 70 per cent of university students in the top ten institutions were keen to get a job in another EU state. Okólski is not simply interested in the demographic consequences of this form of youth drain but also the implications in terms of human capital development, as he argues that most of these students are more interested in seeking employment abroad in order to supplement their income: 'the massive post-accession mobility of university students focused on job seeking abroad and not improving their qualifications or acquiring knowledge abroad' (ibid.: 54). According to his data, the vast majority (80–90 per cent) of undergraduate migrants are hired in posts that need no professional qualifications. The main concern here then is the longer-term effect in terms of the deskilling of mobile graduates with implications for the value of those who do return.

As with brain drain data, the figures on youth drain remain contentious and open to interpretation. Kicinger (2005), for example, urges some caution, suggesting that recent general data on Polish emigration do not lend support to the idea of a youth drain or indeed to the increasing feminization of migrants. Iglicka (2000: 64) similarly notes a 'steady growth in the average age of Polish migrants' in the 1990s, together with a 'dominance of individuals with low levels of education', concluding that 'there were no signs of brain drain in the 1990s, although some 15% of scientists had already left in the 1980s'.

The prevalence of undergraduate mobility emerged in some of the interviews with our respondents. Asked whether the predictions of an increase in undergraduate mobility might be exaggerated, Kiril, a Bulgarian doctoral researcher in the UK, replied 'No, I am not surprised by it knowing how Bulgaria is and how difficult it is to live there in any way, shape or form that can be considered comfortable in comparison to Western European countries'. Kiril argued that this form of movement – of younger undergraduate students – did constitute an important element of the brain drain. For him, the issue was not solely about loss of investment in human capital but also the *potential* loss of contribution. He remains optimistic that recovery will take place in Bulgaria but feels that this youth drain will inevitably slow progress down: 'I would characterize undergraduate mobility as brain drain . . . although Bulgaria hadn't invested much, if they stayed home I think they would have contributed valuably . . . eventually Bulgaria will be alright but it will take two or three times as long because all the people are leaving'.

Violeta, a post-doc, expresses similar concerns about the number of younger people leaving Bulgaria: 'If we don't come back then the situation in Bulgaria will never be better because all the young people are abroad'. Ludwika, a Polish doctoral researcher based in Germany, observes what she sees as an increase in the number of younger Poles moving abroad to study at undergraduate level: 'I think at the moment there are more and more students going abroad to study and I don't know how many of them will stay abroad but I think now it's easier to be accepted for some studies abroad and to get some scholarship or something'.

Two of the respondents interviewed in Poland – Stanislaw and Tomasz respectively – refer to an acceleration in the level of student mobility in recent years in response to cheaper travel and improved opportunities to study abroad: 'I think the very big problem is that most of the really brilliant young people are going abroad and staying permanently'. It is this trend that is perhaps most influenced by accession, especially in the UK, as Poles and Bulgarians are no longer required to pay overseas student fees (Aston, 2004).

This section has summarized some of the literature concerning the volume and scale of highly skilled migration from Poland and Bulgaria into the UK and Germany. Available secondary data on levels of migration and the propensity to migrate is highly unreliable and, in many cases, misleading and contradictory.

On the basis of available data, the sending countries appear to have lost significant numbers of highly skilled citizens and scientists in particular, since the 1990s. However, much of this loss occurred during the initial transition period and losses appear to have levelled off since then. A significant proportion of these losses, however, were connected to the sudden and marked decline in scientific positions, with many scientists moving to other sectors as well as abroad.

The experiences of our respondents would tend to suggest that laboratories and departments in the sending countries have experienced a significant loss of scientific *potential* (as much as established scientists) and that the mid-career generation is often thin on the ground, with important implications for the training of researchers in future. There is also a sense that migration is selective in its effects, resulting in the losses of many high-quality and enthusiastic researchers often in specific disciplines and sub-disciplines.

Just as 'losses' via migration need to be seen alongside within country 'losses' to other sectors, it is also important to consider the demographic trends in the countries concerned. Both Poland and Bulgaria have ageing scientific labour forces and very low and declining levels of fertility. These demographic challenges pose serious problems for the countries concerned. Whilst the 'evidence' on scientific 'brain drain' is unclear and contentious, the loss of potential through increasing emigration of young people at or before undergraduate level is of grave concern.

II PATTERNS OF SCIENTIFIC MOBILITY

The traditional debate around brain drain presumes fairly simple, unilateral and semi-permanent geographical moves. This characterization attributes considerable symbolic importance to return, which is itself often caricatured as part of a two-stage, bilateral process, shaping knowledge transfer in a fairly direct fashion. There is growing recognition that return typologies used in earlier studies of migration are not flexible enough to capture modern mobility trajectories: 'in a transnational era, movement is better described as continuous rather than completed' (Ley and Kobayashi, 2005: 111). Iglicka (2000) observes an incomparable growth in levels of shuttle or pendular migrations from Poland since the 1990s. For Iglicka, shuttle migrations are the moves by people who never went abroad for periods of more than three months. In discussing Polish migration behaviour since transition, she notes that shuttle migration constitutes the largest migration behaviour amongst Poles, with 35 per cent of her sample – many of whom were petty traders – reporting this form of mobility (ibid.: 70). Boswell (2005: 3) also notes the growth of this type of mobility and its usage as 'a household strategy for supplementing the income of families at home'. With specific reference to trends amongst the more highly skilled, Smeby and Trondal (2005) refer to the growth in what they call 'professional journeys' related to conferences, guest lecturing, study and research visits, evaluation work and research collaboration. In a similar vein, Scott (2006: 1119) identifies the growth in hypermobility amongst nomadic young professionals or 'emigration as walk-about . . . initially at least, professional career path migration tends to be temporary . . . and appears to be getting shorter in length'.

Rangelova and Vladimirova's (2004) work on migration potential – drawing on the data from the International Organization for Migration (IOM) – lends further support to the idea that patterns of mobility are changing and that migration from Eastern Europe, and Bulgaria specifically, is increasingly short term. Although 43 per cent of young people and 23 per cent of graduates in the IOM survey were described as potential migrants, only 6 per cent of all respondents aged 18–60 expressed firm plans to resettle (ibid.: 15). Thirty-one per cent preferred to work abroad for a couple of years and 35 per cent for only a couple of months (ibid.). Echoing the language used by Smeby and Trondal (2005), Rangelova and Vladimirova's (ibid.: 18) analysis leads them to talk of the importance of 'dynamic visits' to access business and professional opportunities. Gächter (2002: 10) similarly reports high rates of return and 'substantial coming and going' in both the Polish and the Bulgarian context. The marked increase in opportunities for cheap travel post-accession undoubtedly supports this trend (Ferro, 2006).

The previous chapter noted the shift in emphasis in recent years to the *circulationist paradigm* in an attempt to capture the complexity of flows and their multidirectional quality, particularly in the context of East–West, intra-European migration. There is also a tendency in migration research to focus on the migration decision – or what Baláž and colleagues (2004: 7) describe as 'discrete individual choices' – and the motivational factors shaping whether and where to move in relative isolation from the issue of length of stay. Scientists, particularly in the natural sciences, are on the move all the time in one way or another. This kind of mobility is a fluid and dynamic process, reflecting a succession of decisions that are constantly under review rather than a one-time event. This chapter considers the issues of circulation, return and temporality in the context of our sample of Polish and Bulgarian scientists and explores the relevance of length of stay to an understanding of the impact of scientific migration. It opens with a general overview of the kinds of mobility experienced by our sample, describing the frequency and duration of moves (including returns). For the purposes of this study, the sample comprised Bulgarian and Polish scientists who had spent at least three months at some point in time – and at doctoral level or above – in the UK or Germany.[3] The sample of returnees had been back in their own country for at least three months at the time of interview.[4] Although this single mobility episode was sufficient to qualify them to take part in our study, the majority of the respondents had made other moves often before their PhDs or to other areas outside of the EU. Many had made at least one return and several had experienced a combination of longer and shorter stays. To illustrate the diversity and complexity of moves, the chapter considers in more detail the experiences of two groups of 'short-' and 'long-' stayers.

Table 2.1   Summary of respondents' mobility patterns

Single Outward Move	Single Outward with Return	Repeat Mover – No Return	Repeat Mover – with Returns	Plans to Leave – No Moves Yet
20	3	9	53	4
22%	3%	10%	60%	4%

Sample Trends: Circulation, Return and Length of Stay

Table 2.1 simply shows that only 20 of our sample fell into the single outward move category. Of these, 13 were women and 11 were early career researchers and/or doctoral candidates. By far the largest group (60 per cent) of interviewees were people who had moved repeatedly and whose trajectories often included periods of return to the country of origin.

The majority of our sample can be characterized as repeat movers or circulators (having made more than one international move). Analysis of the host country interviews – which excludes the country of origin (COO) returnees[5] who had by definition made more than one move – showed a high rate of circulation: 68 per cent were repeat movers. Although there were no obvious differences by nationality, women were less likely to be repeat movers: 21 of the 49 repeat movers in the host sample were women (43 per cent of the total sample) and 28 were men (57 per cent of the total sample). The majority of repeat movers (in the host sample) had experienced a stint back home: 35 of the 44 repeat movers had returned at some point. The remainder had spent time in another or other countries. Most of these repeat movers (79 per cent) had moved within Europe only (we are, however, including the ex-Soviet bloc as Europe for this purpose).

Table 2.2 shows the mobility patterns of respondents according to their self-identified career stage. This shows that current doctoral candidates were most likely to have made a single outward move at the point of interview. Twenty-three per cent of intermediate-level researchers had made more than one international move without returning to their country of origin. Although the sample of senior researchers was smaller in the host countries (n = 10), 80 per cent of those had returned at some stage to their COO.

The overwhelming majority of our respondents had experienced return. If we exclude the COO returnee sample, we have 64 respondents (31 women and 33 men). Over two-thirds of these (69 per cent) had returned at some point (Table 2.3).

Women in our sample were less likely than men to return. Analysis of host country interviews (n = 64) only found that 18 of the 31 women we

Table 2.2   Host country respondents' mobility patterns by career stage

Career Stage	Single Outward Move %	Repeat Mover – No Return %	Repeat Mover – with Returns %	Total %	Total
Doctoral candidate (equivalent)	46	4	50	100	24
Intermediate	27	23	50	100	30
Senior	10	10	80	100	10

Table 2.3   Host country respondents' mobility patterns by gender

Gender	Single Outward Move %	Repeat Mover – No Return %	Repeat Mover – with Returns %	Total %	Total
Female	42	13	45	100	31
Male	21	15	64	100	33

Table 2.4   Mobility patterns of COO returnees

Country Based	Single EU Move and Return	Repeat Mover and Return to COO	Non-Mover
In Bulgaria	1	9	1
In Poland	2	9	3

interviewed had returned at some point (58 per cent) compared with 26 of the 33 men (79 per cent).

Like their contemporaries interviewed abroad, as Table 2.4 shows, most respondents in the COO sample exhibited repeat mobility. A minority of cases could be characterized as boomerang movers, involving a single move followed by a return: only one Bulgarian and two Polish interviewees fell into this category. Two of these cases were making efforts to go abroad again, thus highlighting the ongoing nature of mobility. In practice, once mobile most scientists become repeat movers.

The Geography of Moves

This study looked at new dimensions of East–West mobility, bearing in mind that skilled workers usually move to industrialized nations

(Docquier and Marfouk, 2004). A related aim was to explore how competitive European host countries are to scientists when compared with the pull of the US and elsewhere internationally. The European Commission (2007: 34) highlights South-East Asia as the 'new major player' in tertiary education and goes on to argue that 'the US will remain highly dependent on the inflow of large numbers of foreign-born, highly-skilled immigrants' (ibid.: 35). Likewise, a recent OECD paper (Katseli et al., 2006b) reports that skills shortages are already becoming apparent in China and India and suggests that skilled European workers will be amongst the pool that relocates there. It is therefore important to look at the migration trajectories of scientists to understand whether scientists are being retained in the EU.

Lowell, Findlay and Stewart (2004: 7) note the increase in skilled migrants to the US, Canada, Australia and Western Europe and they draw a distinction between permanent settlers and a stream of circulators. The interviewees from our study exhibited a strong orientation towards European locations – for both practical and cultural considerations – and this is borne out in their geographic trajectories. Contrary to concerns about floods out of Europe, our sample had limited experience in the US:[6] only eight respondents (9 per cent) had visited the US during their studies and only nine (10 per cent) had visited during their employment. Only one researcher had worked in Japan. A difference between the COO and host country interviews is apparent here: 14 per cent of researchers in the host country had worked or studied outside Europe, whilst the proportion within the COO sample was far higher (64 per cent).

Analysing the number of foreign countries that respondents had worked or studied in, differences are again identifiable between the sample of returnees in the COO and the host country interviewees.[7] Whereas 45 per cent of respondents in the host country had only worked or studied in one country outside their home country, as demonstrated in Table 2.5, this was only the case for 24 per cent of COO returnees (see Table 2.6). Returnees in the country of origin were more likely to have spread their mobility and visited three countries than the respondents in the host country. This indicates that those scientists based in the home country have more varied geographic mobility. There were no strong patterns in the number of countries visited or the order in which moves were made between countries. Russia and Germany feature in succession in a number of trajectories (but less so in more recent moves). Switzerland also features heavily: this can partially be explained by the nature of the scientific work undertaken, with many of our sample needing access to large-scale physics resources in either Dubna or Geneva.

Table 2.5   Foreign countries worked/studied in by host country sample

	One Country	Two Countries	Three Countries	Four Countries
Cases:	29	23	11	1
%	45	36	17	2

Table 2.6   Foreign countries worked/studied in by COO returnee sample

	One Country	Two Countries	Three Countries	Four Countries	Five Countries
Cases:	5	5	9	1	1
%	24	24	43	5	5

Table 2.7   Mobility pattern of respondents by total length of time spent abroad

Total Length of Time Abroad	Single EU Move	Single EU Move and Return	Repeat Mover (No Return to COO)	Repeat Mover and Return to COO	Non-mover	%
0 prospective leaver	0	0	0	0	4	4
1–6 months	2	0	0	2	0	4
7–12 months	1	1	0	3	0	6
13–24 months	2	1	0	7	0	11
25–36 months	3	1	0	8	0	13
37–48 months	3	0	0	5	0	9
Between 4 and 8 years	3	0	6	13	0	25
Longer than 8 years	6	0	3	15	0	27

The Temporality of Moves: Length of Stay

The findings above indicate a high rate of circulation and return amongst our sample. The next section explores the duration of moves. Table 2.7 shows the total time spent abroad by mobility pattern. Over half (52 per cent) of our sample had spent over four years working abroad at the time of interview, with over a quarter spending over eight years abroad in total. The three boomerang movers who had experienced a single episode of mobility before return had all done so within three years. The nine repeat

Table 2.8   Total length of time spent abroad by stage for repeat movers with return/s

Total Length of Time Abroad	Early Career	Intermediate	Senior
0 months (prospective leaver)	0	0	0
1–6 months	1	1	0
7–12 months	2	0	1
13–24 months	5	2	0
25–36 months	4	3	1
37–48 months	3	2	0
Between 4 and 8 years	2	7	4
Longer than 8 years	0	5	10
Total	17	20	16

Table 2.9   Time abroad current visit

Length of Current Visit	Total	%
1–6 months	4	6
7–12 months	7	11
13–24 months	9	14
25–36 months	9	14
37–48 months	5	8
Between 4 and 8 years	15	23
Longer than 8 years	15	23

movers who had not returned to their COO to work or study had all been abroad for longer than four years.

The majority of the sample (n = 53) were repeat movers who had returned, at some stage, to their home country. Table 2.8 provides detail on the length of stays for this group by their stage of research and shows that more senior researchers had generally spent longer abroad in total (which is an expected trend and correlates to length of career).

If we go on to consider the duration of the most recent mobility 'episode', the sample also shows a skew in the direction of longer stays (Table 2.9).

It is tempting to conclude from these broad trends that East–West moves can be characterized in terms of relatively long stays or settlement. Forty-six per cent of the host country sample had been abroad for more than four years at the point of their interview. More detailed analysis of the migration histories of the sample reveals the level of mobility and the length of stays at different career stages.

Mobility by Career Stage

In total, 39 respondents had spent some time abroad during their undergraduate or Masters degree.[8] For some, this involved spending the whole
undergraduate period abroad. This was not uncommon before the transition in Eastern Europe where long stays of over 48 months often
reflected undergraduate study in Russia or East Germany. In other cases,
and more commonly in recent years, respondents spent shorter periods of
between 3 and 12 months abroad as part of an undergraduate exchange
programme.

Twenty-one of the COO sample had been abroad: six of these had been
abroad during their first and/or Masters degree, ten had been abroad during
their doctorate, and 15 (71 per cent) had been abroad during their professional career. This includes two researchers who had been mobile at all
three stages. Only one respondent in the COO had been mobile during their
first degree and had not subsequently moved again. Of the ten respondents
who had been mobile during their doctorate, five had made a subsequent
move during their career.

In the host sample, a large number of respondents either remained in
or returned to the same host country after this undergraduate experience
(n = 17). This group will be interesting to observe in future years as trends
might be expected to change significantly, with accession resulting in lower
student fees and (potentially at least) greater access to forms of student
finance.[9] At the time of our research very few Bulgarians were able to afford
the kind of tuition fees charged in the UK at undergraduate or doctoral
level. Only 2 of the 17 cases noted above involved Bulgarians staying on for
doctorates. The current German regime – which is also set to change – does
not involve fees and has thus been more attractive. There was evidence that
Polish scientists were beginning to undertake doctorates in the UK
although Research Council rules still limit the payment of maintenance
scholarships to EU nationals (again, this is also subject to change). This situation is likely to have shaped our sample, thus resulting in the higher proportion of Polish doctorates in the German sample and more post-docs in
the UK sample.

Levels of circulation increase at doctoral level. In total, 53 (82 per cent)
of the 64 researchers interviewed in the host countries had been abroad
during their doctoral studies. In 22 cases, this was their first period of
mobility. Once again some quite long stays were evident, often involving
the duration of a PhD in Russia (four to five years) or, more commonly
in recent years, in another EU Member State. The majority of respondents who moved during their PhDs did so for the full duration. Quite a
number of others, however, spent shorter periods abroad, often for three

to six months. The majority of respondents who moved at doctoral level experienced just one or two distinct episodes, usually returning to the same host country. Just over half (n = 26) of the 50 respondents who had experienced mobility at doctoral level had returned home at some point either before, during or after their doctorate (excluding the COO sample).

Post-doctoral stays were more diverse in terms of length, frequency and location. The host sample included only eight people who had not moved earlier in their career (people for whom mobility commenced at a more senior level). If we consider the location of moves, around 15 of the host sample who had moved at doctoral level had moved to a new location at senior level compared with ten who remained at or returned to the country where they did their doctoral research.

Post-doctoral stays in the host sample vary enormously in terms of duration. Some are very short at least in the earlier stages, often culminating in or followed by longer stays. The COO returnee sample showed a strong prevalence of circulators or frequent movers. If we exclude doctoral candidates, all of the Bulgarian and the majority of Polish returnees fall into this category. Many exhibited a kind of shuttle or pendular mobility, spending from one to three or six months abroad at regular intervals. In some cases this was interspersed with longer stays of a year or more. A quarter (n = 16) of the host country interviewees had been abroad during their first degree and/or Masters, during their doctorate and then later on in their career. This subset became mobile in the early stages of their training and show evidence of the trend for continuation into mobile careers.

The following section takes a closer look at two distinct sub-samples in order to explore migration behaviour in more depth: first, it considers the sample of returnee respondents interviewed in Bulgaria and Poland; and second, a group of long-stayers from the host sample.

Circulators in the Returnee Sample

Nearly 50 per cent of the Polish and Bulgarian returnee sample had experienced at least five stints abroad. Seven of these had not moved at undergraduate or doctoral level, with mobility commencing at a more senior stage. Some examples from this group are presented in Figure 2.1 to give a flavour of the location and duration of these stays.

Scientists were found to make shuttle visits where the opportunity presented itself. Dessislava repeatedly visited Italy because she felt that working conditions in Bulgaria had worsened, she wanted to engage more in the international science community and lastly she viewed it as an

Dessislava (Bulgarian 41–60)
No moves at undergraduate or
  doctoral level
1993 12-month fellowship in Italy
Returned for 2 years
1996–99 4 annual 6-month stays in
  Italy as 'invited lecturer'
Thereafter repeat returns
1999 3-month fellowship in France
2000 12-month fellowship in Germany
2003 3-month fellowship in Germany

Total: 45 months abroad

Roumen (Bulgarian 41–60)
Entire undergraduate/Masters degree in
  Russia (4 years) (1960s)
Returned
1972 Entire PhD and teaching position
  in East Germany (7 years)
Returned to Bulgaria
1984 2-year fellowship in Germany
1991 present 5–6 months per year in Germany
Additional short stays in Switzerland
  and the States

Total: 20 years abroad

Yulian (Bulgarian 41–60)[a]
No moves at early career level (but visits
  to other Eastern European countries)
1983 5-month fellowship in the Netherlands
Return
1995 6-month fellowship in France
Return
1997 6-month fellowship in France (as above)
Return
1998 3-month guest professorship in Canada
Return
1998 10-month guest professorship in Japan
Return
1999 4-month fellowship in France (as above)
Returned to Bulgaria

Total: 34 months abroad

Tomasz (Polish 41–60)
1994 and 1995 2 3-month TEMPUS stays
  in the UK (doctoral level)
Returned from PhD
1995 12-month fellowship in Brazil
Returned
2000 3-month fellowship in Sweden
Returned
2001 12-month fellowship in UK
(different institution from above)
Brief return
2002 12-month fellowship in Germany
Returned

Total: 45 months abroad

Bronislaw (Polish 60+)
1968 48 months in Russia (undergraduate
  degree)
Returned for PhD
1973 10-month fellowship France
Return
1978 18-month fellowship Russia
Return
1980 20-month fellowship Germany
Return
1984–95 4 separate stays in Germany of
  3 months and 2 of 5 months' duration
  with repeat returns

Total: 10 years abroad

Agniezka (Polish 41–60)
1992 3-month fellowship in Germany
Return
1992 6 month fellowship in Brazil
Cut short 2-year contract to return
1994–2004 10 annual 3-month stays in
  Germany (as above) with repeat
  returns

Total: 39 months abroad

Note: a. Although he had not spent time in the UK or Germany, Yulian was interviewed in his capacity as a university dean.

Figure 2.1 Shuttle mobility patterns in the returnee samples

opportunity to augment her salary. Scientists often return repeatedly to the same place when they have teaching or research links, they need to access specialist infrastructure or to conduct experiments. This group of shuttle movers is interesting for a number of reasons. First, it illustrates the diversity of situations with some moving for longer periods and to disparate locations, whilst others establish a clear and strong link to a particular institution and make more or less annual stays there for many years. The majority of cases of repeated shuttle migration involve German institutions and often a particular funding body (such as the DAAD [German Academic Exchange Service] or the Von Humboldt scheme). In Agnieszka's case, regular funding to support bilateral cooperation between her group and universities in Germany shaped her migration trajectory. Agnieszka had worked at the Polish Academy of Science for 24 years and first moved in 1992, for three months to Germany. She then took up a fellowship in South America but returned six months into the two-year contract as she was concerned she may lose her position in Poland. In 1994 she was awarded bilateral funding from a university in Germany to build her own research group and began to make repeated visits to that institution. When this finished she received funding from the DAAD to support the mobility of staff and students from her group to another German university.

The motivational factors shaping decisions about length of stay and the specific value attached to shuttle moves on the part of scientists in the sending regions is discussed in more detail in the following chapter.

Longer Stays and Settlement

The pattern of shorter stays among the returnee circulators, as seen above, can be usefully compared with those people who appear, superficially at least, to be settled in the host or returning country. It is often assumed that short stays or circulation bring positive implications for sending countries despite the risk that this kind of experience and the opportunities it generates might precipitate a longer or more permanent stay for some people. The corollary to this, of course, is the association of longer mobility episodes with less positive outcomes and greater potential losses to the sending region. The following section therefore analyses the migration patterns of the group of long-stayers. If we select the cohort of respondents whose most recent mobility episode has resulted in an extended stay of over eight years (n = 15) we get some interesting and highly varied situations, as depicted in Figure 2.2. Six of these cases involve stays in one country alone and three of the respondents based in Germany have remained there following completion of doctoral stays in Russia. The rest have made a variety of moves, with Marek and Maciej displaying the kind of shuttle moves identified in the returnee sample (see above) for some years before securing a permanent position abroad.

Perhaps unsurprisingly the most striking commonality is the issue of permanency. The majority of this group (n = 10) have permanent positions and all but one of those who remain on a fixed-term contract is relatively young. With only one exception (Piotr), the group had occupied a series of insecure post-doctoral positions prior to permanency. During this time the majority experienced a degree of 'within country' mobility between institutions and labs. In Teresa's case, for example, the lack of ongoing international circulation does not imply a lack of mobility since she has moved on three occasions between three highly prestigious and international research groups in the UK's golden triangle. Similarly, Maciej has held positions in six different institutes during his time in Germany.

In practice many of these people, despite their extended length of stay, do not describe themselves – or give the impression – as having settled. Ivanka, summarized in Figure 2.2 below, is a professional circulator, skipping between centres of excellence across three countries and never returning. She describes her reasons for this: 'If you want to be a research scientist it is part of your training to move around. There are no two ways about that'. Ivanka says that she sacrificed having family in order to achieve this and describes her motives as 'purely scientific'. Two key factors shape her decision about length of stay: (1) the fact that she now has a permanent position; and (2) the ability to work effectively in science through accessing 'resources and the environment that allow me to do my best with my skills . . . if it happens to be Britain, then so be it'. She expressed a strong interest in return but only if this latter condition could be met – and she doubted that in the immediate future.

The following two examples are almost a mirror image to the kind of shuttle moves that have been described above. Maciej is a senior Polish scientist who has lived in Germany with his wife and children for many years, holding positions at five different institutions. Although he has been out of Poland for the last 18 years, he still holds a permanent position and spends three months of every year there. He also holds a permanent position in Germany. Maciej's description of his mobility and career highlights the importance of seeing migration as an incremental and reflexive process. It is clear that he did not decide at any point to make a permanent move: rather, it just happened that way. Furthermore, he does not consider himself to have left Poland and settled in Germany. Talking of his migration history, Maciej says he 'got a kind of fellowship and I went every two or three months for the next several years and I

Teresa
Polish female aged 31–40
24 months at undergraduate level (UK)
Returned home to take examinations
36 months PhD (UK)
48 months post-doc (UK)

Total: 9 years abroad

Marek
Polish male aged 41–60
1983–89 4 short visits to UK including
    1 stay of 12 months
1989 16 years in UK (post-doc then
    permanent)

Total: 17 years abroad

Renata
Polish female aged 41–60
1996 UK 9 years (post-doc then
    permanent)

Total: 9 years abroad

Justyna
Polish female aged 41–60
1970s worked in UK (accompanying
    husband)
36 months UK (PhD)
12 months Australia (post-doc)
6 years UK (post-docs then permanent)

Total: 35 years abroad

Piotr
Polish male aged 41–60
12 months MA and 36 months (PhD)
    in US
Returned for 18 months
12 months Switzerland
No return
36 months US
No return
11 years UK (permanent)

Total: 19 years abroad

Ivanka
Bulgarian female aged 41–60
1987 1 year in Germany (prior to PhD)
7 years in Canada (PhD and post-doc)
14 years in UK (post-doc then
    permanent)
No returns

Total: 22 years abroad

Svetlana
Bulgarian female aged 41–60
36 months (US for PhD)
1989 48 months return to Bulgaria
14 years in the UK (post-doc then
    permanent)

Total: 21 years abroad

Magdalena
Bulgarian female aged 31–40
2 months and 6 weeks in Germany
    during Masters
Returned
8 years in UK (PhD then post-doc)

Total: 8 years abroad

Boyko
Bulgarian male aged 31–40
5 years in Spain (MA/PhD)
12 months Austria
36 months UK (post-doc then
    permanent)

Total: 9 years abroad

Rumiana
Bulgarian female aged 41–60
10 years working (accompanying
    husband) in UK
36 months PhD in UK
7 years (post-doc) in UK
(No returns)

Total: 20 years abroad

Antoni
Polish male aged 41–60
1981 36 months Russia (PhD)
1986 Returned to prepare thesis
1993 Returned to Poland for 3 years for
 habilitation
24 months in Germany (post-doc)
Return
12 years Germany (permanent)

Total: 17 years abroad

Maciej
Polish male aged 41–60
1982 12 months Germany post-doc
6 years 'shuttle' moves between Poland
 and Germany
1988 18 years (permanent in industry
 then Professorship)
Total: 20 years abroad

Vasil
Bulgarian male aged 41–60
1977 12 months Russia (PhD)
Return
1985 1 year Germany
1 year return to Bulgaria
17 years Germany ('guest' professor
 then permanent)

Total: 19 years abroad

Figure 2.2   Mobility patterns of the 'long-stayers' sub-sample

worked there so in this way I could do my habilitation'. He then returned
to Poland. Asked whether leaving Poland again was an important decision, he replies:

> Well I would say I never left Poland. I'm a professor in the city all the time. I
> spend I would say about two months per year in Poland. I would say that my
> centre of gravity has moved 1000 km to the West but I never left Poland. My
> family went with me to Germany and it was always for one year, you know, and
> it was not a dramatic decision. It was simply 'the job is there, I'm going, I will
> work and we will see what happens'. Of course after I became a professor the
> situation has changed dramatically. I believe that we will come back to Poland
> after I retire.

Clearly securing a permanent position in Germany had a significant impact
on his perspective. Although he does not envisage leaving Germany to work
solely in Poland, Maciej is fiercely critical of the inference that his extended
stay is to the detriment of Poland:

> I came from the country and I give the chance to a lot of people to be engaged
> in international research. That's the reason I'm forming consortia here with
> sometimes 100 people to work together, so I've formed the German-Polish
> network on an element of technology. So I went to Germany but I counted only
> how much money I have now transferred to Poland and this was several million

euros, so if I am in Poland I would never attract so much money to come to Poland, so that is what people perhaps forget.

Maciej sees himself as effectively working *for* Poland – and science in general – from a temporary base in Germany. His case provides an example of the kind of migrant that Okólski (2006: 57) identifies: 'even when residing abroad, they can have a huge influence on scientific activities in Poland and contribute to the transfer of knowledge and technologies'.

Antoni presents a similar picture. He also lives with his wife (who does not work) and three older children in Germany. He describes his decision to move to Germany:

> It was not very difficult because before moving I already lived for a longer period in two countries. At that point I was not quitting my position in Warsaw. I didn't consider that I'm moving to Germany and spending the rest of my life in Germany, at this particular moment it's optimum to do this. I was, for a couple of years, holding my position in Warsaw but then also I moved here for a permanent position so I had two permanent positions.

Asked how this works in practice he refers to the increasing ability to work at a distance and remotely:

> I'm not very often there I have to say, I go for several months a year but I am permanently in contact and thanks to my activities in this experiment I somehow motivated people in this university to join this project and I'm more or less leading this group, it's possible even without being there very often . . . When you have a big collaboration you quite often meet not necessarily here but . . . we meet quite often on a regular basis and because of the modern communication and you can get the information by e-mail and so on so we don't have to be there to be actively involved in the research.

In other cases, scientists who have been out of the country for as many as 15 years cannot be described as having settled or made a decision not to return. This situation has to be viewed in the context of science careers in general and the extended pre-qualification period, which means that careerwise they are often still at a relatively early stage even if they are in their 30s and 40s (or older). Teresa is a case in point. She had lived in the UK for some nine years and at the time of interview was just commencing her second post-doc. At this point many scientists are still highly mobile. Lucjan is in a similar position. Although he has only recently taken a four-year post in the UK, he has spent 11 years outside his home country since 1995: first during a PhD in the UK followed by an 'unsuccessful' year back home, and then 30 months in Sweden. Asked whether he has considered what he might do next, he replies that he 'doesn't think that far ahead'. In

these cases the lack of permanent positions in the UK is not the sole deciding factor: the scientists concerned are still very much in the mobile early
post-doc period. Clearly securing a permanent position in future might
increase their likelihood of 'sticking' in a location.

Rumiana, on the other hand, is in her late 50s with very little time left on
her contract. Although she has spent the last 20 years in the UK working,
doing her PhD later in life and bringing up two children in Britain, she
cannot be described as settled. Indeed, she talks enthusiastically about
returning should the opportunity arise and was actively searching for
opportunities at the time of the interview even if this meant leaving science
research. As she puts it: 'At my age you always think of going back to where
you are from . . . if an opportunity comes to go back and do research . . .
my project finished this year and I am looking for work everywhere, applying everywhere but there are no positions in Bulgaria'.

It is clear from this analysis of the accounts of our longer-staying respondents that the majority have made a series of moves, often involving a
return at some point. Even where the respondent has been in the host
country for many years we need to take care in interpreting this situation.
Many are maintaining active links and spending valuable time in their
home countries and very few regard themselves as settled. The issue of
employment permanency emerges as perhaps one of the most critical
factors shaping length of stay. The role of contractual insecurity and other
factors shaping migration decision-making processes – and length of stay
in particular – forms the subject of the following chapter.

Long-stayers can also be found in the sample of COO returnees. The
following two cases involve people who appear to have settled in the home
country on return, in contrast to the circulators discussed above. Ewa, a
female biologist, experienced a single mobility experience 20 years ago,
when she had visited West Germany on an 18-month fellowship. During
this time her husband took leave from his job in Poland. Ewa was also
on a sabbatical from her position in Poland and so they returned to recom-
mence their work there while raising their family. In the meantime, the
group she visited closed and she did not experience real triggers to move
again. However, at the time of interview her children were reaching
independence and she was considering putting in an application to visit a
laboratory in the US. Ewa's case illustrates the relationship between life-
course (partnering and parenting) and mobility and also the importance
of specific triggers such as contacts and networks in maintaining
mobility.[10]

The second case of a straightforward single move and return concerns
Jacek, a geneticist who registered for his PhD in Poland but was presented
with the opportunity of working in Germany by his supervisor. He spent

36 months in Germany where he was paid as a technician but also did the experimental work for his doctorate. As he was registered in Poland he was committed to returning to complete his thesis. Jacek also considered the greater job security in Poland to be beneficial and wanted to return to his contract. He felt that to remain in Germany would most likely imply successive shorter contracts. A further factor in his return was consideration for his wife's career, as visa restrictions prevented her from working in Germany. Jacek has now spent five years back in Poland working in a university, but he has recently applied for an Alexander von Humboldt Foundation fellowship to support a further stay in Germany.

CONCLUSIONS

The interrogation of our respondents' situations presented above confirms the complexity and fluid quality of scientific mobility in the EU and breaks down simple distinctions between movers and stayers or settlers and returners. In practice we have seen very few simple unilateral moves and a high degree of circulation in both directions. For the majority of our sample, mobility is an ongoing reflexive process combining shorter and longer episodes. Gamlen (2005) argues that there is little research on actual mobility patterns to support the shuttle migration thesis. Our research with this specific cohort of migrants provides evidence of a high level of shuttle or pendular migration – the kind of short-term circulatory movements that Wallace (2002: 603) argues are 'better described as mobility'. Verwiebe and Eder (2006: 142) make a similar observation in the European context, arguing for the need to reconceptualize intra-European movements of people in terms of 'transnational mobility' rather than 'transnational or intra-EU migration'. Certainly traditional conceptualizations of brain drain – as 'the diffusion of skilled scientific and technical human capital, from home to host country' (Davenport, 2004: 617) – need to be revised in the context of the patterns of movement described in this chapter.

Baláž and colleagues (2004: 7 and 12) describe the distinction between permanent and temporary migration as a 'false dichotomy', arguing that in reality, outward and return moves form part of migration cycles and are often characterized by 'cumulative causation' and 'unintended outcomes'. Nevertheless, their research indicates a relationship between forms of temporary and more permanent moves with initial temporary moves often acting as a precursor to more permanent, economically driven re-migration. This raises the important question of whether the kinds of shuttle mobility identified in recent research does in fact amount to a substitute, thus obviating the need for longer-term moves or eventually increasing the propensity for longer stays. Baláž and colleagues (ibid.: 18 and 21) concluded, in the context of their work on Slovakian return migration, that 'many of those who return are likely, in the longer term, to re-migrate permanently . . . If they cannot match their enhanced skills and aspirations to more rewarding jobs in Slovakia, they may be even more likely to migrate permanently than non-migrants'. To the extent that early short-stay mobility enhances skills and raises expectations, then, it can be expected to increase the propensity for subsequent moves. Certainly the cases presented in this chapter provided some evidence of this process. Yet this is not the only pattern observed. We also found that many returning scientists engaged in forms of repeat mobility using the networks and contacts they had established rather than making more permanent moves. Return is frequently followed by ongoing shuttle moves although the timing of these is often shaped by life-course considerations. Many longer stays are also interspersed with shorter moves and return episodes and those who have not returned often remain committed to the idea of return at some point.

This situation does not exist in a vacuum but is highly context-dependent. Subtle changes in the context might trigger a shift in attitudes towards length of stay, with implications for the countries and individuals concerned. The following chapter considers the factors shaping scientists' migration decisions, identifying a range of push and pull factors. In practice, as our study reveals, scientists are exercising a degree of choice within diverse frameworks of constraint and are attempting to balance their desire for optimum scientific productivity with their family and personal lives.

NOTES

1. Central Statistical Office, 'Population, size and structure by territorial division. As of June 30, 2007', *Statistical Information and Elaborations*, Warsaw. Available at: http://www.stat.gov-p l/gus/45_655_ENG_HTML.htm. Accessed: 21 April 2008.
2. These will be coloured, of course, by a number of factors, including their current location, the length of time since they migrated and the strength of existing connections.
3. For further details see Annex 1.
4. Williams (2006: 590) argues for a flexible definition of migrant to capture 'periods spent working in another country, involving sufficient time for significant integration into the labour force that is, beyond placements of a few days or weeks, or attending seminars or workshops'.
5. We refer here to returnees interviewed in Poland and Bulgaria, which we term country of origin (or COO) returnees. Many of the scientists in the UK and Germany had also experienced a period of return at some point.
6. Although, of course, a different picture might emerge if a sample of US-based Eastern European researchers were surveyed.

7. It is important to stress here that this *does not* directly relate to the number of moves that have been made.
8. In practice it is hard to distinguish these two phases, as in Eastern Europe the first degree takes between four and six years and is equivalent to Masters level.
9. The issue of student fees and its effect on mobility is discussed in Chapter 3.
10. These are the focus of Chapters 5 and 6.

3. Migration processes and their determinants: 'professional' factors[1]

INTRODUCTION

The literature on highly skilled, and indeed all forms of migration, has tended to shift in recent years from a narrow and economically focused analysis of push-pull factors, to a somewhat broader concern with migration motivations. Whilst this development quite rightly shifts the emphasis from an often rather limited analysis of the relative merits of two distinct places or positions (the sending and receiving locations), the emphasis on identifying motivational dynamics continues to characterize migration as an atemporal process and fails to capture the degree of complexity and flux identified in the previous chapter. The majority of scientific migrants move repeatedly, often incorporating returns and re-emigrations in their trajectories as careers and the life-course evolve over time. Mobility of one form or another is almost always on the agenda and under constant negotiation and reflection. Quite often, decisions concern not only whether or where to move (or return) but, critically, for how long to stay and on what basis. Our concept of a migration decision therefore needs to encompass fully the somewhat distinct but related issues of location decision and length of stay. Even in this more fluid context we need to take care in conceptualizing the *decision* itself: the very notion of a *migration decision* implies a conscious and active appraisal of situations by a rational, informed actor or actors – if we acknowledge the involvement of other actors such as family and friends and colleagues in this process – at any point in time. Hadler (2006: 114) illustrates this approach, suggesting that 'migration starts with imaging the new destination, continues with balancing benefits and costs, and ends with an actual move'. In very many situations, migration does not work like this and scientists are catapulted into circumstances that they have had very little time to take stock of or evaluate effectively but which precipitate or trigger an unplanned mobility episode. Serendipity or chance thus plays a critical role in understanding migratory processes. Janina's case, for example, illustrates the role that unpredictable triggers play in migration processes.

Janina had wanted to do a PhD in the Polish lab where she had completed her diploma work and her supervisor was keen for her to do so but was unable to offer Janina a place. Instead she recommended another lab in Poland and put her in touch with the professor there. Janina was accepted to begin her PhD in that lab but circumstances changed within two weeks of starting: 'My supervisor called me and said "Now we are going to have some kind of cooperation with this university [in Germany] . . . it would be good if you could go there". I said, "Okay, why not, but I cannot speak any German!" Within two weeks I was here'. Janina began working on her doctorate in Germany, which took the form of a joint degree and assumed that she would return to work with her supervisor in Poland. However, his sudden death precipitated a new chain of unplanned and unforeseeable events: 'I have got no connections in Poland now . . . Things have changed a lot because this guy I would work with . . . he got cancer and he died, so somehow I had the problem of should I go to Poland or not because I had got no contract there'. Janina decided to stay in Germany where she was in the final stages of her doctorate and was about to commence a post-doc.

Unforeseen circumstances plus opportunities resulting from networks established through supervisors, at conferences or simply through friends were responsible for triggering many moves.[2] On the other hand, scientists who may have fully researched and carefully planned their career and mobility preferences may find themselves unable to put these plans into action for one reason or another. Here, they are motivated to migrate but fail to do so.

This chapter identifies some of the factors shaping the context within which scientists negotiate mobility. Although it does discuss some of the key influences shaping scientific mobility, it also acknowledges the importance that migration triggers play in effecting and, on occasion, instigating unplanned moves. The range of issues identified by our respondents has resulted in a pragmatic decision on the part of the authors to distinguish *professional* and *personal* factors. Although it is useful to make this broad distinction, in practice they are not independent but relational with economic prospects, for example, viewed through the lens of personal and family circumstances. This chapter focuses on the former – *professional aspects* – and Chapters 4 and 5 on the influence of family and personal relationships on migration processes.

This chapter places some of the professional issues raised in this case within a broader discussion of academic employment and career progression. It opens with a discussion of the expectation or valuation of mobility in science careers and the role that this plays in stimulating moves. Although the 'expectation of mobility' places a premium on international experience critical to career progression, in many cases scientists move simply to access a position either because opportunities do not exist in the current location and/or because recruitment systems are not perceived as fair. The interviews draw attention to the relationship that exists between the quality of academic positions (in this case the issue of contractual security) and mobility. Whilst many scientists move in the first instance to take up temporary or fixed-term posts, these positions typically imply acceptance of repeated mobility and, in some cases, may tip the balance in favour of return. Contractual status in the receiving country is also considered in the context of positions back home. This is particularly the case for those scientists who hold unpaid retained positions in their home country – a practice, which although unusual in the West, is quite common in Eastern Europe. In other cases, scientists exercise short-stay mobility as part of their paid work. This was evident in our sample of scientists interviewed in Poland and Bulgaria. The nature and location of their positions often had a significant impact on the type of mobility they were able to engage in and notably on length of stay.

In addition to this range of issues loosely classified as linked to the nature of employment opportunities, scientists identify a range of migration stimuli connected with their ability to work productively and competitively and develop their skills. These include access to resources (human and physical), having time to do research and having the autonomy to develop as independent researchers. As well as scientific skills, mobile scientists are often keen to develop their linguistic skills and particularly their command of written English for publication.

The recent practice by policy-makers of characterizing scientific migrants as *knowledge* rather than *economic* migrants reflects the recognition of the impact of the kind of employment-related concerns raised above on their mobility (DTI, 2002: 12). This does not imply that narrower economic concerns, and pay in particular, are less important. Pay must be understood in relation to expenditure both in terms of the cost of living and also the professional costs of studying and undertaking doctoral research. Finally, the chapter considers the role that organized mobility schemes play in scientific mobility both in terms of 'triggering' individual mobility episodes but also in increasing the propensity for future, ongoing, mobility and 'staying-on' practices.

RESEARCH FUNDING, ACADEMIC LABOUR MARKETS AND CAREER PROGRESSION

We have already referred to the impact assessment of the Marie Curie Fellowship Scheme (Van de Sande et al., 2005). As part of this work, 2918 current and former fellows were surveyed about their experiences of

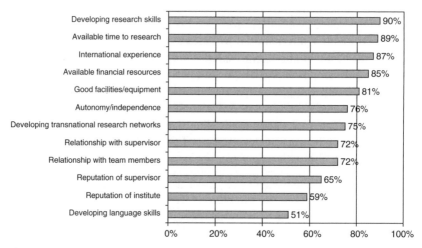

Source: From Van de Sande, et al. (2005: 13).

Figure 3.1   *The relative importance of factors to working effectively in scientific research*

mobility. Figure 3.1 summarizes fellows' responses to a series of questions inviting them to rank the factors that enabled them to *work effectively* in science. The responses provide a useful broad assessment of the importance that mobile scientists attach to different potential stimuli. Marie Curie Fellows placed a very high premium on the value of international experience but also on the opportunity to develop research skills, commit time to research and work in contexts that are adequately resourced.

Valuing Mobility in Career Progression

Eighty-seven of the Marie Curie respondents identified international experience as a key factor shaping their ability to work effectively in science. Perhaps unsurprisingly this is the factor they attach most significance to in terms of the impact of the Mare Curie Fellowship Scheme (which requires an international move). Progression in science careers places a high premium on mobility (Casey et al., 2001; Rothwell, 2002; Ackers, 2003, 2005a; EUA, 2005). Jerzy explains how his supervisor 'always told me that it's just the scientific career – you have to go abroad to meet other people'.

Although mobility is often seen as having some intrinsic value, it is also viewed as a vehicle promoting the achievement of other goals such as international experience, exposure to different approaches and new skills, accessing established centres of excellence and research 'stars' and generally promoting knowledge transfer processes. Dickmann, Doherty and Brewster (2006: 30) identify international experience as key to career progression, arguing that 'individuals appear to focus most keenly on the whole process that can lead to promotions and emphasised the [career] development potential of international work'. In practice, the relationship between mobility and international experience is rarely considered in any detail. More importantly, from the point of view of the present discussion, it is rare to find any consensus or even debate about what forms of mobility are optimal or 'good enough' to achieve these objectives. There is a kind of received wisdom that evidence of mobility, in itself, is evidence of international experience, achievement and career development.[3]

Piotr contrasts the relative stagnation of Polish academic labour markets (with few people moving between institutions) with the value attached to mobility in the UK and particularly in the US, which he describes as 'more sensible . . . so people are basically expected to get a position elsewhere rather than in the same institution'. For Piotr, mobility is an indicator of competitiveness in research. He distinguishes the degree of circulation in the West with the kind of patronage that blocks positions in some countries and institutional settings. For others in the sample, international moves are a vital means of accessing diverse skills sets. Margarita spent six months in Russia during her undergraduate degree and then moved to Germany for her doctorate and first post-doc. She immediately identifies the significance of international and diverse experience, as a result of mobility, to career progression and her prospect of securing a permanent position: 'It is really very important, if you apply for any permanent job in our field, one of the things that are really highly rated is foreign experience because they see that, first of all, you work with different people and different ideas. It's very, very important because if you get stuck in one thing you don't have such a big future definitely'.

Although scientists may become and continue to be mobile during the early and mid-career stages in pursuit of new forms of knowledge and skills, in some cases respondents talked of how this could, in the longer term, generate a momentum of its own, making it harder for them to settle. Fryderyk makes an interesting observation about the unsettling consequences of repeated mobility. He suggests that the lack of academic mobility *within* Poland means that it 'lacks the international exciting atmosphere . . . you don't get the same experience [as London]. But once you've emigrated for some time and moved somehow . . . you're not at home here entirely and you're not at home back there as well. It's quite difficult for people'. Becoming mobile, then, can lead to the kind of nomadic lifestyle described in the previous chapter.

The expectation of mobility in science careers is an increasingly important factor, positively encouraging, in particular, early career researchers to move between countries and experience research in different contexts. For many it is a vital part of a CV-building process and, as Margarita explained above, often the key to accessing a permanent position. In addition to this positive benefit of mobility, however, it is important to remember that the requirement to move repeatedly is also a reflection of the research system and the nature of research funding, particularly in the host countries. Research funding is ultimately responsible for the volume of positions and the type of positions available.

It is interesting in this context to consider the relevance of Williams's (2006) distinction between those groups of highly skilled migrants that move with their employment in 'bounded careers' (such as intra-company transfers, for example) and what he terms 'free agent labour migration'. Although Williams does not specifically cite scientists as an example of this latter category, they would appear to fit the characterization rather well. Describing free agent labour migrants as 'workers who migrate without formal employment contracts, and outside of company frameworks', Williams suggests that these individuals focus on 'their long-term employability security within a career model that implicates mobility . . . Boundaryless careers are constituted of sequences of jobs across organisations and, in the case of international migrants, across national boundaries' (ibid.: 595). This description goes some way towards explaining how the expectation of mobility functions in science careers as a positive mechanism enabling individuals to build a career and their long-term employability (and progression) out of a series of insecure positions. In the context of job mobility rather than geographic mobility, Opengart and Short (2002) refer to the development of 'portfolio careers', with employees shifting their attention from employment security to employability security. Migration, in this light, represents the exercise of agency on the part of the individual as part of a planned and deliberate career-building strategy. Certainly we have seen evidence of this. However it is important, as Williams does, not to overplay the agency dimension and to situate our understanding of agency or choice within the framework of constraints that constitute science careers. Of particular importance here is the lack of employment security, which effectively forces or requires scientists to move whether they want to or not.

Mobility and Employment Opportunity

Unsurprisingly, one of the most important factors colouring the attractiveness of different locations concerns the availability and accessibility of positions. The relatively high number of opportunities and relative open-ness of labour markets and recruitment processes in Germany and the UK encourages inward flows. Marked reductions in scientific funding in Bulgaria and Poland results in a dearth of positions, and the continued existence of more 'closed' approaches to recruitment limits access to those positions that do exist. These differentials together facilitate and direct labour migration.[4] Notwithstanding the contribution that mobility makes to the transfer of knowledge, the UK and German post-doc system is not organized primarily for that purpose. Rather it is a direct consequence of wider systemic issues determining the nature of research funding. The pos-itive characterization of the UK as a 'post-doc paradise' (Balter, 1999), which makes it attractive to foreign researchers, reflects both the availabil-ity of positions and the relative openness of this segment of the academic labour market. The corollary of this, however, is the fact that the over-whelming majority of early and even mid-career positions in the natural sciences are insecure and temporary. The accounts of respondents placed significant emphasis on the relationship between contractual status (in the host countries) and migration behaviour.

In a case that illustrates the relationship between the research funding system, employment contracts and decisions about length of stay, Margarita explains her plans for the future following the expiry of her current position in Germany. Margarita and her partner are both scientists and work in the same institution, so both of their positions are at stake:

> I have a contract for three years until 2007. [Q: Have you thought about what you're going to do after that?] Physics of course, well the thing is that our pro-fessor's going to retire as well in four years so it's more or less simultaneously or shortly after the end of my contract. Let's say until 2007 we are going to stay here definitely and then we were planning probably after that, because if our profes-sor is not here anymore there's no reason, I have to be honest really there is no reason to stay. We were thinking probably even to go to England for some time or go to Italy or go to Canada. I really don't know exactly.

This case is by no means exceptional and illustrates the reliance of post-docs on individual grant-holders – an issue that lies at the heart of many recent discussions about the development of the Researcher's Charter and the Code of Conduct in the European Research Area. Other similar cases include the death of a supervisor or, more commonly, the emigration of supervisors and grant-holders. These events play a significant role in triggering or precipitating mobility. Whatever the cause of the relation-ship breakdown, Margarita's account illustrates the freedom and uncer-tainty the symbiotic quality of the post-doc/grant-holder (or principal investigator) relationship generates in terms of thinking about their next position and where it might take them. Although we have identified a number of cases here where the loss of the supervisor or principal investigator (PI) has generated insecurity for the researcher, in other examples some degree of employment security is achieved by the early career researcher accompanying the PI/supervisor when they move.[5]

The interviews with scientists emphasizse the critical relationship that exists between contractual insecurity, mobility and length of stay. It is clear that permanency probably carries the highest viscosity factor encouraging scientists to stay for longer periods in the host countries and reducing the propensity to return.[6] While contractual security in the host country plays an important role in shaping length of stay and attitudes towards location and future mobility, for many of our sample this is viewed in connection with their employment status back home. The majority of younger respondents who left their home country at pre-doctoral or doctoral stage would not have held established positions prior to their departure. A surprisingly large number of post-docs and more senior scientists[7] in the host countries did retain some form of position at the point of departure, sometimes for many years. In other cases, particularly among the 'returnee' sample, the quality of the position they held and its relationship with their role influenced the frequency and length of stays abroad.

'Anchored Moves': The Effect of Retained Positions on Migration Decision-making

The retention of permanent positions at home are associated with a degree of 'stickiness'.[8] Maciej and Anton's ability to retain their permanent positions played an important role in maintaining their contact with Poland and supporting regular short-stay returns over the years. It also had an important symbolic value. As Maciej puts it, 'I would say I never left Poland'.

For many other people, positions back home were retained for a finite period – often around two years – after which they had to decide whether to return or relinquish the position, and this had an important practical and emotional impact on them. Gill (2005) characterizes this group of scientists as 'anchored movers', contrasting them with 'footloose movers' who either leave without retaining positions or who had no positions to retain. At the time of interview, some 13 per cent of UK-based respondents and 21 per cent of those based in Germany were formally 'on leave' from the home countries (see Table 3.1).

In addition to this, however, a further nine Bulgarians and four Poles in the host countries had at some stage relinquished a permanent position in

Table 3.1   Anchored and footloose movers by country

Country-based	Anchored	Footloose	Non-mover
In UK	4	27	0
In Germany	7	26	0
In Bulgaria	10	0	1
In Poland	11	0	3

the sending country: this represents 62.5 per cent of our sample (40 of the respondents in the host countries had held a retained position at some point during their migration history). Most startling, however, is the fact that 100 per cent of the returnee sample in Poland and Bulgaria had moved whilst anchored to the home country.

The ability to go abroad for a short- to medium-term stay while a post is on hold in their original institution is very attractive to scientists. Elzbieta's case serves as a useful illustration. She is a lecturer based in Warsaw and secured a permanent position very early in her career when she worked as a technician during her doctoral studies. She believes that having a long-term position shaped her attitude towards mobility: 'I had my position for life . . . so I was really relaxed and that's maybe the reason I was travelling so much and working in other places'. Her supervisor granted her three months' leave to visit the UK during her PhD, after which she returned to Poland for two-and-a-half years spending some time also in France. Elzbieta explains how 'leave' works in her position:

> If there is a short-term visit somewhere for up to three months you can keep your position and sometimes you can even have your salary but they call it a scientific break or something like that. Now it changes . . . I didn't keep my salary, it was leave of absence. My position was secure as long as you were coming back and as long as you had approval from your supervisor you always can go back.

One of the most fundamental problems, however, can be managing mobility and a position in the home country. Often there comes a crunch time when the period of leave ends and the scientist has to decide either to return to their position or stay out. In Elzbieta's case she decided to go for a post-doc in America, during which she extended a one-year contract to two and then to three years. This was followed by a difficult choice:

> I knew that at the end of three years I would have to make the decision I'm staying abroad or returning. They [Poland employer] couldn't keep my position longer than three years, I would be asked to leave or resign and I didn't want to so we found somebody to continue this project [in the US].

She regards her decision to return to Poland as 'a mixture of circumstance' involving the balancing of career opportunities with the needs of her partner (who was a post-doc in Canada but returned to a permanent position in Poland) and her mother (who was also in Poland). Eventually, she decided to resume her position and has since remained in Poland (though she has made a four-month trip to the US).

In practice, marked variation exists in the terms of retained positions both between countries and institutions, and scientists were themselves often unsure about how systems operate. Periods of official leave often seem to fall between three months and three years, but can last longer and in some cases leave is indefinite. Lucjan, for example, has retained his position back home for over 13 years. He says the position gave him 'some hope, it's a safe place so I could always come back if anything bad happens I can go on state salary and survive. It is a place to cover a dry period. There is a level of safety in it for me'. Keeping his position at home allowed him to balance the benefits of a secure and permanent – albeit low paid – position with the rewards of working in better funded, higher paid and less secure positions abroad.

The relationship between retained positions and length of stay is interesting and complex. On the one hand, they form a powerful anchor to the home country, serving the purpose they are designed to serve: namely, allowing or even encouraging people to leave for short periods whilst building an umbilical link with them to support return moves and reverse knowledge transfers. In that respect they are highly effective in maintaining links with the diaspora (see Chapter 6 for more discussion of this). On the other hand, their purpose in preventing people from being locked out arguably contributes to the problem of position-blocking and patronage that makes it so difficult for many other expatriates to return and reintegrate in scientific labour markets, thus reducing the volume of positions available for open competition and privileging those people who have previously held posts.[9] According to some respondents, one of the incentives for institutions to offer retained positions was the ability to save money on the salaries: leave was usually unpaid and employers rarely arranged cover for those positions.

The Characteristics of Positions in Poland and Bulgaria

Chapter 2 drew attention to the incidence of short stays in scientific migration patterns. Short stays often act as a precursor to longer stays. In other cases they take place in the period following return as the scientist attempts to retain links and support their research. Interviews with the returnees in Poland and Bulgaria raised a number of issues about the quality of their positions on return and the effect of this on future mobility. Generally speaking, research-only or research-rich positions offer greater flexibility in terms of mobility. In Poland and Bulgaria, research takes place both in the university sector (where roles are similar to those in the UK and the German university sector and typically demand a degree of teaching), and the Academies of Science where scientists are focused predominantly on research (Slantcheva, 2003; Sretenova, 2003). Both of these groups are represented in our sample and their accounts illustrate the relationship between the nature of their positions and their mobility.

Where respondents held university positions, they often had to organize their stays abroad around teaching, examining timetables and administrative commitments. Bogdan talks of having to use his summer vacations for the purpose of short stays abroad. If he wishes to stay abroad for longer periods he will lose his salary. According to Bogdan, this arrangement does not provide sufficient leave for him to function effectively in science:

> There is one bad thing here is that our university has not the right policy today I would say because all the administration was changed and what concerns them most is just to have the person that he/she fulfils his/her duties as a teacher, so number of lessons, number of courses, and for going abroad and doing research so you are left alone more or less. There is no support so they do not give you paid sabbaticals here so you have a certain amount of holidays. Okay you can use these 30 days [annual leave] and if you go beyond those you have to get a leave of absence and without your big salary. [Q: So you don't get study leave as such or research leave?] No, this is if you travel every year for a month there is a rule that every seventh year you can use for this. This sabbatical year and then your salary is kept on a certain level and this is already good but it's not enough to be in time with developing science.

The practice of using vacation time to travel for the purposes of research is not restricted to Poland and Bulgaria. Our previous research on the progression of women in science highlighted the practice across Europe, with many scientists using their leave to conduct research, present papers and attend conferences (Ackers, 2007). In Bogdan's case, however, the need to travel is of particular importance to his ability to function effectively in research.

Yulian's case illustrates the impact of seniority and the administrative duties associated with more senior positions in the university sector, which make it difficult for him to spend what he considers to be adequate time abroad for the purpose of research: 'My visiting abroad stopped for the past two or three years as I am a dean. I have administrative duties [so] I have to get special permission now from my rector. I need to go to France for six months but at this point it is not possible'.

Dessislava, based in the Bulgarian Academy of Science, is not bound by teaching responsibilities but her account shows how she has organized her time abroad around her employment rights, combining vacation leave with unpaid research leave and maternity leave to maximize her flexibility and length of stay without jeopardizing her position in Bulgaria:

> [Q: Did you still have your salary from the Academy during your leave?] No, it depends on the position you have at the Academy. If you have let's say 30 days of holidays, so officially paid holidays, so when I was abroad I was asking for my holidays [to be] officially paid and then these unpaid holidays, so being at the Academy you can have two years like that every five years, but in Bulgaria there is also another trick you can use and if you have a child you receive permission to be absent from the work for three years. I had my second child . . . so I was just going to [an EU Member State] for five or six months but every two weeks I was coming back for a week then again and sometimes with the baby, sometimes not, so I used this for three years. [Q: Did you leave the baby here with your mother and your husband?] Sometimes yes, most of the time I was coming back and they were quite nice and [the host institution] reimbursed my airplane tickets.

Although Dessislava held a research-only position in Bulgaria, she in fact held a teaching position in the host country. This reduced the time she could spend on research during the normal working day but she used her free time there to utilize the resources available, undertake her experimental work and was able to significantly augment her income.

WORKING EFFECTIVELY AND PRODUCTIVELY

Figure 3.1 identified a range of factors that mobile scientists consider critical to effective working in science. These include access to optimal human and physical resources, which, in practice, often implies working in a recognized centre of excellence with established and renowned researchers. In order to work productively and competitively they also need sufficient time to devote to their research. In addition to these resource issues, scientists place a high premium on their ability to work in an autonomous fashion and develop as independent researchers.

Chompalov (2000: 11) argues that the conditions in Bulgaria were 'ripe for migration' due to the 'low salaries, outdated equipment, inadequate capital investment and irregular funding for purchase of materials and substances'. Georgieva (2004: 369) similarly points to the 'intolerable' lack of basic consumables and resources and 'meagre' library and computer support for doctoral students in Bulgaria. In the Polish context, Okólski (2006: 50) notes that the factors pushing scientists to go abroad were low income and worse labour conditions, low prestige and social status of science and education, poor equipment, restricted access to literature, lack of research funds, limited opportunities for contacting scientific circles and also the top quality of Polish education (enabling them to go).

The respondents in this study echoed similar concerns with some – especially Bulgarian – scientists pointing out that experimental science was really impossible given the resources available to them. According to Kalina, 'the problem is really that the conditions for work are not that good and nowadays we don't get new machines and old of course are already too old'. Similarly Vanya, now based back in Bulgaria, explains why she went to the UK during her doctorate: 'Here it's not possible to do really what I wanted to do within the subject on plant metabolism'. Svetlana sheds further light on the situation in Bulgaria:

> I think that there is the basic core support for research which is still there and some of it is decent. There are bits and pieces of equipment which are obviously not there and there are things which are clearly not available there – those are things which you can't easily put on a grant. We're talking about big things, things like micro-rays, these are modern things that are simply not accessible there. It's not unthinkable to get some of the equipment necessary but running costs are a big problem . . . Money is a big problem.

While Svetlana indicates that some equipment could be purchased with grant funds, the more critical problem is the cost of running large machinery or buying other equipment on a routine basis. Additionally, much more basic things such as glassware and access to chemicals can prove problematic. It is perhaps in this area where there seemed to be the most marked differences between the Bulgarian and the Polish contexts. Many of our Polish respondents made comments indicating that everything can be done in Poland, it will just take longer and Sylwia describes her lab in Poland as similar to those in Germany: 'The equipment and everything it is exactly the same as here. So maybe here you have more groups and a little bit less people for the same equipment'. Our work with Bulgarian scientists indicated a more severely limited infrastructure. There seemed to be almost no access to modern equipment and only limited availability of PCs. However, more pressingly, electricity failing in the university and BAS [Bulgarian Academy of Science] buildings seemed a common problem. Todorka articulates the problem: 'There are such poor conditions for work, it is not only salary. It is equipment, chemicals, they are SO expensive'. Our findings concur with that of Slantcheva (2003: 449) who argues that universities are starved of resources, which has led to a drastic reduction in infra-structural investments . . . Obsolete research equipment, under-funded libraries and publishing centres, a lack of teaching technology, and inadequate faculty office space are common facts of life . . . the academic system has been kept on the brink of extinction.

Indeed one respondent, Dessislava, confirms this explaining that in her lab they 'didn't even have money to pay electricity one year'.

ACCESSING PHYSICAL AND HUMAN RESOURCES: THE MAGNETIC EFFECT OF CENTRES OF EXCELLENCE

Given the poor conditions for experimental research in Poland and espe-cially Bulgaria, it is perhaps unsurprising that scientists are drawn to places where they have access to resources that allow them to work much more productively. The majority of our respondents talked of the better condi-tions and easy access to equipment and facilities in the host countries. Boris explains that 'in Bulgaria we haven't good apparatus and systems to do complicated experiments' so he organizes his research in such a way that allows him to carry out the experimental work abroad and analyse and write up data in Bulgaria. This case is not unusual and respondents clearly value the superior infrastructure and access to equipment and facilities pro-vided in Western institutions. In the Polish context, Lucjan talks about what attracted him to the UK: 'What really attracted me was the availabil-ity of equipment, people and methods in one place and the level of research'. Valentina, also, confirms this: 'One of the most important things there is access to the papers we are interested in. If I would like to see a paper here usually I will have to call a friend in Germany and ask them to send a paper'. For Sylwia, the key factors attracting scientists to the West are 'good working conditions. In the case of my boyfriend when he went to Berlin he just was shocked with the laboratory, by the amount of equipment and by the amount of money and the research'.

The sorts of conditions valued by natural scientists often exist in the most prestigious institutions and recognized centres of excellence. Accessing these centres is, however, about more than equipment per se: accessing reputational capital and the know-how of 'top' people acts as a powerful draw (Puustinen-Hopper, 2005).[10] In fact, excellence and reputa-tion alone can be a strong reason for choosing one host country or institu-tion over another. Approaches to excellence vary between scientists. Some, like Jan, focus on the national level: 'With computer science, for example, you look for papers, which universities and who makes what and you mainly come up with three countries, Germany, UK and the USA'. Millard (2005) notes that the reputation of a country in terms of research excellence and research environment plays an important role when shaping scientists' mobility and location decisions but recognizes that the perceived reputation of individual areas, institutions or clusters is more important than that of the country overall. Georgi, for example, said that Heidelberg 'has a very good name for molecular biology . . . I heard for the first time about Heidelberg when I was still at school'. Similarly, the following exchange with Teresa highlights the attractiveness of the University of Cambridge: 'I looked in Poland, I looked in America. [Q: What were you looking for?] I think for excellence mainly. [Q: And money I guess, some sponsorship?] Yes scholarships, yes, although they are the same all over the UK. [Q: In terms of choosing a UK institution?] Yes that was academic excellence'.

Mahroum (2000b) has argued that 'the ability of some countries, regions and cities to attract highly talented personnel from all over the world seems to be enormous'. Our work with the Marie Curie Fellowship Scheme (Ackers, 2003; Van de Sande et al., 2005) identified the specific attraction of research clusters in the UK's golden triangle of Oxford, Cambridge and London. Looking at Germany's research landscape reveals a number of clusters in Nordrhein-Westfalen, particularly in the Düsseldorf, Dortmund and Bonn area, the Mainz and Wiesbaden area, around Munich in Bavaria, Stuttgart in Baden-Württemberg as well as clusters around Hamburg and Berlin.

Mahroum (2000a) talks about scientists moving to gain access to scholarly power both in terms of accessing a high-quality research environment as a whole but also in terms of gaining access to individual professors or groups. So, for Irina: 'I didn't look for a place to go abroad. I was sort of thrilled and honoured to work with this particular professor in this particular area'. For early career researchers the reputation of their chosen institution can be of vital importance for their future career. Puustinen-Hopper (2005) notes the kudos of having a foreign PhD, but there was some indication amongst our doctoral respondents who not only wanted a Western PhD but who were also aware of the relative reputations of specific institutions in their research field. Radka, for example, was fully aware that a doctorate undertaken at a Max Planck Institute would stand her in good stead in the future. Ivan agrees: 'It is very important to be in a good group, to have a good PhD thesis and just to be competitive'. Stanislaw puts it more bluntly: 'You want to start from a very good place, not just a place'. Echoing that sentiment, Dimitar highlights the benefits for him of working at a specific research group in Denmark:

> It is a very motivated centre, it's a leading centre in this area . . . they have a lot of knowledge, people and equipment to do research and they are developing

rapidly. You can have anything you wish for in your studies . . . so you work in a highly educated environment with a very high level of scientist. So you work fast.

Working Productively: The Importance of Time

The issue of accessing human and physical resources is not just important in terms of being able to work effectively but also in terms of being able to work fast, be productive and be competitive. The interviews highlighted that tasks can take significantly longer to complete in the home country or cannot be completed without accessing other facilities elsewhere. Georgi explains the difference between his home lab in Bulgaria and the lab he worked in during an undergraduate stay in Holland:

> For these five months you could really see how much work you can do in a lab and you have the possibility because you have the money for supplies in the lab and to buy basic things. . . There I could see that things which we do for one week more or less or for several days you could do for one afternoon in Holland and this had a lot of impact when you see what is different.

Valentina makes a similar comparison between her work in Bulgaria and that in Germany: 'They have lot of computers and I make computer simulation; if I want to make a test I can run jobs on different computers and it will take two days. Here on our computers I need to run it for a month'.

The examples given by Georgi and Valentina show how inefficient some areas of scientific work in Bulgaria are. Similar views were expressed by Polish respondents. Being able to work efficiently is of utmost important in science as competition between groups working on similar issues is fierce. Hanna, based at a Polish university, explains:

> We did some experiments and we wanted to publish it and I had this result. It was in April or May and the paper was finished in July and unfortunately someone was faster than us. It was one year of my really hard work and . . . I think the other group had good support and was able to write in a very short time so now the paper will probably go to another not as good journal, so the groups in Poland end up with the not so good publications.

Because Hanna's group lacked the resources and support to work fast and efficiently, a Western group was able to publish their results sooner and submit them to the most influential and highly regarded journal, leaving Hanna's group looking second best.

LANGUAGE AND MOBILITY

Chompalov (2000: 2) argues that 'potential emigration [from Bulgaria] is positively affected by knowledge of English'. In a similar vein, Slowinski (1998) notes that mobility opportunities are dependent on language skills and that those university students who do have such skills possess important linguistic capital. Because the language of science is English and most scientific conferences or workshops and key publications and materials are in English, it is important for scientists to maximize their language competency. La Madeleine (2007: 1) points out that 'in science, weak English hinders a successful career'.

Most natural scientists have a good command of English language and moving to, and living in, an English-speaking country therefore does not require them to learn an additional language in order to communicate at work and for everyday life. As Ania explains, 'The UK is in quite a unique position because the language is right. Most people study English and you don't need to learn another language just to stay here. I think that's what makes it easy to start with'. Respondents in the UK expressed concerns about going to other countries, including Germany, because of their lack of language proficiency. Teresa confirms that 'language was one issue' and that she looked mainly for positions in the UK 'because English is the only language I could speak apart from Polish'. Roumen suggests that now that English is the language predominantly learnt at school in Bulgaria, the UK could benefit from that language competency: 'Most people now speak English not German so this could be a strong impetus for people to look in the direction of the UK'. Maria also highlights the importance of improving language skills as a motivating factor: 'I'm thinking about language as well, I'd like to make progress in language'. The chance to work with native speakers of English was valued highly.

Bozena had spent some time in the UK at undergraduate level and her first choice had been to return there for her doctorate. Unfortunately, she could not find appropriate funding and in the end decided to try her luck in Germany. She did, however, share the concerns about language discussed above: 'I was a bit afraid with not knowing German . . . I was more thinking that it might be difficult to feel like a stranger without language and so on. I had this obsession of language but now it's much better'. However, most respondents based in Germany did not have the same worries about language and Bozena herself confirmed that she had worried for no reason. Many respondents felt that they could get by without German. In fact it was the experience of speaking English rather than their native Polish or Bulgarian that was important, even if that was not in an English-speaking country, as Ivan explains: 'The language of science is English so we should have experience of this, so it's better for you [to go abroad] and language is very important you know'. Falagas and colleagues (2005: 655) note that 'the adoption of a universal language in science, namely English, could facilitate communication between individuals from different countries and enhance the timely interchange of ideas among researchers and scientists with potential benefits to scientific advancement and development'. However, they also warn that the dominance of English 'could also lead to poorer outcomes in the field of research and development because of the possible exclusion of those not able or not willing to adapt' (ibid.).

THE ROLE OF FINANCIAL DETERMINANTS IN MIGRATION DECISION-MAKING

In many respects the issue of income and remuneration straddles the professional and the personal. On the one hand, levels of remuneration have a symbolic significance and represent the value attached to scientific research in different contexts. On the other, however, scientists are concerned with the direct, practical relationship between pay and their ability to achieve an acceptable standard of living for themselves and their families. Traditional migration theory has been dominated by rational choice approaches that place significant emphasis on economic – that is financial – determinants. Whilst our research underlines the importance of pay to migration and career decision-making, it does not support the emphasis on narrow profit-maximizing behaviour (nor the assumption that higher salaries will play a determinative role).

Dickmann and colleagues' (2006) work on highly skilled, corporate mobility supports this contention, emphasizing the huge priority many individuals in their survey attributed to career development. They argue that individuals conduct 'complex assessments . . . the data has challenged the predominant argument that financial considerations are a primary motive for expatriates and instead points to the importance of [career] development and family considerations' (ibid.: 25). Jalowiecki and Gorzelak (2004: 300) make a similar point in the context of academic mobility: 'intellectuals are attracted to Western countries by higher salaries, better working conditions, stability and political freedom, and improved educational prospects for their children'. Although financial considerations were also important, for some 'finance appeared to be more of a hygiene factor in terms of the influence on the decisions' (ibid.: 20). However, in the context of Eastern European moves it seems that scientists share common drivers with other economic migrants. As Roman puts it, 'The salary is higher [abroad], it's not just about money, I mean it's about being able to live'.

Table 3.2   Average gross monthly remuneration in scientific research in Poland and Bulgaria as reported by interviewees (in euros)

	PhD Stipend	Post-doc	Senior
Bulgaria	125–150	200–250	300–350
Poland	250	350–400	550–1500

A number of authors distinguish between the motivation to achieve a higher living standard (through higher wages) and economic hardship, like Roman does above. Rangelova and Vladimirova (2004: 9) argue that the main reason for Bulgarian emigration in general is 'economic hardship and high unemployment'. With specific reference to science, they refer to the 'lack of funds for the development of science, education and high technologies in Central and Eastern Europe, including equipment, and adequate infrastructure' (ibid.: 9). Chompalov (2000: 2) similarly identifies the 'the slow speed of reforms and low salaries are the leading reasons for the decision [of Bulgarian scientists] to emigrate'. In the Polish context, our respondent Roman observes that 'each PhD student in Poland that I know prefers to study abroad because they have financial problems [in Poland]'. Kicinger (2005: 32) cites a Polish key informant as saying: 'If we want to encourage good researchers to stay we should make their salaries three times higher'. Although this would still not bring them into line with salaries in Germany and the UK, she argues that this would encourage many more to stay in Poland and in science. Moreover, the same key informant goes on to add that resourcing is more than simply about salaries but concerns also the quality of 'research conditions' and the importance of 'money to set up a lab at the level you have in the West' (ibid.).

Table 3.2 shows current gross salaries in science in Poland and Bulgaria. It is important to note that these salaries are significantly less than the salaries in other comparable professions in the sending countries and do not support a reasonable standard of living. Valentina, based in Bulgaria, says that 'people manage here, it's difficult, it's not impossible. Scientists are some of the lowest salaries'. The respondents in Bulgaria talked of having to take before or after work positions or Saturday employment working in shops, delivering newspapers or driving taxis to augment their salaries. Pay in these areas of semi- and unskilled work was often higher than in scientific research.[11]

Citing figures of €170 per month for a professor and €90–110 for assistants, Slantcheva (2003: 443) suggests that salaries for 'junior faculty are on the verge of poverty. The situation is little better for more senior academics . . . salaries for habilitated staff are barely adequate to cover people's basic needs'.

The tone of the interviews in Poland suggests that the situation there is less a question of subsistence, but more a failure to satisfy relative living standards in the face of increasing prices and also the emergence of more lucrative opportunities outside of science.[12] Kwiek (2003: 469) refers to the 'striking decline' in academic salaries in the Polish public sector higher education in recent years. By 2001, academic salaries in this sector were 95.5 per cent of the average monthly salary – he cites €220 for an associate professor and €370 for a professor – and, according to Kwiek, required academics to 'relinquish expectations of a middle-class standard of living' let alone the 'upper middle class social status' of scientists in the West (ibid.)

The previous chapter has identified the range of diverse patterns of mobility exhibited by scientists. The existence of marked disparities in remuneration, in this context, might be expected to have a complex effect. Whilst in some cases, the prospect of higher salaries might increase incentives to outward migration and longer stays, in other situations the financial incentives might support a decision to remain in the sending region and augment salaries – and permanent contracts – through regular short stays. This also offsets some of the costs of establishing long-term residency in the West.

Salary Augmentation through Short-stay Mobility

The opportunity to augment low salaries in the sending regions through short-stay mobility played a very significant role both in terms of encouraging circulation but also in terms of retaining people in science. Remuneration during short stays abroad is typically in the form of stipends, expenses or honoraria and often on a tax-free basis (although, of course, scientists will have to accommodate themselves in the host state during their stay). We have already seen in the previous chapter the important role that short stays can play in salary augmentation. The following examples further illustrate the impact short stays can have on personal income: 'The DFG [German Research Foundation] scheme pays €2000 per month expenses for stays of up to three months (on top of an average Bulgarian salary)'.

Roumen refers to the attraction of the remuneration associated with mobility and points out that this income forms critical support for dependent family members: [13]

> They would pay an honorarium with no taxes; it's excellent. Something like €2500–3500 per month. A flat sum without any deductions, so it's excellent and very desirable; as a rule I don't get salary [at home] at this time. [Q: How much are you motivated to make these decisions for financial reasons?] Very much so. I wouldn't say this was the only motivation because I love science and am

devoted to what I am doing but I have also other people to support. It's not just me, I am modest in my personal requirements but there are many old retired people in Bulgaria who have no means to improve their living unless someone helps them. My parents and my aunt and uncle who died recently – excellent people with a very high standing in life who fought all their lives for this democracy to come but when it came it was devastating financially. There is no state support. They get about €50 a month for rent and this is not enough even to pay heating – the heating is about €60 per month.

It is worth pointing out that a stay of one month in this context could make a significant contribution to the annual income and a stay of three months may more than double their yearly income. The kind of annual six-monthly visits made by some respondents earning on average €3000 per month would attract an additional annual income of €18 000, often in addition to the local *gross* annual salary of around €3600.

Relative Living Costs and Expenses

Salary differentials in themselves tell us very little. They need to be interpreted in the context of the costs associated with moving and living in the receiving country. Where scientists face the costs of maintaining two households in either location or where the costs of living are very high, salaries in themselves are likely to have a reduced effect. This was evident in respondents' replies to questions about remittances, with one researcher simply saying that he had no surplus income. It is important to take into account both the cost of living in a particular location (and centres of excellence are often located in more expensive urban areas) and any professional costs (such as students' fees for themselves and their children). The UK is generally recognized as one of the most expensive Member States to live in. Housing costs in cities such as London, Oxford, Cambridge or Edinburgh are very high and child care is particularly expensive. These costs need to be understood in the context of migrant scientists' citizenship status and access to social security and welfare benefits.

In addition to general concerns around the costs of living, a key issue raised by respondents concerned the professional costs and, in particular, the dampening effect of tuition fees. Rangelova and Vladimirova (2004: 17) identify Germany as the most attractive European destination to young Bulgarian migrants 'because it offers a range of free-of-charge undergraduate and postgraduate courses which are open to foreign students'.[14] Notwithstanding the commitment of the Bologna process to create a level playing field in the area of European higher education, marked diversity remains between national systems. Of particular significance to the current study is the level of diversity in the status of doctoral candidates. The UK and German systems are quite distinct at the present time with the UK continuing to ascribe doctoral candidates student status and requiring them to pay tuition fees, whilst in Germany the majority of doctoral candidates in the natural sciences have a form of employment status combining paid work with their doctoral research.[15]

One of the most striking differences between the UK and Germany in the context of both undergraduate study and doctoral research is the issue of tuition fees. As Tzonka put it, 'People don't come to the UK because of the fees'.[16] Fees remain a factor at undergraduate, Masters and doctoral level in the UK both for the individual scientist, their partners and their children. While in Germany, doctoral studies have been free and look to remain free even when tuition fees are introduced at undergraduate level.[17] The UK continues to charge significant fees for doctoral registrations. These fees are variable. The UK Careers Service publication, *Prospects*, lists annual international postgraduate fees for science courses as being between £6500 and £9950 in 2006. Moreover, fees at some of the more prestigious institutions – Cambridge, Oxford, Edinburgh and Imperial College, for example – can be much higher and commonly reach around £12 000. With Poland's accession to the EU, Polish doctoral candidates, now EU nationals, pay home rather than international student fees and although that represents a significant drop to around £3000 per year – around €4400 – it is still an amount that might discourage potential doctoral candidates from registering in the UK. Tzonka considers the situation in the light of Bulgaria's accession to the EU: 'Some rich people, yes they will start sending their children . . . because £3000 is one thing and £9000 is another'. However, she clarifies that most Bulgarians would not be able to afford even the home fees, noting that 'it will be still too high'.

Yet there are some suggestions that the reduction of fees could act as a trigger, encouraging more doctoral researchers to come to the UK (Okólski, 2006). Furthermore, changes in the regulations concerning payment of maintenance grants to undergraduate non-UK nationals changed following the case of *R. (Dany Bidar) v London Borough of Ealing and the Secretary of State for Education and Skills* (Case C-209/03) in 2005. The introduction of undergraduate tuition fees in the UK went hand-in-hand with the introduction of a new system of student finance, including loans and means-tested bursaries. Until recently these systems of financial support were restricted to home students. Recent European Court of Justice (ECJ) cases have introduced some significant changes to this situation, which may not only make it financially more attractive to study in the UK at undergraduate level but may also ease the transition into doctoral research (thus encouraging retention). Several Polish respondents talked of significant increases in the number of Polish students interested in studying in the UK since the changes to the fees regime. Ania, for example, has witnessed a change not so much in overall flows but in the career planning of Polish people already working in the UK in semi-skilled positions: 'I think a lot of Polish people who were working here now are starting to think about starting university in September, because they can see there's an opportunity to find a proper job, not necessarily like a restaurant job. People have asked me how university and papers work, all these things'. The ruling in *Bidar* has had a knock-on effect on the Research Councils in the UK, all of which now pay maintenance awards to EU nationals who have lived in the UK for three years as part of PhD scholarships as opposed to the previous fees-only awards. Teresa reflects on these changes and the effect they might have on mobility: 'Now I think it's much easier for PhDs because it's the same as other European countries. Fees are very low and people are eligible for [Research Council] scholarships and everything'.

For the respondents in our study, the *Bidar* ruling came into force too late to have any impact, but our data does seem to suggest that the reduction of fees and the availability of fees and maintenance awards to EU nationals would encourage doctoral candidates to consider the UK as a destination more seriously. The change in fees status for Polish nationals makes undertaking doctoral research in the UK feasible where it was not before (Aston, 2004). It provides more opportunities not only for the candidates themselves but also for institutions trying to find funding for them.

THE ROLE OF MOBILITY SCHEMES AND THE MULTIPLYING EFFECT OF MOBILITY

We have already referred to the attraction of being able to move without relinquishing links with the home country through forms of anchored mobility. Structured mobility schemes and exchange programmes play an important role in triggering and facilitating scientific mobility. European Commission-funded mobility schemes, such as ERASMUS, SOCRATES, TEMPUS or the Marie Curie Fellowships, all increase the overall volume of mobility opportunities and are usually subject to open and competitive applications, thus enabling scientists to plan their career paths and mobility actively. In addition, many of these reduce the risk of scientific mobility, enabling the applicant to retain their position at home. Schemes such as TEMPUS[18] allowed a number of our respondents to spend time abroad during their career. TEMPUS funds joint European projects that aim to increase cooperation and network-building between actors in higher education in EU Member States and partner countries, and individual mobility grants to allow attendance at conferences or seminars (up to two weeks), retraining or study periods (up to eight weeks) and for the preparation of joint projects (up to two weeks).

Out of 31 respondents in the UK, six had experience abroad through TEMPUS (ten respondents in total had used the scheme) and even though the grants offered were typically short term, they have clearly had a significant triggering effect. Irina first came to the UK on a TEMPUS grant for three months and after seeing the conditions of work and facilities, decided to apply for funding to complete her doctorate in the UK even though she had already started in Bulgaria:

> I managed to get in touch with somebody who was quite active internationally and I managed to start my PhD with her. She was involved in a TEMPUS project. The coordinator of this project was a professor and he realized that he needed to give chance to people from other universities not just Sofia . . . and he sort of picked some people and invited them to come to the UK.

The TEMPUS programme effectively triggered Irina's mobility. She had positioned herself in such a way as to be able to conduct research in Bulgaria and had taken the decision not to go abroad for any significant amount of time. The TEMPUS grant changed that for her and she has remained in the UK since completing her doctorate a number of years ago. Irina had no clear mobility strategy and had not developed a plan based on a rational weighing up of the pros and cons of mobility or of particular destinations. She simply took the opportunity offered and let her career develop from there. Tzonka's initial mobility was also triggered by a TEMPUS grant. She met a British professor at a conference and he agreed to act as host if she got a grant: 'He sent me an invitation that said he will accept me in the department to work for three months and the European Union gave me the grant'. Tzonka was later involved in a further TEMPUS grant before eventually securing employment at another UK institution. The exchange scheme provided the initial trigger to help her become mobile and allowed her to build further links, which supported her career and gave her the confidence to apply for a position abroad, thus shaping her future mobility. Both these cases show how schemes can trigger mobility in different circumstances.

THE ROLE OF INDIVIDUAL FELLOWSHIPS

Although many people move in order to access employment positions (applying for advertised positions), fellowship schemes also play an important role in enabling people to move. Schemes such as the Marie Curie

Table 3.3   Foreign scientists in Germany in 2003 by seniority and funding body

Graduates		Post-docs		Academic Staff	
Funding Body	Number	Funding Body	Number	Funding Body	Number
DAAD	5845	Max Planck	1569	DFG	1409
DFG	1558	Helmholtz	669	DAAD	1225
Max Planck	1383	Humboldt	581	Humboldt	1168

Source: Adapted from 'Wissenschaft weltoffen' (DAAD, 2006).

Fellowship Programme not only increase the volume of positions but also support the kind of lower-risk anchored mobility referred to above.

The type of fellowship and the ease with which they are administered are important factors in determining their triggering effect. Fellowship schemes played a particular important role amongst our German-based respondents. In contrast to the UK, Germany offers a wide range of often very generous individual fellowship schemes at all levels. Four schemes in particular provide funding specifically designed to attract international scientists: (1) the German Academic Exchange Service (DAAD); (2) the Deutsche Forschungs Gemeinschaft (German Research Foundation, DFG); (3) the Max Planck Society; and (4) the Alexander von Humboldt Foundation (see Table 3.3).

These funding bodies were all represented within our sample of respondents although not necessarily as individual fellowship providers. The Alexander von Humboldt Foundation was mentioned by a significant number of our respondents and comments were generally very positive and highlighted the Foundation's role in activating and maintaining mobility. This had a long-term influence on individual scientists. The von Humboldt Foundation offers fellowships for foreign researchers to come to Germany or German researchers to go abroad and continues to provide support on their return home. Roumen's case illustrates how the Foundation has influenced his mobility, his career and that of his early career researchers. His first visit to Germany took place in 1984 as a result of a two-year fellowship and he describes the long-term benefits: 'This Foundation really cares, it does everything to sustain very close relationships with people who have been selected . . . they ask you if you need books, literature and equipment for your everyday research and if you say yes and [they] think you are reliable you will get them'. With the help of the Foundation he has made a series of short stays, spending six months of every year abroad. The funding assistant for computing and equipment has also enabled him to work effectively in

Sofia on return: 'Many times I have got computers and equipment from them simply by telling them I need it, many years after my fellowship'.

The individual fellowships offered by the Foundation are relatively well paid but this does not seem to be the main driving force for Roumen:

> It is very well paid, an honorarium with no taxes; it's excellent, something like €2500–3500 per month. But what matters more than the money is the attitude and this attitude goes through the active fellowship during those two years but even more after that because they remember you, they convey the feeling that they care for you, and this bites emotionally.

Importantly, it seems that the administrative burden and formalities that have to be observed are kept to a minimum:

> What matters, to get this is to maintain some visits and scientific contacts to a partner in Germany, if you have someone who would back your request for something, then it is granted with no formalities at all, no lengthy discussions or applications or questions. All this is based on the trust they feel for that person. Now we have such Humboldt clubs in every East European country with regular meetings with fellows from the Balkan States and Greece for example . . . I still have some months left from the Humboldt that I didn't use so if nothing else works I can still call them and use it . . . and if I have a young PhD student or post-doc with me then I can take them too and we both go to a German institution for six months or so.

Roumen highlights the flexibility of the Foundation and the ongoing nature of support. This has had a major influence on his own mobility and career and also, more recently, on his junior colleagues. These sentiments were echoed by other Humboldt recipients such as Vladimir, who refers to the value of the support on return: 'I know a lot of people who got Humboldt fellowships and they went back to Bulgaria and got money from that scholarship to buy equipment and that was quite successful'.

The Alexander von Humboldt Foundation plays a major role in facilitating scientists' moves to Germany. There is no comparable mobility fellowship scheme in the UK, which specifically targets foreign or overseas researchers. The British Academy,[19] the British Council and the Royal Society do offer some schemes for foreign researchers but most scientists must apply for UK-based fellowships and funding opportunities that are not necessarily part of a mobility programme or targeted at foreign researchers. However, the UK does host a significant proportion of the Marie Curie Fellowships, including scientists from Poland and Bulgaria (Van de Sande et al., 2005).

As well as triggering and shaping outward moves, funding schemes in the host countries can also have a significant effect on science in the sending regions. Schiermeier and Smaglik (2005) report on a number of schemes designed to support scientists in Eastern European countries through grants funding infrastructure, salaries and equipment. Schiermeier and Smaglik specifically refer to the Wellcome Trust's International Senior Research Fellowships (ISRF), which, according to its website, fund 'outstanding mid-career scientists wishing to return to or remain in their home countries'. The ISRF scheme was set up in 2000 following a review of the quality of science and research communities in the EU accession countries. The individual flexible grants are available in five fields – mainly biomedical – but are restricted to the four countries with the strongest science bases in the region (Estonia, Poland, the Czech Republic and Hungary). It now funds 23 fellows who have received €750 000 each. A representative of the Wellcome Trust suggested to us that the funding was not an 'aid programme . . . we wanted to create some honey pots to show that it is possible to do top-class research in Central Europe'. Reference is also made to US schemes, such as the Howard Hughes Medical Institute (HHMI) programme, which has teamed up with the European Molecular Biology Organization (EMBO) in Heidelberg to fund installation grants to help young investigators in Central Europe to set up their first lab.

CONCLUSIONS

It is clear from the previous discussion that mobility is rarely, if ever, the result of a single decision: rather it is an ongoing, reflexive and adaptive negotiation that is shaped by a wide range of shifting stimuli over time and place. Professional and personal dimensions intertwine to mould decisions about whether and where to move over the career trajectory and life-course. Although many scientists do make decisions within this context, it is also important to recognize the role that serendipity, chance or non-decision plays in influencing moves and careers. Many people are catapulted into unplanned and on occasion sub-optimal moves by events, sometimes trailing supervisors or partners. In other situations, carefully planned moves fail to take place as the trigger necessary to facilitate the move is absent (such as access to a position, for example).

Underlying the circulationist perspective is the idea that scientific mobility is inherently positive (at the individual level at least) and part of a normal, desirable and selective mechanism responsible for the effective matching of the brightest and best human capital with the available positions and physical resources. According to this view, mobility performs a critical role as the invisible hand promoting the effective operation of labour markets in a global context. The notion of selectivity and the inherent value attached to international experience underpins what we have termed the 'expectation of mobility' in science careers. Mobility increases exposure to new skills and ideas and new ways of working and, as such, forms a critical means of facilitating the transfer of knowledge. The importance of this expectation of mobility and international experience to career progression in scientific research has led to the characterization of scientists as *knowledge* rather than *economic* migrants. The concept of knowledge migrant implies that moves are primarily influenced by the quest for knowledge and the need to access optimal conditions for skills acquisition and knowledge transfer. In practical terms this manifests itself in the pulling power of established and resource-rich centres of excellence, which contain both the know-how and, critically, the know-who that will enhance scientific productivity and individual career progression. These kinds of stimuli were certainly evident amongst our sample of scientists: some individuals developed a conscious strategy that focused on building up their human and social capital through mobility in order to increase their scientific productivity and long-term employability security.

However, more basic economic factors played a critical role in the majority of cases, with moves shaped by concerns around absolute or relative economic circumstances. In some situations scientists faced the prospect of no wages or were struggling with wages that were incapable of sustaining adequate basic living standards (in the absence of 'moonlighting') or wage differentials that supported a significantly higher quality of life. In addition to these concerns around personal income and well-being, mobility was often the only means of accessing the physical resources that enabled them to function effectively at all in experimental research. It was not so much the desire to access optimal facilities but to have access to basic chemicals and equipment and funding for travel. These concerns do not always lead to longer-term moves. Many scientists in Poland and Bulgaria were using short-stay or shuttle mobility as a transnational strategy, enabling them to work effectively in the home country.

Unfortunately the level of mobility in the West, often viewed enviously by scientists in the East as indicative of vibrant and open labour markets and optimal knowledge transfer, reflects not simply the value attached to international experience but the unintended consequence of funding policies. The high level of mobility in UK and German science markets is a direct consequence of the growth in insecure, fixed-term and externally funded employment (Ackers and Oliver, 2007). These positions form the primary access point for foreign researchers, the overwhelming majority of whom occupy temporary, nominally early-career positions (or inappropriately named 'post-docs'). This situation precipitates ongoing, often undesired and unexpected mobility and increases the propensity to return. Mobility in these contexts is not so much expected but rather enforced.

While notions of employability security are becoming increasingly popular in discussions about highly skilled mobility, the stimulus of employment security – in the traditional sense of having a permanent contract – remains evident in our sample. Its effect can be seen most acutely in relation to the impact of retained positions in Poland and Bulgaria.[20] The ability to move for quite long periods without relinquishing a secure and high status, if low paid, position in the sending country had an important anchoring effect, increasing return potential. The nature of employment contracts and opportunities to take research sabbaticals, for example, or spend long vacations abroad, played an important role, more generally, in shaping mobility and length of stay.

Just as employment security plays a significant role in shaping the mobility and career paths of our sample, so too do concerns around open or fair recruitment and progression. The volume of such early career entry positions in the UK and Germany and a powerful perception of transparent and meritocratic recruitment – at least in comparison with the situation in Poland and Bulgaria – are major factors motivating and directing moves. Scientists are both attracted by evidence of objective and meritocratic employment and propelled from experiences of patronage and corruption. This is an important factor not only facilitating outward moves but also restricting return as opportunities are seen to close behind them.

As scientists move they accrue what some authors have referred to as migration capital. Put simply, mobility often has a multiplying effect: moves made early in a scientist's career, perhaps at undergraduate level and in relatively risk-free contexts, increase the appetite for and confidence to move again. They also generate networks and contacts. This increases the probability of re-migration following return often but not always to the same country or institute.

Taken together it is clear that the characterization of scientists as knowledge migrants – at least in the context of Bulgaria and Poland and, arguably, in Italy during the MOBEX2 pilot project – amounts to an inaccurate and misleading generalization. In practice the dichotomy between economic and knowledge migrants fails to add anything to our understanding of scientific mobility. The complex range of push and pull factors outlined above also raises questions about the selectivity often associated with scientific mobility. Many scientists are more pushed than pulled. To the extent that selectivity exists, it is as much about the ability or willingness of the individual to endure repeated moves and uncertainty than innate human capital or ability. This chapter has identified and discussed a number of the professional factors shaping migration processes. The examples nevertheless illustrate the connection between these professional motivators and scientists' personal lives, particularly when discussing issues of contractual security and pay. The following chapter focuses on the impact of life-course and family on migration decisions.

NOTES

1. This chapter has been co-authored with Jess Guth.
2. The role of networks and connections in triggering moves is discussed in more detail in Chapter 6.
3. In many cases, for example, an internal institutional move within one country might facilitate access to a more international environment than a move abroad, but this is rarely acknowledged. This issue is developed in Chapter 7.
4. The characteristics of scientific labour markets and the effects of this on migration potential are discussed in more detail in other chapters and, for that reason, will not be developed here. Chapter 6 discusses the role of connections in recruitment processes and Chapters 7 and 8 report on labour market conditions in the receiving and sending locations respectively.
5. Examples of this are discussed further in Chapter 6 in the context of the role that connections and networks play in stimulating mobility.
6. This conclusion is supported by our other work on the relative impact of fixed-term contracts and pay on the attractiveness of science careers, which suggest that for many scientists – and for women in particular – permanency is more important than remuneration per se (Adams et al., 2005; Ackers et al., 2006).
7. The issue of seniority and career stage is complex. Although we have coded the respondents according to their position in the country of residence at the time of interview, in many cases people who held more senior and established positions in the home countries moved into what appear on the face of it to be traditional post-doc positions in the UK and Germany. In such cases it would be a mistake to categorize these people as early career although their positions might indicate that. The distorting effect this has on labour markets in the receiving countries is covered in later chapters.
8. The retention of positions in the home country and the relationship between these, migration behaviour and knowledge transfer is discussed further in later chapters.
9. This issue is discussed in Chapter 8.
10. The importance of networks and know-who are discussed in Chapter 6.
11. Of course this also impacts on the time available to do research.
12. In the Polish context we were informed that the average price of a two-bedroom flat in Poland is about €300 per month and that a talented graduate going into the business sector could command a salary of about €1250 per month immediately after graduation.
13. It is interesting that this issue was raised in many of the returnee interviews but when asked about remittances, scientists in the host countries rarely admitted to making regular financial contributions to family back home. In most cases they said that their family did not need this additional income.
14. Tuition fees of €500 per semester for undergraduate courses have now been introduced in some German federal states.
15. There is insufficient scope here to embark on detailed consideration of the complexity of national schemes and the benefits of these. For more detail see Reichert and Tauch (2003, 2005), Witte (2006), Crosier, Purser and Smidt (2007). The main concern in this chapter is to consider the financial consequences of these differences and the effect on location decisions.
16. Undergraduate fees in the UK are currently fixed at £3000 per year.

17. See http://www.studis-online.de/StudInfo/Gebuehren. Fees for Masters courses vary, although many are charged at the same rate as undergraduate studies (€500 per semester). Some are more expensive. However, a distinction between Home/EU and international students is not normally made.
18. The TEMPUS programme is a European Commission-funded programme that funds cooperation projects in the areas of curriculum development and innovation, teacher training, university management, and structural reforms in higher education. The partner countries are currently the Western Balkans, Eastern Europe and Central Asia, North Africa and the Middle East.
19. Both the British Academy and the British Council have Researcher Exchange Programmes for early stage researchers. The Royal Society offers funding short visits to the UK for post-doctoral scientists and above for one week to three months.
20. Interestingly, this was not the case in our pilot study on Italy.

4. The impact of partnering on migration processes and outcomes

INTRODUCTION

Traditional approaches to migration theorizing have tended to focus rather narrowly on a limited number of economic determinants and, in particular, the effect of wage differentials in shaping migration and location decisions. The emphasis on the decision has also tended to characterize migration as a one-time event, perhaps followed by a return move. In recent years, research has drawn attention to the role that a much wider range of factors play in shaping what are now conceptualized more accurately as migration *processes* or, in a European context, 'mobilities' (Wallace, 2002: 604). This might include a more holistic appraisal of economic factors to encompass living costs and expenditures and their impact on family resources. In addition to this, research has encouraged us to consider the impact that personal and family relationships and obligations might have on migration behaviour, perhaps generating resistance to the pull of economic considerations or, in other contexts, lubricating mobility. Concerns around spousal employment rights and the impact of dual career situations form the focus of an increasing body of research that reflect a move away from the individualistic and consensual male breadwinner model to acknowledge the effect of dual career relationships on migration decision-making (Ackers, 2004b; Bailey and Boyle, 2004; Raghuram, 2004; Smith, 2004). Boyd (1989: 640) critiques economic rationality models, which he suggests 'emphasise the movement of people as a result of rational calculations performed by individual actors' drawing attention to the role of partners and wives in particular'. In a similar vein, Kofman (2004) notes the emphasis that migration studies have traditionally placed on the individual primary migrant as a factor limiting the scope of research and its ability to recognize and understand the influence of family and partners on migration processes. Raghuram (2004: 303) further suggests that whilst skilled migration now constitutes the 'only acceptable form of migration' into the UK, little analysis has taken place on how this 'shift in the skills of the primary migrant reconfigures family migration'. To the extent that the role of partners has been studied, the work has largely focused on less skilled sectors of the labour market and typically casts women as the victims of migration, as either 'tied movers' or 'followers' of male primary migrants. Raghuram (ibid.) contends that the nature of family migration changes significantly when migrants are skilled, thus resulting in far more complex patterns and relationships. Although she emphasizes the dangers of generalization, even within the skilled category, and the need to take account of the specificities of labour markets, she argues that in certain contexts women 'play a more active role in configuring the immigration or labour market strategies of their households' (ibid.: 306). Raghuram's empirical research with migrant doctors reveals a more multifaceted picture, with women often playing the role of lead migrants because of the 'occupational niches' they occupy (ibid.).

The MOBEX2 interviews highlight the influence that scientists' personal and family circumstances have on mobility. Partnering has a powerful, but not always predictable, impact on career and migration decision-making. Having a partner affects the way people think about moving in a number of respects: it influences decisions about *whether* to move at all or to move again (including *return*); *where* to move to; and for *how long* to stay. The presence of a partner might in some circumstances dampen the willingness to move or stay abroad for long periods. In other cases, it might increase the incentive to remain and not return. Important factors here include the nationality or country of origin of the partner, their employment status and whether they are also engaged in science. The emphasis on the individual in traditional theories of migration – based on notions of economic rationality – has close parallels with the emphasis on individual competition, selectivity and quality inherent in the brain drain debate. The very idea that migration forms a means of employing the 'brightest and the best' rests on the assumption that individual employees respond to the logic of economic differentials (and wages in particular) and individual employers, through the hidden hand of the market, magically select 'the cream of the crop'. This model is based on two faulty presumptions. First, that highly skilled people are equally footloose and able and willing to move. Second, that the mechanisms exist to identify and reward quality in any objective sense (a point we return to in Chapter 7). To the extent that personal relationships might interfere with these migration dynamics, we might therefore expect a distortion in the relationship between migration and selectivity. Selection might be rather more a reflection of the ability or willingness to move than an indicator of ability or scientific excellence. One of the Marie Curie Fellows interviewed in a previous study suggests that mobile researchers share a common interest: 'Marie Curie Fellows are birds of a feather. There is a common theme – they are interested to be mobile' (cited in Ackers, 2003: 58).

This chapter focuses on the effect that partnering has on the migration behaviour of our sample of Polish and Bulgarian migrant scientists and considers the potential effects of this in terms of the impact of highly skilled migration.

PARTNERING, CAREER AND MOBILITY

The migration literature has tended to focus on two dimensions of the mobility/partnering dynamic. First, the extent to which partnering restricts mobility and, second, the extent to which mobility in (heterosexual) couples impacts on employment status, particularly for the female partner (usually the wife). There is a general assumption that younger, single people are more likely to be mobile and that partnering has a dampening effect on mobility. Literature on the characteristics of flows from Central and Eastern European countries would tend to support this general assertion (Haug, 2005). Krieger (2004: 7) concludes her analysis of the migration intentions of Bulgarians with the comment that 'most potential migrants are single'. In addition to this skew in favour of younger age groups, others also point to the emergence of gender differences over the life-course. Haug and Diehl (2004b), for example, find marked gender differences in migration intentions by age group, with younger cohorts displaying similar intentions but a marked over-representation of men emerging amongst the 30–49 age group when about two-thirds of potential migrants are male. She postulates that this might be because 'women are losing or postponing their emigration due to family reasons' (ibid.: 16) In a later paper, however, Haug (2005: 12) finds that 'only one third of all potential migrants intend to emigrate alone and more than one third plan to be accompanied by family members'. Chompalov's (2000: 16) findings are also contradictory: although he predicted that 'never married and divorced scientists will be more prone to consider emigrating', the data he actually presents on Bulgarian scientific emigration do not bear this out. Initial post-transition data (for 1989) do indicate a predominance of single migrants but slightly later figures for 1993 suggest that only one-fifth (20 per cent) of migrants from Sofia were single and the mean age was 41–50 years (ibid.: 25).

Our own data from previous studies would tend to support the general assertion that young, single people are more mobile but partnering begins to impact on migration propensity as people age and develop relationships. One of the key informants in a study on the representation of women in the Marie Curie Fellowship scheme illustrates the point: 'Women are as likely to move if they are footloose and fancy free. They all head off if they are single and without attachments. If not, they don't

Table 4.1   Partnering status and location of partner in MOBEX2 sample

	Partner Living in Same Country	Partner Living in Different Country	Total
Single person	–	–	13
Dual career couples	21	3	24
Dual science couples	34	5	39
Single career couple	9	2	11
Unknown	1	0	1
Totals	65	10	88

go. Guys do though, unless their wives have got jobs – that's a new phenomenon' (cited in Ackers, 2003: 68). Although this study did find that younger, single people were more mobile and that partnering had a particular impact on women, this does not mean that few partnered scientists move. In fact, in the Marie Curie study, which by definition included a disproportionately 'youthful' population of doctoral and post-doctoral researchers, a majority (60 per cent) of respondents had a partner at the time of interview and about 60 per cent of these were accompanied by their partner in the host country.

As Table 4.1 shows, the majority of MOBEX2 respondents were also partnered (85 per cent).[1] The sample was characterized by a very high incidence of dual career situations (again, 85 per cent) with professional couples attempting to manage careers and relationships in a migration context.[2] The majority (62 per cent) of respondents in dual career couples were partnered by someone currently working in science research. The definition of a dual science couple adopted in this project was quite restrictive in that it only included partners who were actively engaged in science research at the point of interview. As such it excluded cases where partners were qualified or had been working in scientific research in the past or were working in other areas of science (such as engineering or school teaching) and also where partnerships had dissolved. It is also likely to underestimate the real proportion of dual career couples due to the tendency of respondents who are not legally married or cohabiting to identify themselves as single even when a significant relationship exists (Ackers, 2004a).[3]

The strong tendency for scientists to establish relationships with other scientists has an interesting effect on mobility. On the one hand, it places an equivalent pressure on both parties to tolerate repeated geographical mobility and, given the highly specialist nature of scientific research, this often implies an acceptance of living apart for extended periods (Wilson, 1999; Rusconi and Solga, 2002; Ackers, 2004a). On the other hand, these

Table 4.2   Partnering status by gender in MOBEX2 sample

	Male	Female	Total
Dual career couple	13	11	24
Dual science couple	17	22	39
Single career couple	8	3	11
Unknown partner occupation	2	0	2
Total partnered	40	36	76
Total dual science couples as % of partnered	43	61	52
Single person	3	10	13
Total	43	46	89

couples are more likely to understand the rationale for mobility and share similar values in that respect (Raghuram, 2004). It also means that language is less of a barrier to mobility and career reintegration as both partners can usually function effectively in their research, if not socially, in English.

Table 4.2 shows the breakdown of partnering status by gender. In common with previous studies (Ackers, 2003), women in our sample were more likely to be single than men: 22 per cent of women compared with 7 per cent of men were single. When women were in a relationship, however, they were more likely to have a partner who was a scientist than the male respondents: 61 per cent of women compared with 43 per cent of men had a partner who was also a scientist. A fifth of partnered men were in a 'single career relationship' at the point of interview compared with only 8 per cent of partnered women.

These figures follow a similar pattern to the findings in recent related studies. Although the specific approach taken to identifying such couples varies slightly in each of these studies – and full data was not always available – together they provide an indication of the prevalence of dual career situations amongst scientists (Table 4.3).

Recent work in the United States has also identified high levels of dual science partnerships in physics, with more than 68 per cent of married female physicists in partnerships with scientists compared with only 17 per cent of males (McNeil and Sher, 1999). The authors conclude that the 'two body problem' has a 'particularly acute impact' on women and the lack of attention to it in policy terms 'contributes to the leaky pipeline of women in physics' (ibid.). A recent German study (von Ruschkowski, 2003) focusing again on physics, found that 86 per cent of female physicists in Germany were in a relationship with another physicist and predicted 'the number to be as high in other disciplines'.[4]

Table 4.3   The prevalence of dual science career couples in related studies[a]

Project	Dual Science Couples as Proportion of Total Sample	Dual Science Couples as Proportion of Partnered Scientists	Partnered Males with Science Partners	Partnered Females with Science Partners
MOBISC[b] (n = 248%)	56	70	64	79
MOBEX1 (n = 56%)	56	69	63	78
TMR[c] (n = 159%)	Missing data	53	Missing data	70
IMPAFEL[d] (n = 2913%)	Missing data	50	Missing data	Missing data
MOBEX2 (n = 87%)	45	52	43	61

Notes:
a. For details of these projects see Annex 3. The MOBISC results are reported in Ackers (2005d), the TMR results in Ackers (2003) and the IMPAFEL results in Van de Sande et al. (2005).
b. MOBISC = Mobility and Progression in Science Careers: Equal Pay, Career Progression and the Socio-Legal Valuation of Care.
c. TMR = Training and Mobility in Research programme.
d. IMPAFEL = Impact Assessment of the Marie Curie Fellowship Scheme.

The following section moves on to consider the effect of this level and form of dual career partnering on migration decisions and also on the impact of highly skilled migration.

THE DAMPENING EFFECT OF PARTNERS: INHIBITING INITIAL MOBILITY

As we have noted, the overwhelming majority of MOBEX2 respondents were partnered. The specific focus of this study meant that we would not have sampled people who had not moved at all for whatever reason, as the sampling criteria required that all respondents had experienced some form of mobility. In practice, we unintentionally interviewed one scientist in Bulgaria who had not moved, as her planned move fell through prior to the interview. Pepka had worked as a physicist in a lab for over five years since her PhD when she applied for a one-year fellowship in Germany. She said that she had not previously applied and now only wished to go abroad for a maximum of one year because she had a partner who worked in a retail company in Bulgaria. Pepka said that her partner would not be able to move with her so it 'wasn't easy' and if she did go abroad she 'would come back and stay in science in Bulgaria'. In this case, then, having a partner reduced the scientist's willingness to leave (in response to scientific or pecuniary motivations), limited the length she was prepared to stay abroad and indicated a higher propensity to return and continue in scientific research in Bulgaria.

Work we are currently undertaking as part of another project has involved work with Eastern European cell biologists, many of whom have not experienced mobility.[5] Preliminary interviews have identified a number of cases of young scientists who are unwilling or unable to move because of their partners. To illustrate the point, one respondent was about to submit her doctorate after completing a first degree in pharmacy in Hungary. Although she was keen to remain in science research, she felt that this was unlikely due to the lack of positions and declining funding. However, she said that she would prefer to move into another field, possibly medical translation or work in a pharmacy, because 'this would give me the opportunity to stay here with my partner'. The interviews with several Polish PhD students – all of whom were young women – revealed a number of similar situations where they 'preferred' to move into another area of work (and potentially experience a degree of de-skilling) rather than migrate in order to remain in science.

MOBEX2 respondents also revealed evidence of the effect of partnering on the propensity to move (either initially or repeatedly) and the distorting effect this had on any direct relationship between mobility and quality. Roumen, one of the professors interviewed in Bulgaria, talked of one of his 'best' post-docs who became 'motivated as a scientist' as a result of a spell of mobility during her doctorate. He went on to explain that she was nevertheless about to turn down 'a very good offer for her to go abroad for two years, and on a much higher salary, that would be a breakthrough in financial terms but now she doesn't want to go . . . because of family I think. She got married a few months ago'. Valentina – the post-doc in question – told us that she would be turning down the offer of a prestigious and relatively lucrative three-year post-doc in Germany as she did not wish to leave her partner again: 'It's a bit difficult for him to accompany me. He would have to stop his work and then after three years start again . . . maybe the best thing would be to go for two months, to discuss, to start working and make plans and then continue working here'. At the end of the day, although Valentina recognized the value of the potential move in both scientific and financial terms – describing it as the 'perfect opportunity' – she felt that she would 'prefer to stay in Bulgaria. We are trying to organize our life now and for me it's more comfortable'. Many other respondents adopted Valentina's strategy of using repeated short stays as an alternative to longer-term mobility, which effectively enabled them to reconcile the demands of their job (and need for income) with their personal circumstances. However, this is only possible when people have managed to access an established position.[6]

In cases such as these it is hard to interpret migration behaviour as the outcome of narrowly selective processes based on merit or quality. Partners may play an important role in anchoring top-quality scientists – and especially female scientists – in the home country. On the other hand, to the extent that partners dampen mobility, this might also be expected to reduce the ability of the tied-stayers to use mobility as a means of investing in their human capital, increasing their productivity and progressing in the home context and this might be to the detriment both of themselves as individuals and the domestic and European science base.

MOVING WITH PARTNERS

In very many cases, as we have seen, scientists may move with their partners, are joined by their partners or form partnerships in the host country. In these situations we might ask whether the existence of a relationship influences subsequent mobility and, in particular, return, perhaps locking them into the host country at least for a time. Important factors here appear to be the employment status and nationality of the partner.

Violeta's partner is also a Bulgarian scientist. She explains how professional and personal motivations have combined to shape her ongoing migration and location decisions. She completed her diploma[7] in Bulgaria and subsequently worked for a government agency there. Her Bulgarian boyfriend then moved to Germany to carry out his diploma work as part of an institutional collaboration. After a year living apart Violeta decided to look for a doctoral position and join him: 'The reason for coming to Germany was personal because my boyfriend was doing his diploma here and also because I wanted to have a little bit more experience abroad . . . I wanted this for him, he wanted this and I thought it was also a good possibility for my career'.

It is clear from her description that this decision enabled her to reconcile professional and personal motives at that point in time. Violeta's partner then commenced his PhD in Germany. At the time of the interview she had completed her PhD and was working part-time as a post-doc after having their first child. Her partner was in the final stages of his doctorate and Violeta explained that she did not want to look for a full-time position elsewhere because they wanted to ensure that they could find positions in the same place: 'Now we are in the same position as before because we have finished our PhD work. We have to choose and look for another job again. I don't want to move by myself. Maybe we can do it together because he's a physicist and I'm a chemist so both of us have to work in science'.

In cases such as this it is hard to begin to identify a primary or lead migrant. In the first instance, Violeta moved to follow her partner but secured a higher-level position. She is also clear that this was to their mutual benefit. Her subsequent decision to stay put in a part-time position rather than move abroad again could be less than optimal in career terms but, arguably, at this point she is simply biding time, waiting for him to complete his thesis and taking care of her child in the process. Violeta echoes the concerns of many other scientists about finding proximate positions at more senior level in highly specialist fields. In practice, scientists often have to manage ongoing mobility or extensive post-migration commuting in order to reconcile these tensions. This situation also has an important impact on location decisions, with scientists preferring escalator regions – such as the South East of England, for example – where the level of scientific concentration increases the opportunities to secure two relatively proximate careers and achieve an acceptable work–life balance. Although they are both Bulgarian, the chances of Violeta and her partner both securing acceptable scientific positions in Bulgaria is quite remote and might discourage their return.

Apart from bi-national relationships, perhaps the strongest evidence of 'stickiness' or propensity to settle for a longer period can be seen in cases where both partners have managed to achieve a level of professional integration and stability in the host state. This is especially so when children are also involved. Rada provides a case in point. She moved in the first instance, accompanied by her scientist partner, and following her mother and younger sister, to the UK. At the time of the first interview both her and her husband were nearing the end of their doctorates (in the same department) and maintained an open and slightly confused mind about their future location. They also had a two-year-old child. A follow-up interview 18 months later, however, indicated a quite different trajectory. Rada and her husband had both managed to secure attractive research positions in the same company and in the same town in the UK and she was quite convinced now that they would settle here more permanently. As she put it, 'Everything is going well here, we think we will stay now, especially for my daughter'.

In such cases, of course, the sending country loses not one but two highly qualified individuals and possibly loses them permanently. In Rada's case it appears that both partners were equally eager to move in the first instance and now to remain. In other cases, the situation was less consensual, with one of the partners assuming the role of reluctant joiner or reluctant stayer, either moving with, or following behind, the primary migrant. Ivaylo gave up his senior permanent position in Bulgaria to join his scientist wife and their undergraduate son in the UK. Although his temporary contract in the UK was better paid and enabled him to play a more effective role in financially supporting his family, the post-doctoral position he is occupying in the UK represents a degree of de-skilling (at least in terms of loss of seniority and his role as a PhD supervisor) and, from the Bulgarian perspective, the loss of a second highly qualified scientist for family reasons. Ivaylo was also very unhappy with the situation and wished to return. This was perhaps a case of financial imperatives overriding personal wishes.[8]

Ania is another example of a reluctant stayer although she made the initial move and in fact met her Polish husband post-migration in the UK. Initially, she moved for a defined three-year period to do her PhD and expressed a very strong desire to return mainly to be with her family: 'For me it was very difficult because I was very, very close to my family, we are all very close to each other. It was really something for me to move 1000 km from my family. I'm phoning every day to be honest'. Although her partner is Polish he wishes to stay longer in the UK: 'Unfortunately in this moment it's not that easy. My boyfriend opened a company here, which means it's definitely more difficult. He doesn't want to return yet'. Although they are both Polish, Ania's partner's business interests in the UK have restricted her ability to return when her personal migration objectives have been realized. This not only restricts Ania's mobility but also, theoretically, Poland's ability to gain from the investment in Ania's human capital that has taken place in the host country.

Even where couples move together – at an international level – this does not imply that they necessarily cohabit in the host country. Teresa's situation is not untypical.[9] Whilst her Polish, scientist partner is in the UK, the fact that they are both on temporary contracts and living some distance apart without children perhaps reduces the 'stickiness' often associated with partnering. Despite the length of time she has spent in the UK (about ten years) and the fact that her partner is also here, she does not regard herself as settled in any traditional sense and talks of moving again in future. Teresa discusses settling in the specific context of having children, which would force a change in the way they manage their dual career situation, 'requiring' them to cohabit. At this point, she can envisage settling either in the UK or back home in Poland. For the time being Teresa and her partner can best be described as *living apart together* – a situation that is quite prevalent amongst mobile scientists (see Ackers, 2004a; Roseneil, 2006). This also underlines the importance of understanding mobility as an ongoing process. Although Teresa has made only one international move she has experienced three post-migration internal moves between different institutions and cities within the UK. This situation is likely to reduce any tendency to settle in the host country in the longer term, particularly if children are involved. As Ouellette (2007: 701) argues 'combining a family with a commuter marriage adds yet more complications' and may trigger a subsequent international move or return or an intersectoral move on the part of one partner as the desire to cohabit tempers professional objectives.

Many dual science couples reconcile their personal and professional needs, at least for a time, through forms of living apart together, effectively enduring extensive periods of separation or 'weekend marriages'.[10] In some cases, however, the situation extends over the life-course and between countries. Tzonka is an example of someone who moved in the first instance on a temporary basis to take up a fellowship in the UK. Her husband is also a highly qualified scientist who has remained in Bulgaria because he has a strong and well-remunerated position there in a government department. Tzonka's own career progression was limited in Bulgaria and she has found her employment in the UK, albeit at a less senior level, to be more attractive. She also has two daughters currently resident in the UK but asserts that 'I am here first and foremost because of myself'. In a follow-up interview Tzonka talks of new plans for her husband to take early retirement and join her in the UK, at least until she retires when they both plan to return home. Although Tzonka will have spent half of her working life in the UK, their strategy has enabled her husband to remain in and continue to make a contribution to Bulgarian science. The fact that she has such a powerful anchor in Bulgaria has also played an important role in enabling her to retain active social and research links in Bulgaria as she spends a significant amount of time there, increasing the potential for effective knowledge transfer.[11] While this type of arrangement limits the human capital losses to Bulgaria, it does so at a high price for the individuals concerned.

THE IMPACT OF BI-NATIONAL PARTNERING ON MOBILITY

Whilst many scientists had been mobile up to a certain point in their career, it comes as no surprise that many form relationships post-migration and often with other nationals. In these situations, particularly when the relationship is with a host national, dual career relationships tend to lock people into spaces restricting mobility and, more commonly, returns. Magdalena, for example, is in a dual science relationship and displays a strong commitment to return. Although she appears to have unusually good professional opportunities to effect this return, her relationship with an English scientist is restricting her ability to do so: 'I am interested in going back but now I've got an English boyfriend so that creates a massive problem [otherwise] I'd go back tomorrow . . . all my family are there and although I've been here for nine years it doesn't quite feel like you're at home'. Her partner works in the same lab as her but doesn't speak Bulgarian and career prospects for him in Bulgaria are very limited.[12] She adds that they are not interested in moving to another country because of her partner's family: 'This is where his family is and we've lived here for a long time so I don't want to go to another country unless I have no other option'.

Magdalena's specific circumstances – her partner's language skills and the lack of employment prospects for him in Bulgaria – coupled with the stickiness associated with his family ties suggest that, whether she planned it or not, she is likely to remain in the UK perhaps permanently. The draw of Bulgaria is also linked to her family ties, however, demonstrating the difficult tensions involved in negotiating transnational kinship over time and place.

Kiril is also in a dual science relationship with a host national. He came to the UK from Germany to do his PhD and then met his partner, who was also completing a PhD at the same institution. The fact that his wife is British and his familial links with Bulgaria more or less extinguished were important factors shaping his decision to remain in the UK. Asked whether he would consider returning to Bulgaria in the future he replies, 'Even if Bulgaria turned around tomorrow and became absolutely amazing and fantastic I would probably not go back . . . because I have set up a family'.[13]

Boyko's partner, on the other hand, is a fellow Bulgarian and he feels that this increases the likelihood of their return (his case is discussed in more detail below). When talking about his potential return, he explains that bi-national couples would have very different attitudes to return compared with people like him: 'Things change very much if your partner is not from your country. I don't think mixed couples will return to Bulgaria'. The influence of international or mixed-nationality partnering on migration processes has received some attention in recent studies. Scott (2006), for example, highlights the significance of the mixed-nationality partner in shaping middle-class migration in the European context. He found that 'a significant number of British migrants were living in Paris to cement mixed-nationality relationships. Mixed-nationality migrants were the most committed to Paris and the most integrated/assimilated and the least transnational in their everyday lives' (ibid.: 1114–15). According to this perspective, mixed-nationality partnerships (with host nationals) facilitate settlement and restrict return. Of course, the category of mixed-nationality couples would encompass situations in which both partners were migrants and this is very common in science given the highly international flavour of many labs and the fact that migrants tend to socialize together in the host country. In such cases one might anticipate a more footloose, transnational, perhaps even nomadic response. In Scott's study, this group were evidently joiners or family reunification migrants. Scott further adds that a 'large majority of these mixed-relationship migrants were female, with women apparently more ready to move overseas and compromise their own social networks and professional and cultural identities than men' (ibid.: 1121).

Kofman (2004: 247) also usefully distinguishes 'marriage migration' as a distinct and growing form of family migration, drawing attention to the rising percentages of bi-national or mixed marriages. She suggests that this form of relationship raises a number of issues around the organization of family and gender relations across international space. With specific reference to Bulgarian migration to Germany, Haug (2005: 8) cites figures from the Federal Statistics Office, which suggest a very high rate of intermarriage: 458 out of the 530 marriages of female Bulgarians that took place in Germany over a given time period involved a German husband.[14] In relation to MOBEX2 specifically, our findings suggest that in many cases bi-national partnering may actually restrict mobility rather than facilitate it. It is not so much that scientists are moving in order to marry but that relationships develop post-migration in the host state. In such cases, the nationality of the partner is likely to influence decisions about length of stay and return.

PARTNER'S EMPLOYMENT: 'FAILED' MIGRATIONS, BRAIN WASTE AND RETURN

In addition to nationality, the nature of a partner's employment plays a significant role in shaping mobility and location decisions. In cases such as Rada's, discussed above, where both partners have achieved an acceptable level of professional integration, this tends to increase the chances of settlement and reduce the potential for return. However, the converse is also true: where partners have experienced difficulties in accessing acceptable employment in the host state, this often increases the likelihood of return. In such cases there is also often evidence of de-skilling or 'brain stagnation' in the host context. Furthermore, it is by no means always clear that such decisions are based on economic optimization, rather, such decisions may be based on quality of life in a broader sense.

Our previous research with mobile scientists has highlighted the influence that dual science career situations have on the retention and progression of women in science (Ackers, 2003; 2004a). The highly special-ized nature of the work, coupled with the fact that both partners face similar pressures to move in response to the 'expectation of mobility' and the lack of secure positions, often precipitates a career change on the part of one partner and, more commonly, the woman. Our conclusions, at the time, were that dual science situations placed significant pressure on the individuals concerned and could be distinguished from previous work on dual career mobility, which indicated less tension on the grounds that female partners often occupied positions in more ubiquitous careers, which facilitated their ability to trail their partners. Some authors identified the importance of gender-based labour market segmentation in 'setting the stage for the female role as the trailing wife' (Cooke, 2003: 339). Echoing the work of Spitze (1984) and Bonney and Love (1991), Cooke (2003: 339) suggests that 'many women enter into such careers as nursing and primary education in anticipation of their future gender roles as mothers who need flexible work hours and as trailing wives who need to have a job that is in demand in any locality'.[15] This would seem to suggest not only that the migration decision itself is carefully planned and rational but also that women were able to anticipate the prospect of mobility at an earlier stage in their education and/or career planning.

Scientists, it seems, do not fall into this pattern: to have reached the level of a post-doc or even doctoral candidate requires a high degree of com-mitment to research and significant investment, which would certainly not indicate that they were actively planning to trail or enter careers conducive to work–life balance. Science careers also appear to pose greater chal-lenges to migrating couples than many other professions because of the very highly skilled and specialized nature of the work and the difficulties of accessing proximate positions outside established science clusters. As a result of this the partners moving with the primary migrant may experi-ence a degree of de-skilling or 'brain waste' at least at the outset (Iredale, 1999; Mahroum, 2001; Kofman, 2002; Sretenova, 2003; and Okólski, 2006). Much of the migration literature, at least implicitly, tends to focus on the primary migrant as an individual. The design of the MOBEX2 study meant that we were unlikely to identify cases of brain waste as such, among our direct respondents, although many were working in more junior positions than their qualifications, experience and age could command (a point discussed in Chapter 7). However, there was evidence of de-skilling, at least during the initial post-migration period, amongst their partners and, as we have seen, it is often impossible to designate these as secondary migrants in the traditional sense. In other cases, the inabil-ity of a partner to secure acceptable employment resulted in a 'failed' attempt to join and the subsequent return of the partner, sometimes along with the children, could mean leaving the respondent alone in the host state.[16]

The next section considers first examples of 'brain waste' or problems of post-migration professional reintegration amongst dual science couples before looking at the kinds of problems some non-scientist partners experienced. Vasil and Nikolina are a classic example of a dual science career couple who have moved together. Nikolina could be categorized as the trailing spouse to the extent that she followed Vasil to Germany, accepting a position with no pay in the first instance.[17] However, she was later able to resume her career and they eventually consolidated their positions, both securing acceptable permanent posts in Germany.

Krystyna is also in a dual science relationship. She had the opportunity to spend time in France during her undergraduate degree but at this point did not wish to leave her partner: 'When I was a student I was very attached to my boyfriend, now he's my husband and I didn't want to go under any Erasmus programmes because it's very difficult to go to the same place together'. However, she subsequently spent two short periods living in France on her own during her doctorate – about nine months in total – before moving to the UK to take up a two-year Marie Curie Fellowship. Her partner then made the decision to follow her, thus leaving a secure position in Poland:

> We moved together because we have been together for so long and we are a certain age. If I moved by myself, I mean it's easier to move by yourself, do you know what I mean? I really appreciate that my husband decided to follow me because he had good work and he was an important person: he had a big office and his own secretary and he gave up everything.

Krystyna goes on to describe their first year in the UK when her husband could not find suitable employment and could not speak English: 'He's a man and . . . he wanted to *do* something so he was working in a warehouse. Of course he hated this job and he complained all the time. It was more than a year before he got a position in science'. Krystyna's experience shows that, despite the general trend identified in previous research for women to follow men in these situations and assume the role of tied movers, this is by no means always the case. Indeed, the MOBEX2 sample included a number of trailing male partners. Importantly, it also illustrates the significance of assessing situations carefully and allowing time for migrants and especially their partners to adjust to the new context. Although initially Krystyna's partner experienced some de-skilling, this was a temporary period and he was able to access a scientific position after a year or so.

Irina similarly describes the impact of her move on her partner who, like her, worked in the field of computing but not in the academic sector. Irina moved to the UK to do her doctorate but found it hard to live for more than a year on her own, leaving her husband and two children in Bulgaria: 'I came on my own and the first year was very difficult because I didn't have my family here because we didn't have funding. Funding [for my PhD] was only for me. I decided at the end of the first year to go back to Bulgaria because I didn't think I could survive. Then my husband decided to come and join me'. Irina provides a thorough account of the process of trying to help her husband secure employment in the UK:

> When I came over here I realized that there was a huge demand for programmers with skills on these machines. His skills became quite in demand and unique so when I realized that I asked him to come over and just try to find a job. I knew that he, as my dependent, would have permission to work in the UK so that would be legal. And then with his skills he could find something. OK, so he didn't want to come because he didn't know the language and for a man it was a big decision. But when I decided to go back to Bulgaria he decided to try. He realized how serious I was. So then he decided to come over and he came without any language at all. So the first month he immediately went to language courses. The [local] university has very good intensive courses. After a month I realized that my husband was not happy because he was only going to courses and he needed to work and he didn't feel confident enough to go to interviews. So he wanted to do any kind of job and we went to the job centre and they gave him things like cleaning and very basic jobs, and he started going to those interviews but because he was not fluent in communicating I went together with him. I was unhappy about him opting for these jobs because I thought that he was quite skilled and he should have opted for jobs that were according to his skills and competences. So what happened is that when we went to those interviews for temporary jobs – to do some washing up and things like that – he would hide his qualifications because they were scared to talk to somebody who is so highly educated for this job. The last interview he had was at the cricket club and the guy looked at his CV and said 'I wonder why you are coming to this type of job, my wife has some of this experience in computer language and she earns so much money'. So my husband then realized that it was probably more likely for him to find a job there than as a cleaner'.

He then secured a position with a computing company but:

> He started with a half salary which was made clear at the beginning because his references were from Bulgaria and they couldn't trust the references. After two or three months though they doubled the salary and he was well appreciated in the company. Initially he was my dependant and then after my PhD finished I was not quite sure what I was going to do but the company at that time arranged a work permit for him as a highly skilled worker.

In Irina's case, it was the male partner who took the risk of tied migration or being the trailing spouse. He was fortunate, however, to be able to take advantage of the legal system in the UK, which permits spousal employment (even though Irina was a 'student' at the time). Although his initial period of employment could be described as brain waste or de-skilling, this period of adjustment and professional reintegration is not unusual and unsurprising especially when people lack adequate language skills and need some time to understand the employment context. Having moved and invested in his career and achieved a permanent position, the follower has effectively become the principal breadwinner and they are likely to remain in the UK.

It might well be that Okólski's (2006) pessimism over the level of post-migration de-skilling among emigrant Polish graduates masks this adjust-ment or transitional period and the extent to which certain unskilled positions are used as stepping stones into more appropriate positions. Although he suggests that 'the vast majority (80–90%) of Polish emigrant graduates are hired in posts that need no professional qualifications such as maids, waiters, kitchen and catering assistants' (ibid.: 58), these kinds of positions are often used as a period of orientation, a means to gain entry, earn cash and learn the language. Williams and Baláž (2005) make specific reference to the use of au pair positions for this purpose.

Irina's case also illustrates the fluid nature of situations and dependen-cies: once Irina's PhD was over and her partner had secured employment and residency, the tables turned and she effectively became his dependant. In practice, she had planned to return after her doctorate but has now been in the UK for over ten years. The professional integration of her partner, coupled with the settlement of her two children, has together reduced the potential for her return to Bulgaria. From the perspective of the sending country, Bulgaria had the potential to gain from the invest-ment the UK had made in Irina's doctoral training (assuming she had been able to secure a position back home). In practice, it was now losing two highly skilled scientists and their children who are now studying at UK universities.

The findings in the current study suggest that dual career situations where one partner is not involved in scientific research but seeks to develop a professional career are often associated with less favourable outcomes. To some extent this reflects the problems in spousal employment rights outside of the UK prior to accession (or arising from transition), the transferability of qualifications and skills and linguistic competences. Whilst Dickmann and colleagues (2006: 24) suggest that dual career situations have a major influence on migration behaviour, they caution that 'this is likely to be mediated by the type of career a spouse may have'. Raghuram (2004) makes a similar observation, drawing attention to the relationship between mobil-ity and the conditions under which different occupational groups move in dual career situations. In particular, she highlights the impact of job security on partner's responses to moves and the value of occupational niches that often provide a way in.

Access to labour markets for partners and family members in both legal and practical terms is something that scientists consider when thinking about moving. Following the EU enlargement in 2004, Polish nationals had access to the UK labour market in the same way as any other EU national and discrimination on the grounds of nationality is prohibited when selecting for employment. In Germany, however, the transitional arrangements meant that access to labour markets was restricted for Polish as well as Bulgarian nationals although some exceptions exist.[18] This disparity in legal systems and employment rights influenced some of our respondents' location decisions, effectively encouraging them to come to the UK at least at post-doctoral level. Alicja's story reflects this. At the time of interview she had nearly completed her doctorate in Germany and was looking for a post-doc position in the UK. Her boyfriend worked as a driver in Poland but was keen to move abroad with her. He had not been able to work in this capacity in Germany but could do so in the UK: 'This is the advantage that we are in the new European Union and he can work there'. This simple case illustrates the problem of Cooke's (2001) notion of ubiquitous careers facilitating partnered mobility when legal barriers restrict spousal employment. In such legal frameworks, highly skilled people are more likely to be able to access positions and, in practice, scientists generally experienced little problems in doing so due to the existence of skills shortages.

Boyko's moves have been similarly influenced by his partner's employment. His wife qualified as a lawyer in Bulgaria but due to his mobility – to Spain, Austria and finally, to the UK – and work permit rules in the first two locations, she has been unable to work for the last five years or so. Boyko details his experience of moving as a partner. His mobility commenced with an application for a position in Japan:

> There was an interview in which they asked very specific questions . . . mostly questions about family and things like this. About family and whether you have a girlfriend, whether you intend to stay with her, mostly personal questions so I wasn't successful . . . they wanted basically people with no obligations. [Q: Did you tell them that you had a partner in Bulgaria at the time?] Yes, so this was obviously a mistake at the interview.

Following this experience Boyko managed to secure a doctoral position in Spain where he lived on his own for the first three years whilst his wife completed her degree and a one-year post-doc in Bulgaria. After this, she joined him in Spain but 'She wasn't allowed to work because of my visa status, which was quite unpleasant so the only option she had was to master Spanish . . . She was two years in Spain without working'. At this point

Boyko moved again to take up a post-doc in Austria: 'When we went to Austria she was learning German . . . because she wasn't allowed to work in Austria with my status'.

Boyko argues that having a family reduces the desire to move frequently and for shorter stays: 'Moving is not particularly attractive for me, having a family, I don't want to move too much because each move is difficult'. It was for this reason that he decided to leave Austria before his contract expired in order to secure a more permanent position and some stability in the UK. The legal framework permitted spouses of third country nationals to work in the UK. His wife was, however, unable to find a job at an appropriate level partly because of her language skills, the specific nature of her qualifications (as a Bulgarian lawyer) and confidence. Eventually she started to work on a part-time, unskilled basis in a local library but soon became pregnant and withdrew once again from the labour market: 'It was quite difficult to get a job with law, so she has been working in a library for three months just to practise her English and to earn some money but this isn't the job she likes . . . she's been looking after the child. She would like a job that will improve her professional and language skills so there should be an element of improvement'. His wife is keen to re-enter the labour market and had applied for some academic positions in law but was disappointed not to have been offered an interview. She felt that this situation was a result of her nationality – although she had no prior experience of working in this capacity. As a result, 'She is not very happy, she's been complaining. A university advertised some jobs in law but I think they were not very interested in foreigners. They needed really skilled people with English law'.

His wife is now considering doing a Masters degree in order to increase her opportunity to return to her own career but at the time of interview she had foreign student status and the fees were prohibitively high. Boyko explains: 'At the beginning I was very enthusiastic that she can start doing a Masters but she couldn't because it was about £8000 per year'. They were expecting these to drop to home student fees when they had been resident in the UK for three years or following accession. Boyko has a strong return orientation mainly because of his wife's professional situation and because his extended family are there, and may return if his own employment prospects improve: 'Many things depend on how my job develops, how my wife's job develops and how Bulgaria develops so there are three factors'.

Boyko's detailed case raises a number of salient issues. First, it highlights once again the repeated nature of scientific mobility and the tolerance of separation that this often demands. Second, it also illustrates the persistence in some countries and contexts – in this case Japan – of explicit discrimination in the allocation of positions. Of particular concern to many of our respondents was the issue of spousal employment rights. Although the majority of our respondents felt that, as individual scientists, they could move quite freely within the EU, at least prior to enlargement both formal and informal barriers continued to exist in terms of spousal employment. In some countries they were simply not permitted to work; in other situations it was less easy in practice to secure employment in fields outside of science where the transferability of qualifications or language skills posed greater problems. Fortunately, relatively few in our sample attributed this to explicit discrimination – unlike Boyko at one point in the interview. Without denying the existence of prejudice amongst employers, it was apparent that his wife did not have the relevant experience or qualifications to secure an academic position and that it was as much her misunderstanding of the labour market and the opportunities available as explicit discrimination that frustrated her ambitions in this case.

Third, Boyko's situation is also interesting from the broader perspective of trying to understand decision-making in dual career situations. His wife's economic prospects and earnings potential were at least as good as Boyko's both at home and abroad and yet Boyko's career has been given priority within the couple, at least until the point of interview (a point he acknowledged). Finally, and of particular relevance to the current chapter, it is clear that the dual career situation, coupled with the fact that his wife is also Bulgarian, is an important factor in shaping their attitude towards length of stay and the potential for return. In a follow-up interview 18 months later, Boyko and his wife are making active plans to return to Bulgaria even if this means Boyko giving up his position and accepting project-based work, as this would, they felt, result in a better overall situation and for them both.

Although the previous discussion has focused on dual career situations and the impact that managing these circumstances has on migration decisions, it does not follow that situations where one partner is not engaged in the labour market at all are necessarily easier to manage. It is important to remember that some scientists have partners who, for a period of time at least, are not actively engaged in paid employment but perhaps caring for their children instead. In a number of cases, respondents talked of the problems of moving with non-working partners who found it harder to settle and integrate socially in the host country. Yulian describes the series of moves he has made. Although his wife accompanied him initially on one of these moves she was not happy and for the most part mobility has implied separation. Eventually Yulian decided to remain in Bulgaria for this reason:

> I was alone (in Amsterdam) as my boys were too young and they were with my wife. [Q: Did your family go with you to Japan?] My wife was there half a year.

She found it difficult. I think that it's very important for scientists to go abroad . . . But we must stay here in Bulgaria. Our position is here. I can say that when I was in Canada I had an opportunity to occupy a permanent position as professor. For me it is not interesting. I want to be around my family and friends here. Of course for many young people it's no problem.

The difficulties partners faced in integrating socially in a new country when they were not at work were evident in Boyko's situation above. They were also cited in some of our previous work as a factor limiting mobility and encouraging return, especially when children were involved (Ackers, 2003).

CONCLUSIONS

Although single young people show a higher propensity to be mobile, most mobile scientists are partnered even at early career stage. The overwhelming majority of partnered mobile scientists will be in dual career situations and the majority of these will have partners who are also trying to develop a career in scientific research. This chapter has considered the effects of partnering, in this specific context, on scientific mobility and its impact.

The presence of a partner can dampen mobility both in the initial stages, preventing people becoming mobile at all, and at later stages in their life-course and career. This is especially true for women. To the extent that partnering dampens mobility, it is likely to have a negative effect on career development, thus limiting scientists' ability to work effectively and productively and, in some cases, causing what Sretenova (2003) calls 'brain freeze' or brain stagnation. This situation may also be to the detriment of the sending regions to the extent that they are unable to profit from the foreign investment in these scientists arising as a result of mobility. On the other hand, the presence of partners in the home country has an anchoring effect, which mediates any direct relationship between migration potential and quality. The prevalence of these situations leads us to question the idea that migration is a selective, meritocratic process. Receiving countries may be selecting from a restricted pool of people who either want to or are able to move as opposed to a pool based on excellence or potential alone.

In other cases, migrant scientists move with, are joined by or form new relationships in the host state. The effect of post-migration partnering also varies depending on a complex array of factors. Where partnerships form with host nationals there is a greater likelihood that the couple will eventually settle in that location. This may reflect the fact that one partner has extended family and support systems (and obligations) in that location but also the restricted employment opportunities that these people would have in their partner's home country. Where both partners manage to secure proximate and acceptable employment in the host country and, in particular where children are present, the prospects of return decline. This is the case for both bi-national and same national couples and, to some extent, reflects the difficulties of reconciling two highly specialized careers in geographical proximity. The more limited scientific density in the sending regions means that one partner will struggle to access a secure and effective position: the chances of two doing so are acutely remote, especially when one is a foreign national.

Where one member of the dual career partnership experiences significant difficulties in achieving professional reintegration in the host state, and the social and cultural integration that goes with this, the pressure on same-national couples to return or move elsewhere is high. In practice, the specific geographical and legal context within which our scientists were moving meant that this was a relatively frequent occurrence given the legal and practical restrictions on employment that remain in some countries. In the majority of cases identified, however, the initial post-migration de-skilling was relatively shortlived and partners did manage to re-establish themselves in the host state, increasing the propensity to settle at least for a critical part of their productive working lives. This might reflect the fact that most partners were also highly skilled and working in areas affected by skills shortages.

The prevalence of dual science coupling raises various questions about the impact of highly skilled migration. In some cases the most able individuals may be anchored into spaces by their personal ties distorting any simple relationship between migration and excellence. What is also very clear from the findings is the importance of recognizing the value of the human capital that is embodied in the partners of highly skilled migrants both in terms of the gains to receiving regions and the losses to the sending countries (Raghuram, 2004). The prevalence of dual science relationships suggests that, in many situations, the mobility of one scientist is likely to lubricate and direct the mobility of another (their partner) and, in the longer term, the potential human capital embodied in their children. To the extent that mobility represents a means of encouraging foreign investment in scientists in the sending regions, dual career situations might also increase the propensity to move and achieve this investment. Our evidence would suggest, however, that partnered mobility in these situations is likely to reduce the potential for return.

The material presented in this chapter emphasizes the importance of understanding the wider context within which highly skilled migrants move and the impact of personal relationships on migration processes. These relationships distort any direct and simple correlation between economic determinants and rational migration behaviour and also between mobility and quality. Migrants, particularly later in their careers, rarely make decisions in an individualistic, profit-maximizing vacuum. The presence of partners might add friction to these processes or lubricate them depending on the specific circumstances. Moreover, such circumstances might change over time and space. The presence of children locks people more firmly in the host state and the following chapter considers the effect of parenting and children's life-courses in more detail.

NOTES

1. This figure to some extent reflected the sampling strategy and our concern to ensure that a variety of age groups and levels of seniority were sampled and should not be taken as a representative figure.
2. Much of the migration literature focuses on the role that family plays in creating the networks and human chains that stimulate and guide flows. This issue is discussed in more detail in Chapter 6.
3. Our impression is that this is most likely to affect the male sample as they were often more reluctant to discuss personal issues.
4. A recent article (Ouellette, 2007) cites other research and refers to a new study of dual career situations currently taking place in the US.
5. These interviews were conducted as part of the E-MeP project and further details are provided in Annex 3.
6. The value of short stays and shuttle moves are discussed in more detail in Chapters 2 and 8.
7. The diploma is the equivalent of an undergraduate degree plus Masters.
8. Ivaylo's case is discussed in more detail in Chapter 5.
9. A high level of separation was identified in a previous study, which found that partnered female scientists were more likely than men to have to move alone (Ackers, 2003).
10. This term was coined by a senior scientist in his 60s during the MOBISC study who lived in London during the week and spent the weekends in Newcastle with his wife.
11. The role of networks in this respect forms the basis of Chapter 6.
12. This might reflect his linguistic skills but also the problems foreigners experience in penetrating the labour markets in sending regions (a point discussed in Chapter 8).
13. Kiril's case is discussed in more detail in Chapter 5.
14. Haug (2005) accepts that this might overestimate the proportion of intermarriage as it does not take account of marriages conducted in Bulgaria.
15. Much of the previous work focused on inter-regional moves where language and mutual recognition of qualifications was not a problem. Access to such professions is far more complex in an international and even European context.
16. Maria's case is discussed in Chapter 5.
17. Raghuram (2004) provides examples of partners taking unpaid positions in medicine as a way in.
18. The German government recognized the importance of spousal rights in attracting highly skilled personnel to the country. The introduction of the Residence Act, which came into force in 2005, allowed the spouse of a highly skilled worker being granted a settlement permit to work in Germany without having to apply for a work permit in their own right (Residence Act of 30 July 2004 (*Federal Law Gazette I*, p. 1950), last amended by the Act on Implementation of Residence – and Asylum – Related Directives of the European Union of 19 August 2007 (*Federal Law Gazette I*, p. 1970) §30).

5.   Multiple life-courses? The impact of children on migration processes[1]

INTRODUCTION

Scott (2006: 113) emphasizes the relationship between mobility and family and/or life-course, suggesting that 'there is then a work–life balance that matches the acquisition of mobility capital against familial priorities'. Although the role of partners has been recognized for some time in migration research, attention to the influence of children has emerged more slowly. Cooke (2001: 419) argues that research has generally 'failed to consider carefully how reproductive, labour market and migration decisions are connected'. Whilst the attention to children in this work is welcome, its focus is primarily on the effect of child-bearing on mothers' employment. Kofman (2004: 243) suggests that the neglect of family-related migration reflects the 'emphasis in migration studies on the individual, a heavily economic focus and an association with female migration based on the dichotomy of male producer and female reproducer. Family-related migration is treated as a secondary form of migration subordinate to and divorced from labour markets'. To the extent that family migration has been recognized in migration research, it has tended to be treated as distinct from and less important than employment-related migration. Implicit within this analysis is the view that women – as wives and mothers – and children are largely moving as dependants and not as major economic players in their own right.

Where the influence of older children is recognized in research, children tend to be viewed as the passive appendages of migrant couples who vicariously weigh up the impact of individual moves on the child's economic and social welfare. The focus remains on the life-course of the adult (and particularly the 'primary' migrant) rather than on the interplay of multiple, parallel life-courses that intertwine over time and space, shaping migration and location decisions.

This chapter discusses some of the issues arising from our interviews with mobile Polish and Bulgarian scientists.[2] As such it seeks to advance our understanding of the influence that the presence of children has on migration processes *in this specific context*. Three key concerns emerge from the interviews: (1) the challenges of organizing child care in a migration context; (2) the influence of children's educational opportunity on decision-making; and (3) the effect of children's social integration on subsequent mobility.

MOVING AND CARING FOR CHILDREN

One critical factor shaping the mobility of people with young children concerns the ability to access and pay for care. In previous research on the impact of migration on domestic caring arrangements, Ackers (2004b: 378) underlines the importance of recognizing the diversity of child care needs among migrant women that depend, to a large degree, on the age of the children and family dynamics: 'Care is a key determinant, emerging and re-emerging over the life-course, often in a most unpredictable fashion to challenge location decisions'. Indeed, each stage of a child's life-course, from post-natal care through pre-school and full-time education, poses new challenges to migrant workers who are faced with organizing their professional obligations around the care needs of their children in the face of limited familial support and a foreign, often inaccessible, welfare environment.

Caring responsibilities generally appear to dampen mobility, effectively locking people into spaces either in the home or receiving country. Rangelova and Vladimirova's (2004: 15) analysis of data on migration potential from Bulgaria found that '78% of respondents who do not wish to migrate cite ties with their family and friends as a reason strong enough to deter them from leaving'. The MOBEX2 sample, by definition, had all experienced at least one mobility episode – or were planning to move. We would not, therefore, have captured cases where child care had prevented any form of mobility. However, many respondents suggested that the scientists left in Bulgaria and Poland were often there because of family responsibilities. Svetlana's comment is quite typical: 'The people who stayed [in Bulgaria], it was mainly through family considerations'. In other cases, caring influenced length of stay or location decisions. When asked why he had only spent short (that is, less than three-month-long) stints abroad, Boris, a senior Bulgarian scientist replied, 'I have family here. I have children. It was impossible for me, now it's possible because my sons are married. I was free [to be mobile] but not to emigrate'. Haug and Diehl's (2004a: 16) analysis of Bulgarian Census data on migration intentions revealed a gender imbalance amongst respondents aged 30–49 (compared with younger age groups), which the authors attribute to 'women losing or postponing their migration plans due to family reasons'.

For Gamlen (2005: 16), caring responsibilities often precipitate return moves, at least temporarily: 'returns . . . are frequently motivated by non-economic factors such as childrearing and care for the elderly . . . and might be called "breather periods" in which the migrant takes advantage of free public assistance with child rearing, healthcare or retirement in their home country'.[3] Whilst Gamlen's recognition of the role of care in precipitating moves is welcome, it is perhaps inaccurate to describe such factors as 'non-economic'. In many cases migrants talk not so much of accessing free public assistance but returning to access – or indeed to provide – informal, family support. Of course, this might reflect the level and quality of welfare support in Bulgaria and Poland at the time of the interviews. Recent work on retirement migration in the European Union would support welfare magnet theory, at least in the context of returns (Peridy, 2006; Coldron and Ackers, 2007). Furthermore, the 'return' that Gamlen refers to might not involve the whole family or even the 'primary migrant': indeed, it could be one or more of the children moving alone.

MOBEX2 revealed cases where concerns around child care and the problems of accessing and financing support had a marked effect on both migration and location decisions. Academic scientists moving on relatively low wages and with little corporate support often express serious concerns around the provision and cost of child care in the host countries (and the UK in particular). Whilst this is a general concern for all migrant workers, the culture of long and unpredictable working hours coupled with ongoing work-related travel (often abroad), make this a particularly difficult problem for scientists (Ackers, 2007). Alexander, a Bulgarian post-doc, explains how the costs associated with having a young child caused him to turn down a prestigious employment opportunity. Alexander had completed his doctorate in Germany and stayed there for a post-doctoral position. He then secured employment in the UK and planned to move with his wife who was expecting their first child at the time. He cites the high cost of housing and child care and the lack of statutory support – as a non-EU national at the time – as important factors precipitating his return to Germany after only one week:

> The major reason, or at least catalyst, for our decision was the financial shock that stunned me from the day I set foot in England. What also didn't help was the realization that although we pay as much national insurance and tax as any British person on similar income – in fact more tax, because we are not entitled to any tax credits, such as working tax credit or council tax benefit – we do not have the right to any social benefits, including any form of child support, such as child benefit or child tax credit.

Although they were still migrants in Germany and lacked the support of family and friends there, they felt that they could manage as housing and child care costs were significantly lower and, according to Alexander, 'In

Germany we get the social benefits related to child support, even though we could have managed without them'. Alexander was fortunate to be able to return to his previous position.

In other situations, respondents 'managed' the demands of a mobile career by leaving their children with parents in the home country and, on occasion, bringing their parents over to care for their grandchildren, yet this was more problematic for non-EU nationals who had more restrictive legal rights (Ackers and Dwyer, 2002). In such cases the mother or father tolerates a degree of separation. Zofia recalls the time when she had to leave her daughter with her mother in order to spend short stays abroad during vacations: 'It was very tough for me but it was possible because my mother took care of my daughter. So, after finishing teaching I went abroad. I spent summer holidays and all the winter holidays and Easter time in such so-called "free" periods I went to Norway to work'. Zofia's ability to rely on informal, family support in the home country enabled her to achieve a degree of mobility and progress in her career but the conditions under which the mobility was made possible implied serious restrictions on the timing and length of her stays abroad.

Agnieszka recounts her own experience of trying to develop her career – and use mobility to enable her to work effectively – as a young mother. For the first 13 years of her career she was unable to move:

> I had children and maternity leaves so that was not a very intensive time in my job. So I didn't travel. Then I got this proposition to go for two years. I didn't know Brazil so for me it was too far away. The children were too small. The younger one was three and I really couldn't find a solution for two years. Then we decided that I will go there at first for half a year and we would see . . . My friends who have habilitation usually did it after longer stays abroad. My stay was only six months so it was too short to make habilitation.[4]

In practice, Agnieszka cut short her stay, returning after only six months, partly because of her children (who remained at home with their father) and partly because of concerns about professional reintegration. She reflects on the impact of this decision, which meant that she could not make optimal use of the opportunity (and complete work for her habilitation). This would no doubt have limited her ability to progress in Poland.

In the two examples above the presence of children made a significant difference to the duration of mobility episodes, permitting short stays only, and this was achieved through tolerance of family separation.

Maria, a Hungarian respondent in another study we are currently under-taking,[5] explains how her mobility has been shaped by family circum-stances, resulting in long-term separation from both her child and her partner. Although she moved in the first instance to the US with her (non-scientist) partner and child, his inability to secure a work permit pre-cipitated a return and subsequent move to the UK where Maria took up a three-year post-doctoral fellowship. Unable to find suitable employment in the UK, her husband returned home leaving Maria in the UK with their two-year-old daughter. Maria endeavoured to manage effectively on her own with her child but ultimately the demands of her position – in terms of extended and unpredictable working hours and regular travel within and outside of the UK – meant that this was not sustainable. The daughter therefore returned home to be cared for by her father and grandparents and Maria has been living apart from her family for the past two years. The sit-uation is unbearably painful for Maria but, for the time being, unresolvable at least until she secures a viable permanent position in either location. Ultimately Maria's situation shows that the child care 'problem' is not reducible to finances (although undoubtedly more money might help her to buy in more flexible child care). In practice, scientists manage the demands of their mobile and time-consuming positions through relying on a combi-nation of spousal, paid and informal support, which people in Maria's sit-uation have limited access to. One 'alternative' to locating and paying for child care in the receiving country was to leave children with their grand-parents and/or other parent in the home country. This practice was quite common especially when respondents were on shorter contracts of less than a year. Rangelova and Vladimirova (2004: 28) argue that the practice of family separation might have long-term implications for individual fam-ilies and the social fabric in Bulgaria as it distorts the 'intergenerational equilibrium' and results in many children growing up away from one or both of their parents.

Of course this situation has a knock-on effect on the mobility of grand-parents, some of whom will also be scientists. Pepka, a senior Bulgarian sci-entist, tells of how her own mobility has been limited by her caring responsibilities towards her granddaughter whose mother emigrated some years earlier following the breakdown of her marriage: 'I prefer to travel only for short times as my granddaughter is with me'. Pepka's case illus-trates the intergenerational dimension of transnational kinship and its effects on individual mobility. At the time of interview, Pepka's husband had ceased working due to illness. Her caring responsibilities towards her husband in the face of the marked decline in welfare support in Bulgaria further restricted her ability to spend longer periods abroad.

In some situations, the presence of young children did not appear to affect mobility to any great degree. In itself, moving children at pre-school or primary school age was not a major problem if one of the parents was not engaged in paid work (interestingly, in our sample, this was always the mother): the problem was locating and financing child care and the impact of this on their employment rather than concerns around a younger child's ability to integrate or learn languages. Krzysztof has two children – one nearly three years old and the other just six months old – who are looked after by his wife at home. Asked whether the presence of his children changed his attitude to mobility he replies: 'I don't think so – we are quite mobile'. He accepts that this might change when the children start school but for the time being Krzysztof is happy to contemplate further moves in future.

Another approach to managing mobility and family life is to delay having children. The challenges that many migrants and especially female migrants face in attempting to achieve an acceptable work–life balance may result in 'decisions' to either postpone, reduce the number of, or decide against having children at all. Teresa has been living in the UK for nearly ten years. Her Polish partner also lives in the UK but their jobs are in different locations so they live apart, visiting each other at weekends. During the interview she suggested that this situation had encouraged her to delay motherhood: 'I think I would want children and I'm kind of pushing it later and later . . . I feel conscious quite a bit because there is a limit to pushing it later and later' (see also Ackers, 2003).

BUILDING HUMAN AND SOCIAL CAPITAL: CHILDREN'S EDUCATION AND PARENTAL MOBILITY

Dickmann and colleagues's (2006: 18) recent study emphasizes the importance of family considerations to the 'complex assessments' that migrants make: 'two of the five most important factors for individuals were family-related including willingness of the spouse to move and children's educational needs'. Katseli and colleagues (2006a) make the point that on the one hand, research indicates a detrimental effect of migration on children's educational achievement as families are separated and traumatized by family disintegration and stress. Yet on the other, increased remitted household income through migration might lead to increased educational attainment. They note that 'in some cases, children might emulate their parents' migration in order to increase their own migration and career prospects, increasing the stock of human capital' (ibid.: 44). Most of this literature assumes that these losses or gains to children are experienced in situ (that is, the children themselves do not migrate in the first instance). Velev (2002: 4), on the other hand, argues that one of the chief reasons for the brain drain lies in the desire to 'obtain a better future for one's children by moving [them] abroad' (ibid.).

Many of the MOBEX2 respondents positively valued the prospects of moving *with* their children and the educational opportunities this might generate for them. Concerned about the economic and political situation at home and recognizing the value of reputational capital and language skills, they often placed a premium on mobility for their children and this increased the incentives to move. The weight attached to these educational opportunities is clearly linked to the specific context within which people are contemplating moves. Dickmann and colleagues (2006: 22), for example, found marked differences in the importance attached to education in their samples of Asian and British migrants: 'Many interviewees from Asia outlined the positive effect a move would have on the education and language capabilities of their family (and sometimes themselves). In contrast, respondents from the UK saw the different educational systems and languages more as a barrier to mobility and perceived a potential disruption of family life'.

Our Bulgarian and Polish respondents were generally much more optimistic about the potential benefits a Western education would bring to their children's future economic and academic/career prospects. Much of this optimism is grounded in positive perceptions of Western education systems and particularly the merits of attaining fluency in the English language (which is seen as the language of the global economy and science). This did not imply that respondents did not value the education systems in their home country: indeed, many believed their home systems to be more rigorous and demanding (see Chapter 7 for details). They were nevertheless concerned for their children to access the reputational capital associated with Western education and, in particular, prestigious universities. The MOBEX2 sample included a number of cases that illustrate the influence that concerns around children's education had on migration processes. In each of the cases presented below the decision to make an initial outward move had already been made, presumably taking into account the presence of children at that point in time. What is interesting is the subsequent influence of their children's educational circumstances in the ensuing period, triggering a re-evaluation of mobility, which often reconfigures family relationships and location decisions quite significantly.

Andrey's first period of mobility had occurred many years beforehand when his two children were much younger. At this time he had reconciled the needs of his then young children and his own career through the relatively common practice of repeated short stays. This enabled his family to remain in Bulgaria – affording them some stability – whilst allowing him to augment his salary and develop his career through regular short stays. The decision to return to the UK for a longer period was influenced by concerns about his 17-year-old daughter's education: 'From a personal point of view

I wanted very much for my daughter to have the opportunity to receive a good education in an English college so we discussed with my wife and we decided that it would be good to apply for this position and to have one of the daughters with me'. Asked whether he might consider a more permanent move in the future, he replies:

> No, I had never considered it mostly for personal reasons because of the family, and my wife is a teacher in biology but she doesn't speak English at all, and she is now in Bulgaria, so I'm here with one of my daughters and my wife and the other daughter are in Bulgaria. Also, my parents live there so I never considered going for a long period abroad.

Andrey's mobility has been shaped by the needs of his partner and the presence of children in his family and illustrates the importance not only of his life-course but also his children's. When his children were young and at school he 'preferred' to make a series of shuttle moves in order to maintain the stability of the family unit. Later on, the perceived benefits to the older daughter of spending time studying in the UK precipitated a longer stay of two years or more. This implied an extended period of separation from his partner and younger child and also from his own parents. He anticipated returning after the two-year period, presumably with his older daughter, although, of course, other events might intervene to modify this situation. He might, for instance, decide that his other daughter would also benefit from a stint abroad, or his older daughter (who would then be aged 20) may decide not to return with him, preferring instead to remain in the UK perhaps for undergraduate study. Alternatively, she might move elsewhere.

Tzonka also made a series of short visits to the UK, on her own, before she made the decision to bring her daughter over with her. She explains how this longer first move to the UK was initially planned as a two-year stay, leaving her husband and older daughter (who was an undergraduate at the time) in Bulgaria. She was accompanied by her younger daughter (then aged 11) as she believed that a short time in the UK to learn the language would be beneficial to her. Asked whether the presence of her daughter increased the likelihood of her staying here for longer, she replied:

> When she came it was extremely hard. I intended to stay for two or three years also to learn the language and I always hoped that things may change [in Bulgaria] so I considered my stay here quite temporary. Until my daughter goes to university I think I'd better be here. She's 15 and she has got her GCSEs now. After that she will have two years A levels and after that university. [I will stay] at least until she goes to university.

Tzonka's original plan to spend a short time in the UK before returning to join her husband and older daughter underwent serious revision as time progressed. The idea of a two- or three-year stay was extended to encompass not only the completion of her daughter's schooling but also her undergraduate study (a minimum of ten years in total). Her husband has remained working in Bulgaria during this time but her older daughter (and this daughter's husband) subsequently moved to join her and were working at the same university at the time of interview. In practice, it is unlikely that Tzonka will return to Bulgaria at least during her working life (she is now in her early 50s). Although her employment contract is only temporary – and due to expire – the prospects of her children, and now grandchild, remaining in the UK for some time is likely to reduce her willingness to return. Some time after the interview she referred to the possibility of encouraging her husband to take early retirement and join her in the UK at least until her own retirement when she plans to return.

Irina was in a similar situation. She came to the UK eight years ago to do her PhD and fully intended to return. As we saw in the previous chapter, Irina had initially come on her own, leaving her husband and children in Bulgaria, but she found it hard to cope so they moved over to join her:

> After I finished my PhD we decided to go back to Bulgaria and my son, who is 20 now but was about 16 at that time, was the one who stopped us and said that he felt happy here and he felt that the environment was very supportive. He had settled down at school and said he wanted to go to university here rather than in Bulgaria. And once we had made the decision that our sons would go to university here we had to support them and we had to be here. When we thought we would go back to Bulgaria it was the kids who were happy here and really wanted us to stay. We still believe that we will go back to Bulgaria . . . the question is when.

Irina's experience reveals the complex and fluid nature of migration decision-making, particularly when children are involved. In the early stages, Irina felt she could not cope on her own and would have returned at that point if her family had not come over. At the time of interview, however, her children had integrated and were now restricting her ability to return home. The final sentence evokes the sense of limbo that scientists sometimes experience as new factors emerge to influence their migration decisions. In a few years time their children might meet partners and establish families, perhaps with other nationalities, which might further influence Irina's decisions.

Ivaylo's case is somewhat different. His move was almost entirely precipitated by the needs of his son. His wife, who is also a scientist, had moved in the first instance to take up a short-term position, leaving her son with Ivaylo in Bulgaria. His wife then encouraged her son to move to the UK to undertake his undergraduate degree at one of the most prestigious universities, presumably to increase his future employment prospects. At the time of interview, Bulgaria had not acceded to the EU and their son was therefore required to pay expensive overseas tuition fees. This put pressure on Ivaylo to leave his permanent, if poorly paid, position in Bulgaria and take a temporary research position in the UK in order to contribute to the costs of their son's education. In response to a question about his plans to return, Ivaylo replies: 'I wish I knew, I wish I knew. Sorry for saying this but we are planning to stay approximately three years more and then we'll see. [Q: Is that mainly for your son?] Yes, then we will see what will happen'. It was evident at the interview that although he accepted the economic imperative of mobility, he very much regretted leaving his home country and was desperate to return.

Whilst such decision-making might be construed as rational and even profit-maximizing to the extent that it supports his son's future economic prospects, it is worth pointing out that the son was in fact going through his second undergraduate degree in the UK, having changed his field. His parents were therefore footing the bill for two consecutive periods of overseas student fees. The future for this family is quite uncertain. Both parents are in temporary employment in the UK and have relinquished their more senior permanent positions back home. They are also in their 50s. In this case there is only one child in the family and it may well be that their future mobility will turn on their son's future plans.

Although moving with very young children, as we have seen, is often not viewed by parents as a major problem for the children at the time, respondents often became reluctant to move again or return home until their children had completed their education, often to degree level. Having older (that is, teenage) children in the family appears to increase the propensity to remain for a longer period and restricts return (Ackers and Stalford, 2004). This confirms Bailey, Blake and Cooke's (2004) findings that older children often act as a constraint on migration, particularly in relation to long-distance moves. Our findings suggest that the strongest effect might be on return decisions.

It is interesting to reflect on the extent to which the concept of *tied stayer* could be extended to some of these cases where parents become immobile as a result of their children's needs or plans. This description would seem to fit Ivaylo's situation and also that of Vladimir. Vladimir came to the UK with his wife and child. The fact that they have settled well in the UK is placing pressure on Vladimir to stay even though he has not been able to secure a permanent position:

I came first, so they came shortly after me and my son was five then so now he's finishing primary school and going to secondary [aged 11], and in a sense he's more British than Bulgarian, because in fact a big part of his conscious life was spent here. My wife was a PhD student in Bulgaria when we came here so she had to give up. She started a new one here and just finished this year and found a position. [Q: So really you're quite settled aren't you?] I'm quite settled but that's unsettling for me. Because at the moment ironically I have the shakiest position in the family; my son is quite happy, he is enjoying his school activities and friends and my wife has a permanent position and I have a one-year contract! It's closing very much my options because I can always go to another country and there are a lot of openings there.

This case is yet another example of the fluid nature of mobility and the ways in which power dynamics within families might also change over time and place. The initial outward move was very much motivated by Vladimir's professional interests, even to the detriment of his wife's position, who came to the UK as a *tied mover* or *trailing wife*. Six years later the tables have turned and his son's integration, coupled with the greater security attached to his wife's professional position, have tilted the balance in favour of remaining in the UK, even if this restricts Vladimir's ability to move again and achieve career progression and employment security. At the time of interview he could perhaps be described as a tied stayer with migration decisions, at that point in time, largely determined by his child and wife's needs.

In most of the cases discussed above, the parents were attempting to negotiate some kind of compromise between their own needs and the needs of a child or a number of siblings of similar age (and educational needs). However, it is increasingly common to see significant differences in the age of siblings as people try to reconcile the demands of work with family life. This presents mobile families with even more complex challenges. Dessislava is a case in point. She has two children and her approach to managing parenting and mobility has changed over time as their lives and needs have evolved. In the first instance she moved to Germany alone, leaving the children with her mother and husband (who split his time between the children in Bulgaria and his wife in Germany). As her older son approached 14 she decided to take him to Germany with her 'because they had good programmes for foreigners in the schools . . . a kind of international school with special classes to learn German . . . it was a really nice experience'. During this four-year period her younger son remained with his grandparents in Bulgaria. This configuration enabled Dessislava to resolve her problems of finding child care for the younger child whilst also enabling her older son to access the educational opportunity associated with mobility even if the solution implied long-term family separation. Ferro (2006: 177) argues that the migration of 'some but not all family members can constitute an important risk-reducing strategy'. Although she is referring to the potential value of adult family members 'allocating resources in different labour markets', the same case could be made in relation to the family as a whole and the needs of both adults and children.

AFFECTIVE TIES AND SOCIAL 'INTEGRATION'

Through focusing on the influence of care and education on mobility, the previous discussion runs the risk of over-emphasizing 'practical' issues. It is important to recognize the contribution that other considerations make to migration behaviour. Although Peridy (2006: 5) welcomes extensions to human capital approaches to migration theory, which take into account the fact that such decisions are made by families and not individuals, he suggests that the analysis remains primarily economic and profit-maximizing: 'It is assumed that the family objective is to maximize the household income'. This is not the whole story. In practice, decisions at any point in time are not always 'rational' from a narrowly economic perspective and may, at least temporarily, limit the opportunity to maximize family resources. Ferro's (2006: 182) work on the migration of knowledge workers identifies the importance of 'affective ties', which 'can actually curb plans . . . and also because one's migratory plan might not match that of partners or family'. Although she is referring here to the sending country as 'home', in many cases the children might take a different view on this, especially when they have spent as much time or a critical period in their childhood in another country (see Ackers and Stalford, 2004).

Some respondents in our study expressed more general concerns about the impact of moving on their children's identity and sense of belonging. Kiril's migration history is quite complex. He first moved as a child with his father to Germany after his parents' relationship broke down. He then came to the UK to do his undergraduate degree and has remained here since. Kiril's experience of moving as a child himself has increased his desire to settle permanently and form a 'stable' home for his own children. Language has clearly played an important role in shaping his attitude and sense of belonging. Asked whether he is planning to remain, he replies:

> Yes, because of the family, I've lived now in three countries for almost ten years each and I can say you lose a lot when you're moving. For example, I don't feel like one country's my home, I feel global. I think every country's my home and I think I have a much stronger sense of all people being the same. I see it as a strong positive, but one negative thing is the language. I do not see myself as knowing any language well enough to write a book or poetry or anything like this. I could never master English well enough as someone who has learnt it from birth and I don't know Bulgarian that well because I left when I was ten . . . I

learnt German for ten years and went to school there so I learnt the language very well but I would not feel confident with any of those three languages sufficiently to say I'm a native speaker . . . Also I don't speak any language without accent. People do understand me but Bulgarian people laugh at me because I have a German or English accent and my sentence structure is funny. In Germany everyone thinks I am foreign, in England everyone thinks I'm foreign. That's not necessarily a bad thing but I do find that I would have been happier if I had been in one language, not necessarily in one country throughout life. [Q: Does that shape how you think you'll feel about your own children?] Yes, I would like them to be in one language. That's one of the reasons to stay.

Later in the interview Kiril was asked whether fellow Bulgarians might return if economic conditions improved there. He replies:

That I doubt . . . Because people set up lives and why would they want to go back? Like I have now set up a family. Even if Bulgaria tomorrow turned around and became absolutely amazing and fantastic I would probably not go back. We have started making friends here with people and okay, our daughter is only 18 months old, but she's starting to have her friends and in a few years time she will have formed her friendships for life . . . we are part of the community now and that's where our home is now . . . for me it's important to have a home.

This reference to belonging and the importance of having a home raises important questions around the role of identity, and in particular here, of concerns around children's identities, in shaping migration processes. Kofman (2004: 248) talks of how family mobility, in a European context, acts as a catalyst for a new citizenship, generating a 'crucible of multiple belongings'.

It would be a mistake to give the impression that people who have experienced a period of mobility as a child, as Kiril did, generally endeavour to 'settle'. In many other situations, early experiences of mobility would appear to create a disposition for subsequent moves, perhaps whetting the appetite for mobility, increasing confidence levels or reducing the ability to 'settle' in one place. The findings of a number of studies suggest that mobility may have a multiplying effect, encouraging future moves (Ackers, 2003; King and Ruiz-Gelices, 2003; Ackers and Stalford, 2004).

A number of our respondents were experiencing the stage in their own and their children's life-course where, after a long period of 'settlement' in the host country, the children then become mobile themselves, leaving the country to move elsewhere. At this point the respondents became more footloose again and began to contemplate return (albeit often at retirement). Vasil and Nikolina first experienced mobility 20 years ago when Nikolina had the opportunity to work in Moscow. At this time their first son was only three years old and Nikolina had to leave him behind with her parents. According to her husband, 'We had a difficult time and the child was without parents . . . it was very difficult for Nikolina because she was almost three years apart from them'. They later moved to Germany when their children were quite small and remained there during their education: 'It was a privilege to come here. We are all very happy and also for the children for learning the language, it was not difficult'. Following graduation, however, their two children both moved to the UK where 'they now want to stay. They like London'.

Such moves extend the geographical canvas of family relationships and the challenges of transnational kinship. Rumiana tells a similar story. She moved to the UK to accompany her partner along with her children (then aged 11 and 13) who were educated to degree level in the UK. Asked about her future plans and whether the presence of children increased the prospect of her remaining in the UK she replied that 'they are old enough now to take care of themselves . . . at the moment the elder one is moving to Belgium so she will be moving around as well'. Rumiana was beginning to explore the possibilities of returning to Bulgaria even if this meant she might not be able to remain in science research due to the lack of opportunities.

CONCLUSIONS

This chapter has illustrated the influence that the presence of children has had on migration processes in our sample of Polish and Bulgarian scientists. There are no simple conclusions. The influence is context-specific and constantly in flux. In some situations the presence of children appears to dampen either outward or return moves, locking people at least temporarily into spaces. In others, it adds incentives, lubricating mobility and shaping location decisions. The dynamics of family relationships can change markedly over time. They may shift completely from a situation in which the partner and child play the role of tied movers, to one in which the 'primary' migrant parent becomes the tied stayer. It is also important to remember that families often do not move together as a coherent unit but tolerate a degree of spousal and sibling separation in order to manage careers and kinship across international space.

Kofman (2004: 249) alludes to the importance of the parents' life-course as a key determinant of migration decisions and experiences, proposing that we understand migrant families in 'a different way . . . as fluid and constantly being re-constituted and negotiated, adapting across spaces and through time'. It is also necessary to consider the effect that the presence of children and the evolution of *their* life-courses has on how parents manage mobility, career and kinship transnationally. Not only do children exercise significant influence on the mobility and career decisions of their parents, they are also economic actors in their own right. They move as dependents at various stages in their life-course but, as we have seen, many of them have the potential to make a major contribution to the labour market, which constitutes the 'motor of international migration' (ibid.: 248). The findings presented in this chapter lead us to question the validity of the distinction that dominates migration research between family-led and employment-led migration. In practice, all forms of highly skilled migration are simultaneously influenced by both family and employment considerations with the balance shifting over time.

NOTES

1. This chapter is an updated version of a book contribution jointly written by Louise Ackers and Helen Stalford and published in *Social Policy Review 19*. It is used here with the kind permission of Policy Press (Ackers and Stalford, 2007).
2. MOBEX2 did not include interviews with children as such although many of the adults interviewed were the children of scientists. For more general work on the impact of migration on children see Ackers and Stalford (2004).
3. The role that care plays in retirement migration processes is developed by Ackers and Dwyer (2002).
4. The 'habilitation' can best be described as a second doctorate and is a prerequisite for progression to a full professorship in Bulgaria and Poland (Slantcheva, 2003).
5. For details of the E-MeP study see Annex 3.

6. The role of networks and connections in shaping migration processes and effects

INTRODUCTION

This chapter considers the role that networks and connections play in scientific migration. Existing literature tends to polarize the debate into two distinct positions. The first stance suggests that networks make migrants, lubricating and channelling migratory outflows with a multiplier effect. The second stance – found in a growing body of literature with a focus predominantly on developing countries – identifies the potential that scientific diaspora present as critical compensatory mechanisms, enabling sending regions to benefit from the enriched human capital of their expatriates through forms of 'disembodied' knowledge transfer. This chapter explores the relationship between networking and migration/knowledge transfer processes. It considers the relevance of the concept of diaspora in the context of scientific communities, the quality and function of connections and the factors shaping connectedness in that specific context.

The first aspect of the migration/knowledge transfer process concerns the contribution of networks to the physical movement of scientists, both in terms of outward and return flows. To the extent that knowledge is embedded in scientists, this process of mobility might be expected to involve a high degree of knowledge transfer. It cannot be assumed that knowledge is transferred in any perfect or complete sense, however, as this rather depends on the context within which the scientists are accruing and applying their skills. The second process concerns the importance of networks to 'disembodied' or 'reverse' knowledge flows. In other words, transfers of knowledge that take place in the absence of physical migration. Once again, it is important to remember that these are rarely unidirectional and partially mitigate the effects both of outward movements (on sending regions) but also to host countries who 'add value' to incoming human capital and endure losses in terms of retention.

The chapter describes the kind of connections that the migrant Polish and Bulgarian scientists in our sample refer to. Our interest here is both in the volume and the quality of networks, the kind of people they have contacts with and how active they are. We are therefore concerned both with the tenacity and continued relevance of pre-migration networks (in both locations) and their renewal or substitution over time and place. It is useful to distinguish between three intersecting dimensions of community: (1) the traditional diaspora (that is, the local expatriate community); (2) the scientific diaspora (such as knowledge communities organized along expatriate lines); and (3) and international scientific communities (such as knowledge communities clustered around scientific interests and identities). Each of these communities has a role to play in the knowledge transfer process shaping the impact of scientific migration.

CONCEPTS OF 'COMMUNITY' IN THE CONTEXT OF SCIENTIFIC MOBILITY

Many forms of migration – especially amongst less highly skilled and more contested and involuntary types of movement – facilitate the emergence of localized ethnic communities.[1] Processes of chain migration and the desire to locate in close proximity to other expatriates result in certain localities being closely associated with specific migration streams. As these communities achieve institutional completeness the process multiplies, with areas often acting as magnets to new arrivals. Haug's (2005: 12) analysis of Bulgarian migration potential – notably based on migration intentions – suggests that some two-thirds of Bulgarians who plan to settle abroad have relatives or friends working abroad, compared with only one-third of those who have no intentions to migrate. She consequently suggests that migration networks play a major role in the development of chain migration 'and the establishment of a migration system which will influence migration processes in the future' (ibid.: 19). Boyd (1989: 638), too, notes the importance of family, friendship and community networks that 'underlie much of the recent migration to industrial nations'. She describes personal networks as 'conduits of information and social and financial assistance [which] shape migration outcomes, ranging from non-migration, immigration, return migration or the continuation of migration flows' (ibid.: 639). While Boyd's work draws attention to a neglected dimension of migratory processes, her empirical work focused on the role of networks in less skilled forms of migration and also in the small business sector where 'the labour force is drawn extensively from the same ethnic community using kin, friends and ethnic ties', resulting in the formation of 'ethnic enclaves' (ibid.: 653). Boyd acknowledges that personal networks may 'fail to emerge' (ibid.: 655) amongst highly skilled migrants. The role of networks in scientific migration and recruitment processes can be expected to operate rather differently. Johnston and colleagues (2006) argue that although studies highlight the explosive effect of chain migration in increasing migrant flows and producing what Boyd terms 'ethnic enclaves', in most cases they focus on relatively low-status occupational groups. Their own research with skilled migrants in New Zealand found that 'personal contacts were of limited value to migrants . . . they were not an important source of specific material about qualification recognition and or job prospects, nor indeed did they play a prominent role in financing the move or in finding housing and/or jobs for their friends/kin' (ibid.: 1231). They also identified the role of 'impersonal sources' and 'prior visits' in reducing the need for these kinds of support amongst the highly skilled. Puustinen-Hopper's (2005: 21) research on doctoral mobility concludes that whilst personal contacts played an important role in the recruitment of researchers and PhD students, 'these contacts are more likely to be of a professional nature than family links or cultural clusters'.

These views are certainly echoed in our work, which emphasizes the role that previous mobility, often via organized schemes, plays in easing and directing moves. Scientists are generally attracted by highly international environments and 'global cities'. The very specialized nature of their work and the ongoing, peripatetic quality of scientific mobility implies an emphasis on different forms of recruitment, equally linked to international scientific networks and expatriate ties. Furthermore, their relative social and financial status insulates them, to some degree, from the need to locate themselves within the defensive space afforded by expatriate communities.

Networks based on local expatriate communities and family ties – although evident in some areas – appear to play a relatively minor role in shaping migration flows and employment opportunities for scientists. In a small number of cases, complex forms of chain migration linked to family relationships resulted in a degree of local clustering. In comparison to our previous studies on scientists from the EU15 Member States, a high proportion of the respondents in MOBEX2 had family who were also scientists, perhaps reflecting the historical emphasis in some Eastern European countries on science and the strengths of their education system in these areas. It was quite usual to find partners, parents and/or siblings who were also scientists and sometimes working in a very closely related field. Rada's experience illustrates this, showing how family relationships and the practical help that families can offer may channel scientific migration. Rada moved from Bulgaria with her husband to join her mother in the UK and started her doctorate. All three of them work in the same area of science and in the same institution. They now live together in her mother's house with her cousin, who is also doing a PhD, and her cousin's husband.

According to Rada, her cousin 'expected that my mum will help them so they came'. Family and friendship ties were occasionally referred to by other respondents, especially in relation to the practical aspects of moving, such as housing or negotiating the education system for their children, and 'settling in'. These perhaps provide examples of what Peridy (2006: 7) identifies as the benefits of human networks in terms of lowering migration costs, which has the effect of increasing the emigration rate.

Several other cases illustrate the close relationship that exists between family/friendship and professional networks. Hanna's mobility came about through a link with a close friend who had moved to Germany. Hanna started her doctorate in Poland while her friend Sylwia moved to Germany. During conversations with Sylwia, Hanna began to realize how much more she would be able to achieve in Germany and arranged a stay with Sylwia during her summer break. She explains the role that her friend played in stimulating her mobility:

> Yes because of Sylwia. In fact she called me and I was complaining about my work and my professor and Hanna said 'You can come here and it is a very nice group'. I sent an e-mail to the group leader . . . I said I don't have enough money to pay [and] he proposed to pay for my stay.

Hanna had firm plans to stay in Poland for her doctorate and said that she had not wanted to leave her home environment. Nonetheless, the poor working conditions and difficult relationship with her supervisor led her to start thinking about possibilities abroad. Sylwia's presence provided a safety net that gave her the confidence and security to move. She also supplied the critical contact that triggered her initial move and is now likely to facilitate a second, longer-term relocation.

Elzbieta's experience also highlights the influence that diasporic networks can play in shaping mobility. Her first experience of mobility arose as a direct result of her friend's move to the UK. Her friend moved to Manchester on a Tempus exchange and Elzbieta felt 'kind of curious'. She therefore applied for a Tempus fellowship herself to visit Manchester because she 'thought it would be kind of easier for me when I arrived in the city'. She then returned home and two years later spent time in France as part of her PhD programme. Later on she returned to the UK to do a post-doc 'with another Polish friend of mine . . . It wasn't very long but my friend had a lab there and she desperately needed some help to finish an experiment and asked me if I could come for a few months'. Cases like this lend support to the emphasis that Williams and colleagues (2004: 30) place on the role that 'ad hoc networks' play in the migration decisions of academics including, 'self-recruitment, recruitment through networks of friends and family, recruitment from student mobility and "staying on" practices'.

Meyer (2001: 94) makes a similar point, arguing that highly skilled migrants' informal networks are less likely to be kin-focused but extend to 'more extensive and diverse networks consisting of colleagues, fellow alumni and relatives'.

Although in a minority of cases respondents' moves were triggered by family or friendship ties, it was quite rare for scientists to refer to local, community-based expatriate associations in the context of their own migration or employment. Michal is aware of the existence – and growth – of expatriate community groups but suggests that these do not constitute important conduits for scientists. He also displays some concern about their role in relation to other occupational groups:

> Most of the people I met are through the university . . . at work. There are Polish clubs in [the city] and now there are more young people in them – it used to be people who came after World War II. But these can work the other way. Some of these people are trying to take advantage of people coming in, offering them money to say they can get them a job and then you are left with nothing, but this is at lower levels. Its not the case in academia – in academia you can speak English, get a job and take care of yourself. It isn't so important to scientists.

The study provided more evidence of scientific diaspora in the sense of knowledge communities organized along expatriate lines or national identities.[2] This is somewhat different and harder to pin down: it is rarely geographically focused although clusters of scientists are evident in some research-intense institutions. This concentration is not a simple and direct reflection of networking, however, but an indirect consequence of the research funding system, which results in a high proportion of temporary and insecure research-only positions in certain institutions.[3] In practice, this meant that four or five Bulgarian or Polish scientists might know or be aware of one another's presence in an institution or region and might, on occasion, meet socially, although this largely depended on the presence of one active agent willing to organize events. For Piotr, the Polish community is primarily social. According to him, there is insufficient concentration of Polish scientists in the UK to begin to make a meaningful scientific community, although he suggests that this potential exists in Paris. Piotr's perception of a general lack of structure or organization is backed up by Kicinger (2005)[4] who reported that she could not find any information on the Polish scientific or highly skilled diasporas. Key informant interviews she undertook in Poland revealed there were no formal networks of Polish scientists abroad: 'There are no formal organizations. There may be some small groups of a sociable character . . . but there are no formal structures' (ibid.: 20).

Séguin, Singer and Daar (2006a: 1602) define the scientific diaspora as 'self-organised communities of expatriate scientists working to develop their home country'. They argue that such structures present enormous potential as a partial solution 'to the often crippling effects of emigration' (ibid.). In practice, although their empirical work with migrant scientists in Canada identified 'embryonic linkages', they found little evidence of 'organised mechanisms' and 'very little systematic S&T interaction with their [home countries]' (ibid.). This leads them to suggest that such networks are often not sustainable and regularly collapse or become outdated.

Whilst connections between expatriate scientists in the receiving countries seem haphazard and appear to play a minor role in their professional lives, operating primarily on the social level, it is interesting to consider whether these migrant scientists have specific connections with Bulgarian and Polish scientists *in the home countries* and, if so, how these shape mobility and knowledge transfer. Although MOBEX2 found little direct evidence of what Gamlen (2005: 5) refers to as 'value clusters, value webs and value networks' or 'non-geographical models of industrial clustering', it did indicate significant *individual* links and identified a number of factors influencing the volume and quality of contacts with scientists back home.

SENIORITY AND CONNECTIONS

The issue of seniority (at the point of emigration) emerged as a significant factor shaping the volume and value of connections. People who move at an early career stage are generally less likely to have established extensive and durable networks in the sending countries. There appear to be a number of reasons for this. The first relates to the career stage itself and the fact that a scientist's social capital builds up over a period of time starting usually at doctoral level. This gradually accelerates during post-doctoral and permanent employment as they begin to develop as independent researchers, join professional associations, present their work at conferences, publish, engage in research collaborations and experience mobility. Researchers who left their home country at undergraduate or Masters level are less likely to have established active links with established scientists in the home country prior to their move.

Those who complete their doctoral research in the home country generally have more concrete links, typically deriving from their supervisor. Doctoral supervisors in the sending regions play a critical role in encouraging their students to seek opportunities abroad and enabling them to move through their own more developed *international* – as opposed to diasporic – networks. Avveduto's (2001) research emphasizes the role that a doctoral student's networks play on subsequent migration and location decisions. Supervisors play a major role in generating opportunities to gain international experience and mobility and often provide the initial trigger for an outward move. Having moved abroad either as part of their doctoral research or subsequently, many researchers maintain close links with their supervisors 'back home'. Indeed, this was often the only concrete link that they had retained and was highly valued. Active investment in this anchor frequently kept the door open for them to return and re-establish themselves in national labour markets. The influence of this relationship increases with the seniority and status of the supervisor. Where supervisors held senior or leadership positions, their networks were often more highly developed and influential both abroad and in the home labour market, thus increasing the potential for return.

Krystyna's experience illustrates the importance of links with supervisors in stimulating both mobility and active, bilateral knowledge transfer:

> My supervisor in Poland knew my supervisor in the UK so he recommended me. He has been over four times to visit. I told him about a fellowship scheme and so they invited him so he could obtain this prestigious fellowship and he came for three weeks and could make more links and possibilities for students. We have been doing some experiments and we published in the most known Polish journal in English . . . That example is very good because it ties in all the links . . . even though you're out of the country you still have your name circulated in Poland.

The level of reciprocity in this case is interesting and points to some very positive experiences, including joint publication and teaching collaboration. It provides a useful illustration of the ways in which networks evolve over time and space, resulting in the kind of 'interdependency and reciprocity' that Boyd (1989: 641) refers to.

Many respondents referred to the benefits that accrued to them by virtue of their supervisor's social capital, which, in turn, reflected their own mobility and international experience. Marek explains how his supervisor's international networks enabled him to become mobile and gain a position in the UK. Following his degree in Poland, Marek started a joint doctoral programme in conjunction with a French institution. This opportunity arose as a result of his Polish supervisor's 'personal connections in France – so he proposed me to go there'. Towards the end of his PhD, his French supervisor then put Marek in contact with a professor in the UK. He explains that although he had not met her in person, he had 'received her card' from his French supervisor and subsequently forwarded his CV 'and so she invited me to come and discuss the possibility of the collaboration'. This led to his post-doctoral appointment in the UK. Marek is keen to return to Poland at some stage. When asked about the importance of maintaining networks to facilitate his re-entry he says: 'I have retained links so I am quite sure that I'm going to be able to go back and set up a lab'. He describes 'a close collaboration' with his supervisor in Poland – who is also head of the division – and with the director of the institute, involving 'common research projects . . . actually I'm trying to obtain some samples from Poland and test those samples here . . . so that it would help on papers and so on'. Marek also retains an unpaid position in Poland, which helps to keep his contacts live – a point we elaborate on later. This case illustrates a number of issues. First, the critical role that supervisors play in facilitating access to networks and shaping both outward and return moves. It is important to note that the initial contact (in this case through the simple exchange of a business card) is often quite incidental. Second, it illustrates the potential that such networks offer as conduits for genuine and meaningful bilateral knowledge transfer and research collaboration.

Many early career researchers are reliant upon their supervisors to initiate their mobility. Quite often the supervisor's own mobility is developed through international and not expatriate connections but they can then use these connections to facilitate the mobility of their supervisees, effectively channelling migration. Todorka had spent a series of short periods abroad in three countries. Since returning, she has been actively engaged in stimulating the networks she established for the benefit of her research team. With reference to a new Swiss collaboration she says: 'I will travel there for short periods and organize for my young people to go there to change their opinion about science'. Unusually, this new project provides funding for equipment, chemicals and travel, which she divides between the research team to enable them to travel and work there and exchange activities and return. Todorka explains the benefits of this collaboration to the Swiss team: 'I know the professor very well. I worked there and achieved results and when I got back I prolonged my activity. We exchange results and share them and write papers for journals'. As part of this collaboration she is currently organizing an international conference in Bulgaria that will provide opportunities 'for everyone in our institute to meet people from different countries – contacts are very important'.

Ania describes a similar situation involving an international collaboration between her Polish supervisor and a Hungarian scientist working in the UK:

> My supervisor in Poland when I was doing my MSc, had met my [Hungarian] supervisor [in the UK] a few times before, which means they became friends ages ago. When [the Hungarian researcher] was looking for a PhD student he asked my supervisor in Poland 'Maybe you have someone, we never had a Polish PhD student' and that's how I came here. A year later another Polish PhD student went here and another PhD student from the same supervisor went to Manchester.

Ania's case illustrates the relationship that exists between expatriate and international connections. Although her Polish supervisor is playing a major role in stimulating the mobility of his supervisees, the critical connections are not based on national ties as such. Roman's explanation of how he became both mobile and involved in science research emphasizes the role that supervisors and their networks play:

> Actually I wanted to be a computer scientist after completing my Masters degree so I didn't think about going abroad or even about studying for a PhD in Poland. However, my old supervisor told me about the UK opportunity so I had an interview with the professor [from the UK] who came to my university and asked for one person and my university chose me. He asked me to come here and it's a very good opportunity.

Roman is a very good example of supervisor networks triggering mobility where there was previously no intention to be mobile or even to commence a doctorate. In the rather different context of Romanian IT workers, Ferro (2006: 186) describes the sort of mobility experienced by Roman in terms of 'unexpected and desired aspirations'; highlighting the unplanned and rather spontaneous quality of many scientific moves.

Although the majority of cases cited above involve initial outward moves arising from supervisory connections, Puustinen-Hopper (2005) argues that the same individuals can then use the opportunity to broaden their networks, reduce their reliance upon their supervisor and achieve independence that might have proved difficult in the absence of mobility: 'By going abroad into a research environment that is better equipped generally and in terms of international collaborations and links, the PhD candidates avoid merely taking on their supervisors' networks'. The nature of the research systems in Bulgaria and Poland throw a specific slant on this relationship between career stage and connectedness. The organization of research in what is effectively a binary system, with research taking place both in universities and the academies of science, shapes the volume and quality of networks. Although research does take place in the university sector, the academies are historically associated with a higher level of research intensity (Chataway, 1999; Georgieva, 2002; Slantcheva, 2003; Dabrowa-Szefler, 2004). Where candidates are registered wholly within the university sector, respondents suggested that they are likely to have access to fewer networks. Doctoral candidates based in the academies have had, at least until recently, greater access to international networks through their supervisors and research teams. Magdalena explains how fortunate she was to have managed to get a supervisor during her Masters degree in the Bulgarian Academy of Science (BAS) rather than a university:

> Unless you've been lucky to go to the Academy where there are more people doing international projects, you wouldn't necessarily come across anybody that you could collaborate with . . . if you come out of [Bulgaria] with a Masters degree then definitely you could do Masters only with people from university and then you wouldn't have established any links.

Ivaylo makes a similar point, suggesting that 'people in the universities do not do scientific work. They prefer to deal just with the teaching. In the BAS there is concentrated science potential'.

It is important to note, however, that perceptions of the existence and impact of this distinction varied, with some respondents arguing quite forcefully that research links in the university sector were as strong as they were in the academies.[5] The greater impetus for student and staff exchanges arising out of EU enlargement might encourage the growth of new forms of networks in the university sector, which might stimulate researcher mobility. Georgieva (2004) presents figures that appear to reveal a shift in emphasis. According to her findings, the proportion of research taking place in the BAS has fallen markedly from 1980, when it amounted to 90 per cent of all research, to 60 per cent a decade later. She attributed this trend to the growth in research productivity in the university sector and the pressure on BAS employees to 'moonlight' and take second jobs (ibid.: 365). She also notes that universities are now the main setting for doctoral enrolments, which have doubled since 1998.

A further contextual factor, linked to the issue of seniority and status – which operates at both the psychological (symbolic) and practical level – is the tradition of allowing established staff who secure positions abroad to retain unpaid positions. We noted earlier how Marek had retained an unpaid position in Poland, despite now working in the UK. Respondents spoke of about a third of staff being away on such positions at any one time. Asked whether this caused serious problems in terms of human resource management in the affected institutions, we were told that this expectation was built into the planning process and also that it was a means of saving money in the short term. These positions create a formal, institutionalized anchor to the home country and, perhaps, a motivation for retaining contact, building collaboration and sharing knowledge. Andrey explains the role that retained positions can play in maintaining networks and supporting collaboration:

> I'm now on leave from BAS. My position is reserved there and I will be able to contact people in my group almost every day. Currently we have three joint projects [in the UK, Spain and Russia] . . . this year I am going to visit Spain and I am also going to use my leave [from the UK] to stay in Bulgaria as a host to the Spanish colleagues when they come for the next stage of our joint research.

Lucjan had been on leave for 13 years and outlined the benefits of the system for the sending institutions and the individual scientist:

> It gives them a chance of being in contact with Western research institutions. It keeps affiliation and this was the case last year when my funding [in another Member State] had finished and I was unable to secure another position for four or five months. Then I had affiliation in the Polish university, which is essential if you want to publish. You cannot publish without affiliation, so that's another extra that came up. I went back home for nearly one year.

The ability to retain a formal position is clearly useful to the scientist on an individual level, enabling them to balance the risks associated with temporary contracts whilst retaining a permanent, if low-paid, position back home. The retention of contacts also increases the propensity to return and provides active avenues for reverse knowledge transfer to the benefit of sending institutions.

In the final example, Andrzej holds two permanent positions, one in Germany and one in Poland, and has been able to use this situation to the mutual benefit of both parties. He points to the increasing potential that technology offers to moderate the relationship between physical mobility (or presence) and knowledge transfer:[6]

> I'm not very often there I have to say, I go for several months a year but I am permanently in contact and thanks to my activities in this experiment I somehow motivated people in this university to join this [joint] project and I'm more or less leading this group; it's possible even without being very often there . . . because of modern communication you can get the information by e-mail and so on, so we don't have to be there to be actively involved in the research.

The practice of enabling emigrants to retain positions would seem to play an important role in maintaining active and effective research connections and increasing the potential for knowledge transfer.

SENIORITY AND AGENCY (AUTHORITY)

In the examples above we have seen how international and expatriate connections have been used to support forms of doctoral or post-doctoral mobility and research collaboration. The most effective networks in this context are typically between highly established professors in the respective countries and are primarily characterized by international – as opposed to expatriate – relationships. The interviews also sought to determine the extent to which Polish and Bulgarian scientists in the receiving countries played a role in actively stimulating or supporting moves from their own countries. Two key issues emerged here: first, the issue of seniority and the authority that respondents possess to influence recruitment processes in the receiving countries; and second, their desire to do so.

The study found relatively little evidence of direct action to attract and employ same nationals in their workplaces. When asked about the help they had provided for fellow Bulgarian or Polish scientists to come to the UK and Germany, many respondents replied that they were not in a position to influence such decisions. Often they were simply not in senior positions where such decisions were made. Most of the respondents – and indeed the wider population of Polish and Bulgarian scientists in Germany and the UK as a whole – occupy temporary, research-only positions funded by external contracts and were *employed* rather than *employing* staff. This situation raises important issues about career progression in the receiving countries and the clustering of foreign scientists in more vulnerable positions.[7] As such they are less likely to be grant-holders or involved in making academic appointments. Michal, a Polish post-doc, puts it simply: 'I am not at the stage to recommend students to [my boss]'. Vladimir, a Bulgarian post-doc, makes a similar point: 'I'm not in a position here to be decisive on those things. My influence is not very much existing but it is only the case if I persuade somebody that those people are worthy to be involved in the project'. Although Rumiana, a post-doc, has been unable to play an active role in helping fellow Bulgarians to find positions she tries her best to provide practical help, support and contacts:

> I'm not in a position to do that but I always try to help Bulgarian colleagues if they need something. I'm sending them literature and contacts and I'm giving my contacts to them or directly to the person they are interested to contact. When people come here and they know that I'm Bulgarian, then they contact me and ask for help and I'm helping them here.

Scientists also talked of feeling awkward about advertising opportunities back home and using their contacts to do this as this might be seen to actively encourage emigration. One respondent said that when he had tried to inform his colleagues back home about available positions, he felt that the advertisements had not been disseminated for this reason. There was a degree of embarrassment about the perception that they might be lubricating further losses. In addition to this, there was a general perception that scientific opportunities in the UK and Germany were based on more transparent and meritocratic processes than in the sending countries and, as such, were far less reliant on or responsive to what could be called 'reputational prestige' or 'prestige by association'.[8] Indeed, it might be rather awkward for them to be seen to be promoting their own colleagues in this environment.

Although expatriate connections have an important role to play, most respondents made it clear that it was their international *scientific* networks and not expatriate links that had the most significant effect on their careers and mobility. Many expressed a degree of surprise at even being asked about connections with other Polish and Bulgarian scientists, as this was not the critical issue for them, perhaps reflecting the kind of awkwardness referred to above. Although Stefan is acutely aware of the importance of networking in science, the most critical networks, for him, are of a scientific nature and not directly related to nationality: 'It's not extremely important to establish them with people from your own country, I also have collaborations with people elsewhere'. Asked whether networks are more related to scientific identity than nationality he replied 'Nationality doesn't play almost any role in this'. This reluctance to accept that nationality is an important factor in scientific networking is also made by Justyna. Asked whether the collaborations that she has with scientists in Poland are related, in part, to the fact that she is Polish she replies 'No, I think it's mainly the area and mainly the project . . . It just happens they are Polish, I am Polish'. Alina, a lecturer in the UK, similarly suggests that the nationality of her contacts (and the fact that two of her post-docs are Polish) is incidental: 'It is not at all important where they come from. It just happens that they are from Poland. It's nice on a personal level . . . and as far as I know they have full intentions to go back'. Her final comment about return perhaps indicates her concern to show that employing these Polish researchers would not contribute to the 'brain drain'.

Although there was little evidence of the influence of expatriate networks in actually filling positions in the receiving countries, expatriate scientific communities do play an important role in increasing awareness of research and employment opportunities and assisting people with application processes (including knowledge of how the system works) and initial contact. In some cases this might take the form of emotional support and encouragement or practical help with accommodation and advice. At this level, more junior scientists were also actively engaged in disseminating information about opportunities to their peers. Magdalena explains the importance of expatriate contacts to her progression:

> At the end of my Masters degree I went to a conference to present my paper and met a Bulgarian who's doing a PhD here. He told me you could try to find a PhD course in England – a month later he sent me an e-mail saying there is this PhD scholarship. I said okay and applied and some time later I got a letter saying you are accepted.

Magdalena's migration was triggered by a relatively brief and chance encounter. Rumiana, for example, had been approached by young scientists actively seeking out expatriates for advice: 'This boy contacted me because his project is [in my area] and he thought that my name sounds Bulgarian and he wrote me an e-mail and that's why he got in contact'.

The retention of active connections with senior scientists in the *sending* countries played a much more significant role and was often pivotal to successful return and reintegration, particularly for those who did not have retained positions. In general there would appear to be less emphasis on transparency with fewer openly advertised positions and greater scope for making and awarding positions to people via closed forms of competition. Teresa describes the importance of networks to progression in Poland compared with the UK:

> In Poland, the professor controls the hierarchy and the professor has some doctors under him and the doctors would have PhD students and the PhD students have Masters students and it's all a hierarchy and quite political. It's not even a question of money, I think it's a question of structure in the entire place, the kind of culture, the way appointments are made. I think here so far, this is what I noticed, it's relatively fair because I came here from a different country and I don't have personal contacts and I think the fellowships are relatively fair, whereas in Poland it's more who you know and it's better to be there all the time under your professor. If you are a Masters student and you're just there for all your life you can go up to be a professor. If you want to come from another side, people will not take you very easily because they would feel maybe that you are a competitor to them because you might know more because you travelled around. [Q: Do you think that might be a problem if you wanted to go back to Poland?] Yes, I think basically it would be a bigger problem than the salaries.

The complex hierarchy that Teresa describes so poignantly implies a level of risk associated with mobility. One way of minimizing the risk is to stay home and stay close to supervisors and senior staff who hold authority. This was a powerful factor inhibiting mobility in our Italian pilot study MOBEX1 (see, especially, Morano-Foadi and Foadi, 2003; Morano-Foadi, 2006). For those who do take advantage of mobility, on the other hand, but wish to preserve their ability to return at some point, it is absolutely essential to maintain or build strong connections in the home country. Eugenia expresses concern about her ability to return in the absence of effective and established contacts. Although she has retained links, she feels that these are not sufficiently senior to enable her to secure a position in Bulgaria: 'I have my good friends and a lot of them are scientists and a lot of them are people I know from my university years . . . but I don't think I've got links that I could get a job through. Most of my friends are not in the position to do that. A few of them just stopped doing science altogether'. Ania is more confident about her ability to return and secure a position because she has retained powerful connections: 'I think I would be able to, only because of my supervisor in Poland, he has huge connections, he's a huge name [so] I think I could'.

Although this impression came across quite strongly, it is important to acknowledge an alternative perspective. Marek has retained close links with senior scientists in Poland, which he feels could be influential should he wish to return. Nevertheless, he feels that many positions are 'open' to outsiders:

> My former head of department kept inviting me, sometimes a few weeks, the longest was maybe two months but it was on four or five occasions between. So it would be difficult [to return] but I have a link with the Polish Academy. I sit on the editorial board of a leading journal there . . . Polish people and the Academy are very open-minded compared with here where people are narrow-minded and fight each other.

Whilst networks may prove an important factor shaping the ability of scientists to return and secure scientific positions, they may also increase the propensity to move again in the future. Baláž and colleagues (2004) identify the importance of scientific networks to subsequent, post-return outward moves (what may be termed re-migrations). Their work explored the existence and quality of returnees' networks and concluded that 'the creation or recreation of international social networks is therefore important in permanent migration' (ibid.: 18). The 'international' networks that the authors refer to here are generated primarily through scientific connections and not expatriate ties as such.

THE IMPACT OF EMIGRATION AND SCIENTIFIC DECLINE ON CONNECTIONS

The extent and quality of networks in the sending country to some extent reflects the wider consequences of emigration and scientific investment. The wholesale exodus of a significant proportion of scientists from a country or scientific field destroys scientific communities, dislocating networks and the opportunity for repair and regeneration. Although examples of this were common across all age groups and both sending countries, it was most marked in the context of Bulgarian scientific emigration over the past decade.

Most of Boyko's colleagues were living outside of Bulgaria as 'many of them left for other countries just after finishing [their degrees]'. At the time of interview he was trying to locate some of these people through the Internet and renew links. For him, positive experiences and attitudes towards return would have encouraged him to consider such a move.

The perceptions of this group – the scientific diaspora – were more influential than speaking to colleagues who had not moved: 'I'm thinking of establishing these links. There are databases in which you can find details of your colleagues . . . because contacts are important and then I would like to see how others feel about Bulgaria and about returning there . . . it would maybe convince me and give me more information'.

Davenport (2004) advocates the development of diaspora policies specifically aimed at helping people like Boyko. Providing expatriates with greater knowledge of their professional community, she argues, will encourage them to reintegrate and actively consider repatriation. Whilst a large cohort of respondents identified emigration as a factor shaping the strength of contacts back home, an equal number said that their peers who remained in the home country were no longer working in science or at least in their area of research. Asked whether he had retained contacts with scientists, Stefan said: 'The area in which I'm working has been slowly deteriorating in the BAS. Contacts are possible and effective only in productive research collaborations'. Rumiana had a similar experience: 'Half of the colleagues who used to work with me have changed to different jobs. They closed the research centre and the factory was privatized. There's nobody left there'.

Whilst this is a general pattern it is important to consider the specific situation in disciplines and sub-disciplines. In some fields, the sending regions are doing rather better and this is reflected in better links and a greater circulation of knowledge. In others, and especially in those areas where greater infrastructural and human investment in the host countries has effectively left the sending countries behind or where new areas and approaches are emerging, the networks decline along with the science base. This raises difficult questions about the relational quality of skills as emigrant scientists learn new approaches and move into new research areas, increasing what might be termed as the 'knowledge distance' between themselves and their contacts back home. Changing research field or method is commonly cited as a factor shaping the existence and efficacy of contacts.[9]

Michal, a Polish post-doc, has retained mainly personal relationships with his ex-supervisor: 'We are basically working in a different area now so we can't publish in the same journals – it's more social than personal'. The same situation applies to Alina, another Polish post-doc. She emphasizes the importance of establishing active working relationships prior to leaving: 'I don't have strong links because I've never done anything specifically with what I'm doing now. I certainly know people from that time but I've never worked with them'. In other cases where strong connections had clearly existed in the past, their dependence on one key individual renders them vulnerable and transient. Although Barbara had experienced a very strong ongoing collaboration with a Norwegian research group, including one visit of two years and four subsequent short stays of four months each, the change in personnel (and loss of the group head) more or less extinguished the connection. It is important to remember, however, that opportunities for new relationships do arise as pre-migration contacts lose their significance and poignancy. Renata has developed contacts in her new research area, partly helped by a British Council grant:

> I haven't maintained professional contacts [but] I've got new contacts with other Polish people. I moved to a slightly different area so my ex-colleagues don't work very much in it. I've got contact with other people who are interested in the same subject. We had a three-year grant from the British Council last year. They visited here and we went there . . . we got quite a few publications and some conferences too.

Ivaylo relinquished a senior position in Bulgaria to take up a post-doc but remains engaged in supervisions in Bulgaria, having been in the UK for less than two years. This case illustrates the problems of changing field post-migration but also the potential that joint supervisions offer as a mechanism for continued links and knowledge transfer. It is clear from the tone of Ivaylo's comments that he is frustrated at not being able to provide more concrete assistance:

> I still have two PhD students there [but] they're doing something which is not directly related with our work. I just provide some assignments and samples but this is very simple . . . I still maintain relations with many people in Bulgaria but what can we do? We can send them some papers because they have very little access to the journals especially to electronic journals. We are doing some common calculations – but this is not regular, it's just like a hobby.

The problem of declining synergy as a result of field changes reflects a number of factors. In some cases it is simply the fact that the position they have secured in the host country takes them in a different direction and may, sometimes, involve an intersectoral move. In other cases it is related to the nature of the methods and techniques used, raising issues about the relational quality of skills and the effect of this on the exchange of knowledge. Put simply, colleagues back home might not have the equipment or training to benefit from the new skills. In other cases, it reflects the pace of scientific development and the emergence of new research fields in the host countries. Whilst moving into these new areas offers a degree of excitement and, of course, potential in terms of funding opportunities, it might limit the prospects of return. Piotr, a post-doc in the UK, is acutely aware of this problem and is keen to build networks as the basis for the establishment of a new research area (and his eventual return):

> I've been trying to establish [networks] all the time since I've been here. Trying to keep in touch with Poland partly because I'm trying to get some sort of position . . . especially when I become more established in my field, which is a very popular field and completely unrepresented in Poland. For the last several years I've been trying to sort of influence people in Poland to build up this kind of field because there are conferences in the field where I go to and there are people there from Italy, from France, from the UK, from the United States, from Germany and Russia but nobody from Poland. Poland has very good research in physics in several areas but not in this one. It's a long-term process; basically you need to have somebody local interested in doing this . . . somebody senior enough who would have enough power and influence and at the same time somebody junior enough who wants to do something.

Piotr's situation emphasizes the importance of viewing networks as a kind of living organism: they must constantly evolve in response to changing contexts in order to retain their value and impact. This issue of field is clearly important to the propensity for knowledge transfer. The importance of an industrial link can be critical for a number of reasons. It sometimes implies a greater level of investment potential in the sending countries but also perhaps reflects the incentives that EU funding schemes offer to industry–academia collaboration and intersectoral knowledge transfer. Once again there were mixed messages in this respect. Some respondents spoke of the parallel decline in industrial R&D as a factor limiting collaboration, whilst others identified specific pockets of activity that spawned partnerships. In the example below, Magdalena had worked in industry in Bulgaria prior to moving. Her continued contact with a fast-growing software company provided an ideal partner in subsequent research collaborations although she acknowledges that this is unusual:

> I still keep in touch with everybody I knew there in the university and the company. We now have a joint EU project. It's led by a British company. They were looking for some companies that are doing work in this particular research area . . . It just happens that one of those is from Bulgaria but in general there aren't that many companies.

Although some new industries were emerging, Ivaylo suggests that these were rarely involved in R&D activities: 'New companies are coming but they're using only the human power – they are not keen to have research and development departments in Bulgaria'. This clearly restricts the opportunity for meaningful contact with colleagues in industry in the sending regions.

THE DURABILITY OF NETWORKS

One might reasonably anticipate a time-decay element in the relationship between migration and connections. Although the previous section has shown how changes in field or discipline as a result of migration and new working environments might reduce the value of connections, the findings do not indicate a great emphasis on time itself (although respondents may have felt this was too obvious to state). It was not clear to us, however, that people who had left many years ago necessarily had fewer and less active links: this very much depended on their situation and the factors identified above. It is also important to remember that migration is a process that takes place over the life-course: it is not a 'one-time' event. With that in mind, one can often identify a stronger urge to rekindle old ties or generate new links as the life-course evolves and scientists become concerned about ageing parents or their children's education or simply wish to return home. We have already seen in the example with Boyko above how a person can begin to seek out networks – in this case amongst expatriates in other countries – some years after migration. Irina moved to the UK eight years ago and has recently taken a more active interest in rebuilding an international network of Bulgarian scientists as the basis for effective knowledge transfer. It is interesting the way she describes the transition from her initial caginess about developing more explicit links to her current view that this international community could improve the image of Bulgarian science:

> One thing I realized lately was that I should probably try to keep my professional links with Bulgaria. I have a lot of international links and not too many links with other UK researchers but few of them are Bulgarian. But I realized that if you look like how Italians or Germans, especially in my field, support each other – they go to different countries but nevertheless they build a network and work together and I wondered why we Bulgarians don't do that. Why are we ashamed to cooperate with other Bulgarians? There are Bulgarians in other countries so why not cooperate? So we tried now and that woman I was meeting yesterday she is Bulgarian and she left before me and has established a technical university in the Netherlands, so with her we started a joint project between Britain and the Netherlands and that was very successful. I was myself resistant to work with other Bulgarians in other countries because people would say 'Well you Bulgarians, you only collaborate with Bulgarians' and then I realized that I shouldn't think like that. I came on Friday from a big conference and we were four Bulgarians there but none of us were in Bulgaria now and we realized that we are now building a critical mass and start to create a positive impression of Bulgaria and people start to know about Bulgaria and start to respect the Bulgarian education system. One of the researchers, a Canadian professor, is going to spend her sabbatical in Bulgaria to build links.

This case illustrates the importance of recognizing the potential that exists in terms of developing new contacts some time after the initial migration and even when the person has few firm links at the point of emigration. Irina is talking about building the kind of self-organized community that Séguin and colleagues (2006b) believe holds significant potential for sending regions.

Irina identifies the importance of conferences to this process. Scientific links are often spawned through formal fellowship schemes, joint degree programmes, attendance at international conferences and study visits (see Van de Sande et al., 2005: 12). These types of initiative often form the basis of critical networking and act as a migration trigger. Awareness of the opportunities available and the ability to attend are themselves, however, often achieved through contacts. Access to funding to attend international events is a very serious issue for all scientists: for scientists in the new and acceding Member States the costs of travelling to and attending such events often constitutes an insurmountable barrier. For Eugenia, securing funding to attend a short course precipitated a new contact and significant potential move: 'I went to a microscopy course in Heidelberg last September and met a professor from Prague who was doing the course and she wrote to me around Easter to say that she has a five-year post-doc in Prague'.

In many cases scientists have to raise their own funds to enable them to attend conferences abroad. The paucity of funding to enable migrant scientists to return to their home countries to develop research collaborations or present their work is also a factor restricting reverse knowledge transfer. When asked whether they had been able to participate in seminars or conferences in their home country, respondents commented either that few took place in those locations or that they had limited funding to access or organize these types of event. Where funding was available in the host institution, the priority was to target the most prestigious scientific events in order to present their work and not to use these funds to develop events in their home countries, which some argue might be difficult to justify on purely scientific grounds. Respondents were conscious that this situation impedes their ability to network with scientists in their home countries and support effective scientific exchange. Asked whether he was able to use his expertise to inform science in Bulgaria, Vladimir replied:

At the moment no. Each year they have these schools and symposiums which are organized on a local level. My institution [in Bulgaria] is doing this and if I have a chance to go there to present a lecture and to have contacts that might help but I can't because I have no funding. The only way to do it is during my holidays and sometimes I do it. I did it two years in a row – I paid for my own ticket. [Q: Did you not have funding from your lab then to attend conferences abroad?] I do but I can't say, 'Okay pay me to go back to Bulgaria'. This knowledge has nothing to do with this project and it's particularly weird to do that if the project is funded by the EU because you have to report back why this person was sent somewhere but it has to be something with the project or he's just having fun probably. There should be something which is more organized, probably the Bulgarian government should do it.

Although researchers expressed a keen interest in spending more time, on a professional level, in their home countries this often implies using their vacation leave and spending their own funds on travel. Séguin and colleagues (2006b: 78) conclude their study of the scientific diaspora in Canada with the recommendation that developed countries should 'make the diaspora option an integral part of their international development policy'. They advocate a series of measures including funding for 'initiatives facilitating the return of expatriate professionals for short periods [and] policies that would help postdoctoral fellows spend time in their home country without harming their careers' (ibid.). They also propose that sending regions 'establish an inventory of the skills base within the diaspora and develop programmes that facilitate the transfer of skills and knowledge' (ibid.).

CONCLUSIONS

This chapter has examined the kinds of contacts that exist within traditional diasporic, scientific diasporic and international scientific communities, identifying the factors shaping the growth and effectiveness of these connections. Our findings suggest that whilst traditional diasporic connections linking expatriates together in geographical proximity in the host countries do exist in some cases, these kinds of contacts are not particularly strong or significant to the professional lives of mobile scientists. Links with other scientists from their home countries – the scientific diaspora – are more prevalent and influential. However, it is useful to distinguish links formed with expatriates in the host and in third countries from those retained or established with scientists in the sending countries. The former are less developed and less active than the latter, which often play a more social role. There was some evidence of a renewed interest in establishing and reinvigorating links with the scientific diaspora but it was not clear that these networks currently played a major role in shaping migration patterns or reverse knowledge transfer. Connections with scientists in their home countries, on the other hand, play a very critical role in both respects. It is absolutely clear that connections shape the propensity to return. Here the branches are indeed very sticky. Without established and carefully nurtured 'anchors' with scientists in the sending regions, scientific labour markets can become more or less impenetrable to potential returnees. Where such networks exist, and particularly where the contact point in the sending country is highly established and active, the links have strong potential to shape both return moves and support reverse knowledge transfer. These contacts are primarily individual or personal, however, and do not link up communities as such. It is perhaps more appropriate to refer to them as individual connections rather than networks, which implies a wider and more formal web of interaction.

On the basis of the experience gained in this project it would seem that expatriate networks do play a major role in stimulating and channelling initial *outward* migrations but this works most effectively when linked into broader international scientific networks. Connections achieved through the social capital of supervisors play a particularly influential role. Meyer and Brown (1999: 2) make a similar point, arguing that 'the resource' lies not solely in the individual expatriate but also in 'their socio-professional networks'. For the majority of scientists, networks based on the science of what they do and not their national ties are perceived as both more legitimate and more effective. Moving through these international scientific networks does facilitate mobility but in a less spatially defined way, with scientists moving across international space. This limits the potential for the development of the kind of localized diaspora that are conducive to the kind of chain migration evident amongst other groups. So, international networks do 'make migrants' but not in the traditional diasporic sense.

To the extent that it is possible to generalize and reach some broad conclusions on this highly complex issue of networks and connections, it would seem that international scientific networks play the most critical role in stimulating and facilitating outward migration, and expatriate connections with the home country play a critical role in shaping return moves. The interface of these connections between the scientific diaspora and the wider international scientific community has the greatest impact on migration and represents the greatest potential for effective knowledge transfer.

The opportunity exists for a more positive 'back-flow' of knowledge and expertise. Nevertheless, serious barriers restrict its effective transmission. The dislocation of networks through continued emigration, retirement and scientific decline restricts the potential to retain active links. It would appear that the practice of permitting scientists to retain unpaid positions in the home country during their stays abroad has an important anchoring effect that maintains live connections between the researcher and their home institution. Increasing the funding available to expatriate scientists to spend time in their home countries on research visits and for conferences and seminars – and for scientists in the sending regions to attend international events and make short visits abroad – might improve opportunities for active networking and knowledge transfer.

Analysis of the findings on networks has encouraged us to reconsider the relationship between seniority and brain drain. Although losses of more senior and established scientists, on the face of it, might be predicted to have a more serious impact, not least because of the level of investment that the sending country has made in these individuals, the potential for reverse knowledge transfer in such cases is much higher. Early career scientists generally have fewer or less effective networks. Their migration may, in some respects, imply a more permanent and unilateral loss of knowledge and expertise. On the other hand, it is, of course, important to remember that networks consist not only of pre-migration contacts but also new contacts generated post-migration, perhaps in new fields and with new institutions. Fixed or frozen social capital is unlikely to have significant effect: it is important to the knowledge transfer process that networks evolve in response to changing research environments, in both locations.

This area of knowledge transfer represents enormous potential for all parties concerned and for European science as a whole. The increasing opportunities to conduct 'research-at-a-distance' – using networks to access large-scale research facilities and access data online – reduces the need for regular and extensive travel and enables scientists in the sending regions (where the opportunities to conduct the kind of research that requires significant capital investment remains in decline) to function at an international level. Ferro (2006: 183) concludes her study of the Romanian IT sector by talking about the potential that 'virtual transnationalism' presents in terms of keeping migrants and non-migrants connected across international space. For her, information technologies play a critical role in allowing the 'virtual employment of so-called "brains without a body"' (ibid.: 173). Davenport (2004: 617), with reference to the New Zealand context, is similarly upbeat about the potential for harnessing the scientific knowledge embedded in the diaspora, suggesting that it is not so much a brain drain as 'a world-wide-web, a well-placed global network ready to help New Zealand'.[10] Although Williams (2006: 600) questions the tendency of some research to 'essentialise the role of proximity in knowledge transfer' – and cites Amin's (2000) view that 'intimacy (or trust) may be achieved through the frequent and regular contacts enabled by the distanciated networks of communication and travel'. Amin (2002) echoes other researchers' comments that 'relational proximity is unlikely to overcome the barriers of geographical distance'. It was clear from our work that Bulgaria and Polish scientists were increasingly able to communicate and, importantly, conduct research at a distance. Ultimately, harnessing the potential of the scientific diaspora and international research community demands the existence of a critical mass of powerful anchors in the form of human and physical resources in the home country.

NOTES

1. This is also true of more 'privileged' flows such as retirement migration (King, Warnes and Williams, 2000; O'Reilly, 2000; Ackers and Dwyer, 2002).
2. There is insufficient scope in this chapter to consider the extent to which a *European* scientific community is developing. Recent research (Van de Sande et al., 2005) shows evidence of a strong European identity amongst scientists shaping location decisions.
3. This issue is discussed in more detail in Chapters 3 and 7.
4. Kicinger was the Polish partner in the MOBEX2 study and it is her Country Report – produced as part of that study – that is referred to here (Kicinger, 2005).
5. Although the binary divide has technically disappeared in the UK, a clear hierarchy of institutions is recognized according to research intensity and prestige. Centres of research excellence are magnets for international migrants and will generate significant opportunities for networking.
6. It was clear from our work in Bulgaria that scientists were increasingly able to communicate and, importantly, conduct experiments at a distance.
7. This discussion is taken up in Chapter 7.
8. Of course, it is not as simple as that: reputational capital and contacts remain highly important in all countries, not least in the refereeing process for grant applications and publications.
9. Interviews with scientists as part of our Marie Curie Impact Assessment (Van de Sande et al., 2005) emphasized the importance of 'change of field' as a factor stimulating and shaping migration behaviour.
10. Gamlen (2005: 26) is also optimistic that 'shared enculturation rather than geographical and institutional proximity, may bind knowledge communities'.

PART II

Assessing impact: the experience of receiving and sending countries

7. Brain gain? Assessing the value of scientific migration to receiving countries[1]

INTRODUCTION

The EU is committed to increasing research capacity and sustainability through improved retention and international recruitment (EC, 2001; CEC, 2004). This concern is echoed at national level, with recent policy initiatives focusing on the twin objectives of improving the recruitment and retention of home-grown[2] scientists in national labour markets and augmenting this through international recruitment. The received wisdom, implicit in the brain drain debate, suggests that receiving countries are the net beneficiaries of highly skilled migration, capable of skimming the cream of employees in competitive global markets (Williams et al., 2004: 38). Peridy (2006: 6) takes a somewhat broader approach, suggesting that analysis of 'migration demand, from the host country perspective' should take account of 'the needs of the local labour market, the quality of the migrants, the expected welfare effect of migration and possibly the attitude of natives toward immigration'.

This chapter uses the UK as a case study to demonstrate the impact of highly skilled migration on receiving countries. It opens with a brief discussion of the importance of international recruitment to meeting skills shortages in academic labour markets. The chapter then moves on to consider whether the ability to recruit from abroad goes beyond simple vacancy-filling to enhance the quality of human capital through improved competition, effectively enabling the receiving countries to pick from the 'brightest and the best' as is often suggested.[3] In addition to improving the volume and quality of recruitment, it has been argued that highly skilled migration (HSM) adds to the breadth of knowledge, drawing in new forms of know-how, skills and approaches. Internationalization, in itself, is often ascribed some inherent quality. For Mahroum (2005: 225), 'internationalization, in terms of academic and research personnel, programmes, students and project collaboration, is perceived as a prerequisite for sustained participation in, and access to, global science'. Although the discussion here implies an intrinsic and positive relationship between mobility and internationalization, it is rare for research or policy to distinguish these phenomena as the basis of a more careful assessment of impact. Just as it is important to question the association between HSM and optimal recruitment, we also need to consider whether the human capital embodied in migrant scientists can be and is, in practice, expended in the new employment context. Are the skills that migrant scientists bring to the receiving country relevant and transferable and does the environment permit their effective utilization?

Employing highly skilled migrants also implies some incurred cost by host countries. In many, if not the majority of cases, the receiving country will make significant further investment in these employees. The extent and cost of this will depend on many factors, including the individual in question, the stage at which they migrate, the nature of their work and the length of stay. This leads us on to another area of difficulty: the issue of retention. Discussion of the retention of foreign scientists is often awkwardly avoided in policy debates where awareness of concerns around brain drain and the impact on sustainable development (in the sending regions) raises complex ethical issues. Nevertheless, in situations of acute dependency on foreign labour, discussions around risk and investment demand open and dispassionate debate not least because the alternative to retention might be migration to a third country and not return.

Finally, it is useful to turn the debate full circle and ask the sensitive question of whether a relationship exists between foreign recruitment and longer-term sustainability in the receiving countries. Put simply, does the ability to continue to recruit high-quality foreign researchers into relatively insecure and low paid positions exacerbate forms of internal brain drain or intersectoral losses on the part of home-grown researchers?

In many respects, the debates in this chapter mirror the concerns expressed in the context of the impact on sending regions where the presumption is one of net loss rather than net gain. One of the objectives of the MOBEX2 study has been to add nuance to these somewhat polarized zero-sum debates in order to support a more sensitive and effective policy response. The study was designed to capture the perceptions of mobile Polish and Bulgarian scientists and did not include interviews with principal investigators and employers in the receiving countries (unless, of course, they were Bulgarian or Polish). In practice this has made it difficult to capture information about the demand for and quality of labour. In order to present a broader view, this chapter draws on other related studies conducted by the research team primarily in the UK context.[4]

MEETING SKILLS SHORTAGES THROUGH MIGRATION

We have already referred to the emphasis that Peridy (2006: 6) places on the 'needs of the local labour market' in shaping migration demand. Ferro (2006: 13) adopts a similar approach, suggesting that 'raw' labour market demand is mediated via migration laws and policies to reflect the 'willingness of the potential destination countries to accept immigrants . . . Demand for foreign people and immigration laws decide which part of migration potential becomes effective'. The role of labour demand as a key 'pull' factor shaping the volume and direction of migration flows has long been recognized and applies to most forms of labour migration. Increasing attention to the needs of the 'knowledge economy' have, however, focused attention on more highly skilled migrants. As Ferro (ibid.: 172) suggests 'globalisation and the advent of a knowledge economy has created a new context for labour mobility, expressing a greater need for qualified professionals'.

The UK government recognizes the importance of migration, particularly of highly skilled people, to economic growth. A recent report (Home Office, 2005: 11) argues that 'like most developed countries, the UK needs migration for economic reasons. There are gaps in our labour market that cannot be filled by the domestic workforce. Skilled migrants, students and visitors bring major economic benefits, with net inward migration contributing 10–15% of forecast UK trend economic growth'. Specific concerns over recruitment in the science and technology sector led to the establishment of the Roberts Review to address 'serious problems in the supply of people with requisite high quality skills . . . which could undermine the Government's attempts to improve the UK's productivity and competitiveness' (Roberts, 2002: iii). The causes of skills shortages in the UK are highly complex but contributory factors include losses due to out-migration, the progressive expansion of higher education coupled with the demographic ageing of the scientific workforce and declining rates of transition from compulsory schooling into undergraduate science courses and subsequently into doctoral research and research careers (HEFCE, 2006).[5] An annual survey of recruitment and retention of staff in higher education (Thewlis, 2003) found that almost 30 per cent of universities reported difficulties recruiting younger academic staff and almost 25 per cent in retaining them. This concern is reflected in the White Paper on *The Future of Higher Education* (DfES, 2003: 14), which concluded that 'we need to consider how to attract and retain the best researchers internationally, and how to maintain a steady flow of the brightest and best young people into research'.

Identifying growing concerns around the ability to generate home-grown supply, the Review acknowledged the contribution of international migration as a partial solution to skills shortages, emphasizing the importance of 'being able to access scientific expertise from abroad' (Roberts, 2002: 17). Whilst it concludes that the UK 'appears to be a net beneficiary of the increasing migration of science and engineering talent – enjoying a "brain gain" rather than "brain drain" ' (ibid.: 185), it also acknowledges a degree of risk in over-relying on these sources of supply. The Review alludes to the elasticity of flows of science migrants, which are highly sensitive to changes in demand and conditions in the home and receiving countries and the broader European and/or global context.

Concerned about the continued existence of skills shortages in the scientific sector and keen to assess the effects of policy initiatives arising out of the Roberts Review, the body representing the joint Research Councils in the UK (RCUK) commissioned a study in 2006. The research was directed by Professor Ackers and took place alongside MOBEX2.[6] The wider emphasis in this study on problems of recruitment and retention in British universities translated into a research strategy that included interviews with a wider range of actors involved in recruitment processes – principal investigators, research directors and human resource managers – in addition to doctoral and post-doctoral researchers. The study found widespread evidence of recruitment and retention difficulties. In the areas covered by the Biotechnology and Biological Sciences Research Council (BBSRC) and the Engineering and Physical Sciences Research Council (EPSRC), difficulties were evident across the board with some specific problems in certain sub-disciplines. Although postgraduate tutors and supervisors expressed serious concerns about doctoral recruitment and retention, the most acute problems were seen at transition into post-doctoral research. Online surveys suggested that 17 per cent of supervisor respondents (n = 206) and 35 per cent of principal investigator respondents (n = 235) had recently experienced significant difficulties in recruiting suitable researchers. Qualitative interviews indicated similar concerns and confirmed the trend identified in other work (Ackers and Gill, 2005; Bekhradnia and Sastry, 2005; and Metcalf et al., 2005) of an increasing reliance, within UK academic labour markets, on applicants from abroad. Respondents referred to a decreasing proportion of UK applicants for many positions. The significance of internationalization to recruitment is evident in the following illustrative comments from the RCUK study:

> PhD students, no there's not a shortage. However, of my group, typically the majority of research students would come from countries other than the UK.

Certainly British student numbers have declined dramatically. When I first came here in 1976 we would have taken on something like 14 or 15 British students in our area and now we're down to two or three.

I estimate 80–90 per cent of PhDs we train at the moment are non-UK.

Less fashionable areas were even more reliant on foreign nationals:

It depends very much on the area. In an area like crystallography which is not that fashionable . . . if I put an advert out for a post-doc I get no applicants from Britain, none whatsoever, and that's been going for years.

Most graduate students in my field leave. They either go back to their home country or the British students go into banking . . . it's been years since I've had a post-doc from Britain.

Higher education statistics provide further evidence for these observations. A recent UK government report (Home Office, 2005: 15) specifically acknowledges the contribution that student mobility makes to the 'economic sustainability of many of our educational institutions'. For sure, inter-nationalization at undergraduate level influences internationalization at postgraduate level and in scientific employment through its impact on sub-sequent migration, staying on practices and location decisions. The UK and Germany host over half of all reported tertiary-level foreign students in the EU (Wilén, 2005). At taught postgraduate level too – Masters-level pro-grammes – the UK is witnessing increasing levels of internationalization: only 45 per cent of all Masters students in UK higher education institutions (HEIs) were UK nationals, and corresponding figures for biological and physical sciences were 56 per cent and 49 per cent respectively (HESA [Higher Education Statistics Agency] data). Masters programmes act as feeder routes, channelling students into doctoral research and shaping their location decisions (Ackers et al., 2006). It is difficult to make a meaningful comparison of these figures with the situation in Germany as the introduc-tion of the separate Masters degree is relatively recent.[7] Yet, recent data shows that the proportion of foreign students completing Masters in 2005 is much higher than in any other course type (Statistisches Bundesamt, 2006b). Masters-level study thus forms a key entry point for many foreign researchers into both the UK and Germany. As for internationalization at doctoral level, data shows that in relation to the UK, 59 per cent of total doctorates awarded to full-time students between 2003 and 2004 were to students who were domi-ciled in the UK prior to their PhD and 41 per cent came from abroad (HESA, 2005).[8] In Germany, the level is lower: 13.7 per cent of all doctorates were awarded to foreign nationals (Statistisches Bundesamt, 2006b).

There is also data showing the level of internationalization amongst staff in UK universities: in 2003–04, just over a third of all staff categorized as researchers come from abroad (HESA, 2005).[9] If we disaggregate these figures by discipline, a higher degree of internationalization is apparent: 47 per cent of all bioscience and 50 per cent of all physics researchers in UK HEIs over the same period were foreign (HESA, 2005). There are also institutional differences here as well (see Ackers et al., 2006): at the University of Cambridge, for example, UK nationals make up less than half of researchers in the biosciences (HESA, 2005).

From the most recent data available, we see much less reliance on foreign staff in German HE institutions: in 2005, 86 per cent of all academic and research staff were German nationals (Statistisches Bundesamt, 2006b: 37). There is some suggestion of higher internationalization in the areas of mathematics and the natural sciences: 81 per cent of all academic and research staff were German nationals here (ibid.: 191–4). Institutional-level data on internationalization is not available for Germany.

We have given a flavour of the levels of internationalization within UK and German HEIs to show that there is high and increasing reliance upon foreign recruitment from degree level upwards and particularly in the natural sciences. The overwhelming majority of international employees in UK universities are occupying fixed-term positions (Ackers and Gill, 2005; Ackers and Oliver, 2007; Court, 2004) and this may have important implications in terms of retention. Unsurprisingly, research has found that 'staff on non-permanent contracts are significantly more likely to leave UK HE than their colleagues on permanent ones' (Stevens, 2005: 32).

INTERNATIONALIZATION AND THE QUALITY OF HUMAN CAPITAL

The RCUK study referred to above (Ackers et al., 2006) identified problems both in the volume of applications for positions but also, critically, in the quality of applicants in the UK. A general consensus existed that the quality of home-grown researchers making the transition into doctoral and subsequently post-doctoral research was in decline. The following two excerpts from interviews with principal investigators are typical:

> We don't have problems getting candidates to come forward, it's getting good-quality candidates. I can usually fill a position [but] I've stopped now just filling positions. If I can't get a good enough candidate, I won't fill it.

> It's all very well having home applicants but if they are crap . . . then you are wasting your time.

Assessing the quality of foreign scientists is highly problematic. The reference to research stars in much of the literature and policy tends to focus attention on the movement of a small number of very established researchers.[10] Our research would largely support Bekhradnia and Sastry's (2005: 11) conclusion that, rather than attracting such senior research stars in any numbers, 'migration is overwhelmingly a phenomenon affecting junior staff . . . The absolute numbers of emigrants and immigrants at senior levels are not high and migration rates are low'. In practice, at least at the present time, flows of scientists from Bulgaria and Poland would appear to be mimicking flows from other EU Member States with an emphasis on early career positions.[11]

The previous section has evidenced the high level of international recruitment in British and German universities, especially at doctoral and post-doctoral level. Foreign scientists clearly play an important role in filling vacancies and rendering positions and scientific projects viable. The literature around scientific mobility and brain drain often goes a step further than this in assuming a direct relationship between levels of internationalization and individual excellence or quality. With echoes of implicit social Darwinism, authors use the language of the 'brightest and the best' (Mahroum, 1998: 17), 'the youngest and most able' (Salt, 1997: 23) and 'skimming' and 'poaching' (Wood, 2004) to describe these processes. There is also a direct link with the idea of competitiveness. As Meyer and colleagues (2001: 309) state, 'flows seem always to go from the less developed "haemophiliac regions" to the more competitive places'. So, it is not simply that employment opportunities exist in the receiving regions, albeit often in the less lucrative and desirable segments of the labour market, but that the relative attractiveness of these regions enables employers to be more selective and cherry-pick across global markets. Of course this implies both that excellence is mobile – that scientists are equally footloose – and that recruitment processes can recognize it and operate efficiently and effectively.

The pressure to attract the best international students and staff is evident at national level in both UK and German policy initiatives. The UK White Paper on *The Future of Higher Education* (DfES, 2003: 14) emphasizes the 'need to consider how to attract and retain the best researchers internationally'. Similar sentiments are expressed by the German Federal Ministry of Education and Research (BMBF, 2005: III): 'only countries that train sufficient numbers of highly qualified persons, and that are attractive for foreign specialists, can succeed in the international competition for the best minds'. Both countries, therefore, are making a link between international recruitment and excellence – an idea supported in a recent UK Higher Education Policy Institute (HEPI) report (Bekhradnia and Sastry,

2005: 12): 'Mobility is associated with high quality: not all migrants are high quality – a significant proportion who migrate do not subsequently pursue an academic career – but a high proportion of those who become senior academics have migrated at some point, usually early in their careers'.

This statement conflates the valuation of mobility amongst returning home nationals (who have spent some time researching abroad) with the specific quality of migrants moving into the UK. In the German context, Hilgendorf (2005) outlines the importance of internationalization to the HE system in two respects. First, she argues that hosting foreign students promotes long-term collaborations once the students leave Germany. This relationship, between mobility and collaboration, is echoed by the UK government, which talked of the value of undergraduate mobility in terms of 'enabling bright young people from abroad to develop lifelong ties with the UK which are of long-term benefit to the country' (Home Office, 2005: 15). Second, Hilgendorf (2005) argues that the ability to attract researchers from abroad plays an important role in asserting the credibility of German research and, as such, 'dissuades highly educated Germans from seeking better professional and academic opportunities overseas'. Internationalization almost becomes a benchmark of competitiveness and excellence, although its specific relationship with quality remains implicit. Ferro's (2006: 179) work on the mobility of information technology (IT) professionals questions the received wisdom that mobility is in itself an indicator of excellence: 'the IT profession generates the social expectation that the best IT workers are those who leave, being recruited by the international market. Because working abroad means being a successful person, emigration means high professional achievement'. Ferro provides examples of people who have not been mobile either because they do not wish to move or have family reasons for staying put, but nevertheless experience powerful social pressure on them to leave.[12]

With reference to undergraduate mobility, Altbach and Teichler (2001) further question the relationship between mobility and quality. Although patterns generally show students from less-developed countries moving to industrialized countries, they argue that mobility is becoming more commonplace and less selective, regardless of ability:

> In recent decades, the international mobility of staff and students has become a normal part of academic life, involving perhaps 3 to 5 million people annually. Although mobility is more likely for the most able students and staff, it has become a normal option for staff and students. (Ibid.: 8)

More recently, Kelo, Teichler and Wachter (2006: 3) subtly distinguish two approaches to internationalization at undergraduate level, arguing that 'many governments have started campaigns which market their countries' higher education institutions worldwide, to attract as many students as possible from other countries and regions, in some cases, or to attract the best ones'. The inference here is that the emphasis in some contexts on volume might actually detract from quality. Hatakenaka's (2004) review of internationalization in UK HE goes a step further. Identifying 'market orientation' as 'the new driver of international trends today', he concludes that 'internationalism that is purely market-driven may be inadequate to support the scientific research training of high calibre international students which could bring benefits – both to the UK and the sending countries' (ibid.: 6). Kinnaird (2006) makes a similar point in his analysis of the Australian context, questioning the wider impact of market-driven policies promoting internationalization of student recruitment on migration flows and national labour markets.

The historical association of Eastern European countries with scientific investment, lengthy and rigorous training and the relative comparability with European systems increases their attractiveness as a reliable and convenient source of scientific labour. Member States in the old Eastern Bloc do not simply imply a wider potential pool: they present distinctive opportunities. Although economically weak in comparison to existing Member States, they are characterized by high levels of post-compulsory education (Bekhradnia, 2004; Dabrowa-Szefler, 2004; Kicinger, 2005). Indeed, in some countries the proportion of the population with tertiary education exceeds the EU average: Bulgarians are twice as likely as Portuguese and Italians to have experienced tertiary education, for example. Bulgaria, Poland and Slovenia also have a very high and increasing proportion of science graduates – higher in fact than Portugal, Italy, the Netherlands and Greece (see Gill, 2003). The pool of scientific labour in Poland and Bulgaria thus represents an important potential resource for existing Member States and a different context to previous accession phases. Aston (2004: 7) predicts that accession will precipitate an increase in recruitment at undergraduate level in 'shortage areas such as maths, science and engineering-related subjects because of the disproportionately high number of applicants from the accession countries for these subjects with strong qualifications'. Raising important questions around the problems of relying on such flows to meet skills shortages and bolster university recruitment (and the sustainability of internationalization in this context), however, Aston also emphasizes the volatility of these flows and the extent to which they are influenced by push factors in the sending regions as much as the pull effects of UK and German policy. Of course, this situation makes it more difficult for the receiving countries to manage these processes.

QUALITY: THE PERCEPTIONS OF BULGARIAN AND POLISH RESPONDENTS

The interviews with Polish and Bulgarian scientists included questions designed to gauge their perceptions of the value of mobility to the receiving country.[13] There was a common consensus among the Polish and Bulgarian respondents who had been educated in their home country that the standard of higher education was higher back home than in the host country (at least up to doctoral level). From their perspective, this situation enabled the receiving countries to tap into a better-quality undergraduate pool. Boyko, for example, speaks proudly of the quality of mathematics and computer science education in Bulgaria, arguing that 'in the last five or six years Bulgaria has been in the first five places in the world in mathematics'. Piotr, a senior physicist, expresses his impression of the relative quality of UK and Polish education:

> I think it very much depends on the university. When I compare my education at Warsaw University with the kind of education that students get here or in most British universities then there is no comparison whatsoever. They are two levels below . . . [In Poland] they are much better prepared. At the end of the Masters' five-year programme it's much higher than what you get here.

Svetlana, a Bulgarian Principal Research Fellow, reflects on her experience of recruiting from Eastern European countries: I look at their degree and I know that many science degrees from former socialist countries are five-year programmes, which have a lot of chemistry, physics and maths in so the scientific background is really good. Even Kiril, who came to the UK for his first degree, views the Bulgarian system as more strenuous:

> [Bulgarian scientists] know a lot more than a lot of people who have graduated from here or other Western countries. The education system is very, very hard pressure and you learn huge amounts, far more than you learn here or in Germany . . . In Bulgaria you have to learn off by heart, book after book.

Respondents often talked about how theoretically strong Eastern European scientists are. Justyna, a Polish microscopist, argues that migrant scientists from Eastern Europe are 'usually very good. Theoretically they really excel'. For Alexander, the strength of theoretical training and basic skills in Bulgaria, coupled with the lack of resources, support a more problem-solving approach to learning:

> I believe the training I received during my studies was very good, particularly in terms of theoretical background. I did not have the chance to do as much

practical work as students in Germany and some of the equipment I used was obsolete. Nevertheless, the theoretical grounding I received in the principles of the methods was solid, often more solid than I have observed in the case of some German students, who are quite skilled at using high-tech kits, but lack an understanding of what goes on inside the tubes.

Alexander's comments, together with those of other respondents, did not indicate any major issues in terms of the relational quality of skills from the perspective of the receiving countries.[14] Although we gained the impression that their undergraduate training placed a greater emphasis on these theoretical skills and, in many cases, respondents spoke of the lack of equipment and facilities in their home laboratories, most argued that this increased their adaptability and indicated that the skills they had were transferable. They just needed some time to familiarize themselves with new equipment. Lech's fairly pragmatic response is typical:

> Generally, talking about Polish people not about myself, we are quite good scientists because our level of education in Poland is quite good. We don't have such good equipment but when you go to the lab you just learn how to use equipment. We are very good scientists so I'm sure that they will produce lots of excellent results and publications.

Like Alexander, Jerzy suggests that the challenges of working in a resource-poor environment encourage Polish scientists to be more innovative: 'When you try to work in Poland or Russia you don't usually have enough money for research so we try to use our knowledge to avoid the most expensive things. It's very useful because sometimes you have to use your knowledge, not prepared kits, for example'.

Quality is a rather elusive concept in itself and cannot be measured simply in terms of qualifications and scientific skills. It was clear from the interviews that respondents took a broader view of the contribution they made to science in the receiving countries. In some instances they referred to the value of different kinds of experiences and approaches more generally and also to the scientific networks they bring with them. Asked about the benefits of international mobility to the UK, Teresa states: 'I think it's quite international so when I look at our group, it's people from Italy, from Argentina, Spain and I think it's nice because it brings different experiences. People who travel a lot have completely different knowledge . . . and they are better scientists'.

For both Teresa and Renata, internationalization is associated with forms of knowledge diffusion and exchange that increase the quality of both teaching and research: 'There's a lot of people from Europe in our department from Russia and outside Europe, it's a very international group and I think they bring something different and a different approach to teaching students and this makes life richer'.

In other situations, the question about their contribution to science in the receiving countries encouraged respondents to talk more generally about commitment and attitude. By taking the decision to move abroad for work purposes it is already clear that mobile researchers are committed to doing science. Eugenia believes that some talented Western researchers fail to fulfil their scientific potential and are perhaps less driven:

> People from Eastern Europe are a lot more qualified to survive . . . in a very general sense . . . what we bring encompasses a very active fighter-type attitude. I don't know why a lot of people [here] are actually lacking this. Maybe because they didn't have to survive anything. They've been born into a fantastic social state whereby even if you don't work you're fairly well supported and they never felt that they had to actually fight for anything.

For others, the idea of a greater sense of commitment was expressed in terms of working hard:

> I personally work very hard. I know that I must defend my position and I must prove myself so I put much more effort in. I didn't see many colleagues during the weekends and I was here every weekend.

> The people who leave [Poland and Bulgaria] are usually more motivated and more hardworking people, which of course benefits wherever they're going to.

> It's a bit like grabbing the best opportunities because for us it's such a difference in an institute like this, the facilities . . . you have this big motivation to work.

This association of migrant status with commitment or a work ethic raises a number of issues. For many scientists, research fellowships abroad represent a critical period in their career, during which they can avoid the tensions of combining research with other duties (such as teaching) and really focus on research productivity (Van de Sande et al., 2005). We have also seen how the overwhelming majority of early career researchers occupy fixed-term positions, which places them under pressure to demonstrate productivity in order to secure a subsequent position (Hasluck, Pitcher and Simm, 2001; Bryson, 2004; Ackers and Oliver, 2007). None of these factors are exclusively linked to the migration status of the post-holder.

Other work has identified a strong relationship between the amount of time scientists spent on their research and their migration status (Ackers, 2007). Mobile scientists, at least during the early stages of migration, are often living as single people in the host country (either because they are in fact single or because their partners and children are not living with them) and are less integrated in social networks. This situation, coupled with their desire to prove themselves in a finite amount of time, often results in them working around the clock in the host institution. Buchinger, Gödl and Gschwandtner (2002: 126) coined the phrase 'working time without borders' to describe typical working hours in an Austrian study on the reconciliation of work and family in science careers. Similar patterns are reported by MOBEX2 respondents and particularly those making short stays abroad.[15]

The specific context within which migrant scientists find themselves might thus result in extended patterns of work and associated productivity. It is doubtful, however, that this lies in some inherent quality of migrants but rather the context within which the migrant operates and should not be interpreted narrowly in terms of commitment. Indeed, current debates at European and national level about the attractiveness of research careers and the importance of ensuring that such careers are seen as viable and compatible with a reasonable quality of life lead us to question the impact of this approach to work on working cultures in the lab. Internationalization, to the extent that it encourages a culture of excessive and often unremunerated over-hours working, has the potential to reduce the attractiveness of science careers and the transition of young people in the receiving countries into science.

Although we did not identify any cases of scientists moving directly into established senior positions in the UK and Germany, our impressions from the interviews would support the contention that the pool of scientists in Bulgaria and Poland represents real opportunities for the host countries in terms of scientific potential. The question remains as to whether universities and research groups in the host countries are able to harness this potential.

SELECTION AND QUALITY

As discussed above, perceptions about competitiveness were not only linked to the quality and volume of the potential recruitment pool but also to recruitment processes capable of identifying and rewarding excellence. Although many senior scientists are able to fill vacant positions through international recruitment, this process is not without its risks and costs to employers. The RCUK study (Ackers et al., 2006) identified serious concerns that many posts (especially those on websites) were attracting high-volume, blanket applications, many of which were time-consuming and difficult to assess. Ivanka, a Bulgarian senior lecturer in the UK, talked of being overwhelmed by foreign applications: 'When I advertised the position I had 150 applicants for one post-doc from all over the world. The UK is a magnet for many students and post-docs. . . We are absolutely over-whelmed with applications for post-doctoral fellowships from Germany, Italy and France'.

Selection problems are compounded by lack of familiarity with and confidence in overseas qualifications systems and the quality and relevance of training. Identifying the brightest and the best in these circumstances is often rather difficult. One might argue that the experience of being over-whelmed by the volume of foreign applicants might actually detract from quality appointments. Our research with Marie Curie Fellows (Van de Sande et al., 2005) highlighted the importance not only of the quality of applicants but also the ability of recruitment processes to identify and ensure a genuinely competitive and objective appointment process. In the main, the UK emerged as one of the countries with the strongest reputation for objective and meritocratic recruitment (see also Bekhradnia and Sastry, 2005). Many of the Bulgarian and Polish scientists in MOBEX2 specifically identified the importance of the openness of labour markets and transparent and fair recruitment as one of the attractions of working in the UK and Germany, compared with their home countries where patronage continues to distort the relationship between ability and opportunity (some examples of this are presented in the following chapter). Evidence of effective, merit-based recruitment processes in the host countries would tend to support the association of internationalization with competitiveness. Teresa reports that about half of the post-docs in her lab are from abroad. Asked whether she considers this a benefit to UK science she replies: 'I think so because all of these positions are completely on the competitive level so at least directly the person who gets it is the best person applying. Of course if someone applied from abroad they would have to be better than someone who is English'. The point she makes here about foreign applicants having to be better than host nationals is interesting and might either reflect her own experiences and observations or institutional employment policies that required universities to fill positions with appointable EU nationals before appointing third country nationals.[16]

Many respondents anticipated an increase in the volume of flows – particularly at doctoral and undergraduate level – in response to changes in the financial regime. The costs of studying in the UK were generally felt to be prohibitive to young scientists from Poland and Bulgaria prior to accession (during which time they were required to pay overseas students fees). The introduction of the non-discrimination principle post-accession would significantly reduce these costs but nevertheless the introduction of general fees for UK nationals and their recent increase to £3000 per year at under-graduate level (coupled with the high cost of living in the UK) still acts as a barrier for many Polish and Bulgarian students. In practice the application of the means test might mean that the majority are not required to pay fees at all.[17] It remains to be seen whether the relaxation of overseas fees results in weaker students coming to the UK. Arguably the pre-accession provisions constitute a form of rationing based not on merit but ability to pay and as such bear little relationship with scientific potential. However, the possibility of increased numbers of younger movers does raise questions about the nature of the process in general in terms of the investments made by the sending regions.

Teresa's comments about having to be 'better than' host nationals in order to secure positions resonates with the perceptions of many scientists in response to a question about the impact that EU enlargement can be expected to have on the volume and quality of scientific flows. Quite a strong sense emerged from the interviews that prior to enlargement the requirement to satisfy these harsher employment conditions meant that only the best quality (or most eager) applicants from non-EU Member States could gain access to scientific positions. Provided they possessed the necessary skills and qualities most respondents did not experience serious problems in securing a position for themselves.[18] EU enlargement and the deregulation associated with it, some suggested, might dilute the quality of potential migrants.[19] Michal, a Polish post-doc, explains how he had to compete for his post with EU nationals prior to accession and was only awarded the position if no suitably qualified EU nationals applied. Since accession, he says, it is 'easier to get a job because before we had this rule, you had to be very good in the field, better than EU nationals, and give them more reasons to employ you rather than the others. Now if you are the same, the same knowledge and experience, then you have equal chances. Before we had to be better, now you have more chances. Lots of people are leaving now'.

Although none of the scientists interviewed reported serious difficulties in terms of accessing employment themselves, some suggested that life would be a little easier and less bureaucratic and they might feel like full rather than second-class citizens. Several respondents said that pre-accession visa rules tied them to individual employers whereas full EU membership would enable them to move more easily between institutions and also, importantly, between sectors into industry. Rumiana felt that this change would increase employment opportunities for Bulgarian scientists in the UK: 'It wasn't a problem [to get a work permit] but you are coming to work for a certain company or for the university and you rely for your work permit on the establishment who is asking for the work permit . . . If your base is bigger then your applications will be more diverse and this will help'.

Jerzy said that the UK had made a strategic move in not implementing transition measures that enabled it to have first pick of the best scientists, suggesting either that some people had been prevented from moving in the past or that the approach generated a symbolic positive encouragement to come to the UK: 'It was good that the UK opened its borders compared to the rest of Europe. It was very clever because the first people moving to the UK will be the most highly educated from Poland. Whereas, when France or Germany open to receive workers they won't be the best'. He goes on to predict that following accession Poland was 'going to lose all its scientists', suggesting that volume rather than quality might be the issue.

Perhaps of greater concern was the view expressed by some that EU enlargement might actually reduce the quality of flows both at scientific level but also in less skilled, non-scientific sectors. Some felt that the legal requirement for employers to fill vacancies where possible with EU nationals and make a strong case for the employment of non-EU nationals, prior to accession, encouraged a highly selective process, enabling the receiving countries to cream off the best applicants. It was quite common for respondents, such as Kiril, to refer to the influx of unskilled migrants from their countries, post-accession, and to view this as potentially problematic: 'Initially it will help too many people to leave and I'm afraid of that . . . I think with science and highly skilled people because they're sought after in the West, their employer here will do everything to get them so I don't think this will help them that much but it will make it very easy for anyone to leave'. Eugenia drew a link between what she saw as less desirable flows of unskilled workers and the quality of the environment for migrant scientists, and predicted a rise in the level of racism and intolerance, which might encourage both her and her engineer husband to leave:

> At least until now [migration] has been mainly highly qualified. I'm beginning to be slightly worried about the whole immigration issue. In one sense probably that might have an impact on me making up my mind about [moving to take up a job offer in] Prague because I think the balance has tipped slightly towards more negativity towards foreigners. Some people are genuinely worried that the UK will be swamped by foreigners and there's no jobs for British people. To be honest with you even going to the supermarket I can see why they think so because there's so many people from Italy or people from ethnic minorities who have probably not had the best options in life anyway like gypsies and I've seen many of them now in the UK. Obviously there could be problems.

Eugenia's comments highlight the importance of understanding the links between different forms of migration. Although, as we have argued, it is useful to distinguish specific occupational categories in order to understand the conditions and motivational forces at play, as highly skilled migrants do not live in a vacuum and are influenced by broader migration processes.

THE SUSTAINABILITY OF INTERNATIONALIZATION: REALIZING THE POTENTIAL OF MIGRANT SCIENTISTS

Within the scientific sector, internationalization and high levels of skilled mobility are generally viewed as unproblematic and positive indicators of competitiveness. Bekhradnia and Sastry (2005: para. 9) argue that because 'overall figures for migration are heavily influenced by a large group of postdoctoral researchers who spend (and possibly intend to spend) only a limited time in the UK . . . migration of this type would be unlikely to have a disruptive effect upon UK academic departments'. This leads to their main conclusion that 'the very great majority of movement takes place among junior postdoctoral staff, and this is entirely positive for this country' (ibid.: para. 28). These views are echoed in a recent report by the Higher Education Funding Council for England (HEFCE, 2006: 40). This assumption – that the inward movement of large numbers of post-doctoral researchers is 'entirely positive' – is not based on any evidence and fails to consider a number of critical issues: first, the issue of retention and progression and whether the receiving countries are realizing the full potential of highly skilled migrants; and second, whether there are any policy externalities or unintended consequences associated with such high levels of international recruitment, which threaten the long-term sustainability of academic labour markets.

The introduction to this chapter referred to the awkwardness that surrounds any attempt to discuss the retention of foreign scientists, especially those from less developed countries or regions. This reflects the embarrassment associated with the brain drain debate and increasing concern about its impact on sending countries. To the extent that scientific migration continues to take place on an individual level, through the hidden hand of free market liberalism (as opposed to specific policy inducements), it can be conceptualized as a natural process and any attempts to intervene to restrict it raise serious equality or non-discrimination issues. In many respects this reflects the implicit tension between the development agenda and economic agenda or, put differently, between the promotion of sustainability at home and sustainability abroad. Although the language of sustainability is now entering debates about labour markets in the receiving countries, the discussions – about sustainability in receiving and sending countries – remain discrete and their relational quality stand implicit. The recent HEFCE report on the academic workforce in England (HEFCE, 2006) is a case in point. Whilst the document as a whole refers to sustainability in the context of national labour markets at various points, the links between this and the issue of 'ethical migration' – which is only discussed in the context of the migration of health care specialists and primarily in relation to developing countries – remain entirely distinct (ibid.: 41).

Respondents are more ready to identify these policy tensions. Radoslava, a Bulgarian doctoral researcher in Germany, immediately identifies the kind of conflict referred to above and the potential costs of this form of mobility to the receiving countries:

> I don't know any students who stay in Bulgaria. If they go back after that it's perfect. I cannot understand it because from the point of view of Germany why they give the opportunity to so many Bulgarians and they give them everything for free and then after that they just lose them?

Although some mobility schemes focus explicitly on training for development purposes and as such do not encourage retention,[20] Suter and Jandl (2006: 5) point to a growing emphasis on retention, suggesting that 'foreign students who have graduated from domestic institutions of higher education have come to be seen as a privileged source of qualified permanent immigration and policies to retain foreign graduates have become a standard instrument in selection systems for highly qualified migrants'. The increasing reliance on foreign recruitment described above raises key concerns around retention and sustainability. Recognizing that encouraging entry is only one dimension of the challenge, the UK Roberts Review cautions that the positive effects of science mobility may be mitigated by the propensity to return. This sentiment was echoed by respondents in our study on academic pay, which reported 'some concern amongst the academic community that substantial, and increasing, recruitment from overseas may potentially lead to a problem in the sustainability of UK academic staffing' (Ackers et al., 2006: 103). In practice, the evidence on retention and return is limited and often contradictory. A recent study by the UK's National Institute of Economic and Social Research (Stevens, 2005: 31–2) indicated limited retention amongst EU nationals:

> Academics from other EU (and EEA) countries, Australia, New Zealand and the US are more likely to leave UK HE than UK (and other foreign) academics. Our results support the hypothesis that these staff enter academic employment in the UK after completing a higher degree in the UK, but ultimately intend to return to their home country. If this is the case, such staff will only represent a short-term solution for lower-level jobs in UK higher education unless they can be persuaded to remain in the UK.

These predications are backed up by other recent studies that show that many researchers later return to their country of origin or move elsewhere, raising concerns about retention and the return on investment (Bekhradnia and Sastry, 2005; Metcalf et al., 2005). A recent survey of European graduates who had studied in UK institutions found that only 27 per cent were working in the UK six months after graduation (Suter and Jandl, 2006: 65). Data from the impact assessment of the Marie Curie Fellowship Scheme shows that for respondents who had completed post-doctoral fellowships in the UK, 55 per cent (n = 145) had returned to their home country and 30 per cent (n = 85) remained in the UK (Van de Sande et al., 2005: 20). The fact that Marie Curie Fellows are moving within an organized scheme with fellowships of a fixed duration can be expected to increase levels of ongoing and return mobility. In any event, retention rates of 25–30 per cent could be interpreted as quite high. Research on post-PhD retention in the United States suggest much higher retention rates, with 74 per cent of foreign science and engineering doctoral recipients planning to remain after completion (National Science Foundation, 2006: 6).

Certainly a critical factor shaping length of stay and retention is the temporary quality of most early-career research positions. One of the attractions in moving to the UK or Germany from Eastern Europe is the wide availability of post-doctoral positions and their relative openness to foreigners. For migrants who only initially want to relocate for one or two years, fixed-term positions are often favoured, particularly if they offer the opportunity to focus exclusively on research and generate outputs (Van de Sande et al., 2005; Ackers and Oliver, 2007). However, for migrants who later contemplate staying longer, the lack of permanent positions (and the difficulties in the transition into permanent positions) may encourage them to leave.

Viktor, a Bulgarian post-doctoral researcher, comments that it is partly out of necessity that migrant scientists take fixed-term contracts, as they have few other options for positions in host countries, at least at the onset of mobility: 'For me choosing Germany was quite a matter of coincidence and chance. I was searching for a job here and there. It's hard to get something other than a post-doc when you are coming from Eastern Europe or any foreign country for that matter'. He goes on to explain the significant stress that contractual insecurity causes:

> Life like this is under huge stress; my longest contract was when I get Marie Curie Individual Fellowship for two years. Most of the time I was on all these temporary contracts for one year . . . and you cannot plan your life. My last contract is until the end of this year and I was specifically told that I will not get a single day extension and this is something which really makes me angry.

Piotr reports a similar experience: 'I had a permanent position in Poland . . . In Germany it is limited in time because of high unemployment; it's very difficult to obtain a permanent position here and my contract is permanently prolonged for half a year and so'.

Whilst it is not surprising that many early-career migrants move initially into insecure positions, respondents expressed concern about their future in the host state and, in particular, their ability to progress into permanent and more senior academic positions. This is not only a concern for them as individual scientists and citizens but also a partial indicator of the contribution that scientists can make to the receiving country. As we have noted, at least in our research, evidence points in the direction of the UK and Germany's ability to attract large numbers of high-quality doctoral and post-doctoral researchers rather than the high-flying research stars that attract so much media and policy attention. It is important not to forget that post-docs are also highly productive, as Teresa points out:

> The post-doctoral years are the most productive because you already know what you are doing after the training of the PhD and then it's before you are loaded with teaching and administration, so actually the people who really do the work are the post-doctoral researchers. Even if they come at this post-doctoral time they give a lot of this work at the time which is the best time to research.

Certainly in MOBEX2 we were not aware of any specific attempts by UK or German institutions to approach and recruit established research stars from Poland or Bulgaria in a proactive fashion. That said, the pool of migrant doctoral and post-doctoral researchers represents enormous potential to become the stars of the future yet conclusive evidence of progression is absent at the present time.

A number of respondents expressed the view that their progression in the receiving countries was somehow blocked by a glass ceiling, echoing the debate about the progression of women. Although Marek had achieved a very senior permanent position in the UK he nevertheless felt that he had suffered discrimination: 'I feel that my qualifications, experience and work are not valued in the UK because I am Polish. There seems to be an undercurrent attitude of "British is best, East European education and science is inferior, East Europeans should be grateful for any employment we offer them"'. Viktor, a Bulgarian post-doc, echoes that perception, suggesting that foreign migrants are welcome in Germany but only on a temporary basis:

> I very much want to stay. I never, in the beginning especially, felt treated like a foreigner here, there was no kind of double standard on the estimation of my results or performance for being a foreigner. Everybody was very polite, my performance and results were gradually acknowledged. However, every time I also felt like I'm a guest researcher who is here working for a limited time and performing very nicely but I do not belong to them here. I didn't feel I had all the opportunities like finding a permanent job – that is the main thing.

Ludwika, a Polish doctoral candidate in Germany also has the impression that it's easier to progress as a native. Asked why he is considering returning to Poland, he replies: 'I have a better chance to have a better career in Poland than here because in Germany there is very big competition and also it's easier maybe to be a native German to find a good job here'. Other respondents in the UK expressed concerns about their ability to progress and further their careers and research. Ivanka had held a succession of fixed-term contracts in a single UK institution over a period of ten years at the time of interview: 'This is a burning issue. I cannot describe how difficult it is to move on after you have done your post-doctoral positions'.

In practice it is difficult to interpret some of these experiences. Although the perception might be of discrimination in favour of nationals, it is clear from our work that many early-career researchers, both foreign and home, have limited awareness of the reality of academic career progression and the prospects of achieving a permanent position in the natural sciences where the proportion of fixed-term positions significantly outweighs the proportion of permanent positions especially in the prestigious institutions that attract many foreign post-docs. Whether the problem lies in the research systems of the receiving countries in general or in specific treatment of 'foreign' researchers, MOBEX2 suggests that retention and progression remains a serious concern for our respondents and arguably reduces the contribution that they can make to the science base in the receiving countries.

THE SUSTAINABILITY OF INTERNATIONALIZATION: THE IMPACT OF MIGRATION ON NATIONAL LABOUR MARKETS AND THE ATTRACTIVENESS OF SCIENCE CAREERS

The increasing reliance of the UK on foreign scientists is evident from the discussion above. This section considers two related questions: first, the issue of sustainability and risk inherent in this approach, given the volume of flows and their potential volatility;[21] and second, it questions whether a relationship exists between the decline in home-grown supply chains – reflecting the attractiveness of academic careers – and the continued ability to draw on foreign sources of labour.

Alison Richard, Vice-Chancellor of the University of Cambridge, has recently stated that

> universities will be dominated by foreign academics soon unless more British graduates are persuaded to stay in higher education. Over a quarter of the staff

at Cambridge and 53% of post-docs are from overseas and this raises the prospect of universities depending increasingly on foreign academics for regeneration. (Cited in Blair, 2006)

Professor Richard's concerns are echoed by Professor Drummond Bone, former president of Universities UK, who cautions that 'the danger of relying wholly on non-British researchers in some subjects is not only that they go home, but also that the lack of home-grown talent spirals downwards into less interest in schools' (ibid.).

With reference to the continued ability of the UK to attract these international researchers, Hatakenaka (2004: 5) urges caution, suggesting that such recruitment is 'volatile' and has been 'rising at a rate that will be hard to sustain indefinitely'.[22] Dr Cotgreave, former director of the UK Campaign for Science and Engineering (CaSE), welcomed mobility but expressed concern that the UK may become over-reliant upon international recruitment and vulnerable to the ebbs and flows of international labour markets: 'It's not about being a little England, science has always been international, people have always moved round but there has to be a sort of net equilibrium . . . the overall result has to be that you can sustain the numbers that you need' (cited in Ackers and Gill, 2005: 288).

The reference to sustainability is interesting here as is the notion of 'net equilibrium'. In practice it is rare for people to discuss in any explicit sense what an optimum balance might look like and at what point reliance on foreign labour becomes excessively risky. The following comments were made by a labour economist interviewed as part of our Research Council study (Ackers et al., 2006). Although he is referring specifically to his own discipline he raises more general concerns around the sustainability of labour markets and the management of risk:

> There is a crunch coming along if we don't do something. It's global – we are not attracting home students to renew the profession. It's OK to say 'yes, attract them from the EU and elsewhere' but there are issues about the ability to do that and the composition of the faculty. If everyone was from overseas, OK, that's very international but it's like saying we can do without manufacturing industry. Surely we need to be able to renew this important area from within our own resources – it's a key issue . . . we are not replacing ourselves. It would be foolish to rely totally on people from overseas. It will feed through in terms of research performance and many return home. It's complex and we have got to be careful and it takes us into an area where people think you are saying 'home people are better'.

It is perhaps significant to note that at this point in the interview the respondent requested that the tape be switched off, aware that such views might be construed as problematic and potentially discriminatory. His comments nevertheless draw attention to serious and valid concerns around the declining rate of transition of home-grown young people into scientific research and the longer-term implications of this.

A recent editorial in the *Times Higher Education Supplement* (THES) describes the increasing reliance of UK universities on foreign student fees as 'unsettling news, as it demonstrates growing dependency on a volatile income stream' and goes on to add that with 'the immigration debate intensifying, it is only a matter or time before the spotlight falls on supposedly lost opportunities for home students' (THES, 2006: 12). Two weeks later the same newspaper included an article on what opportunities there are for the UK to learn from Australia's policy of granting residency visas to foreign graduates in designated shortage fields. According to Kinnaird (2006: 21), the policy has 'delivered huge increases in the number of foreign enrolments and in revenue to universities, but it has been an abject failure in terms of domestic impact'. He argues that it has injured the employment prospects of home graduates and led to lower numbers of local enrolments in information technology, where the foreign students are concentrated: 'nearly a third of local graduates could not find work at a time when the visa programme increased graduate labour supply by 80%. As a result registrations for IT courses among home students fell by 50% between 2001 and 2006' (ibid.). Kinnaird further suggests that the new work visas could 'lead to more competition with national graduates, perhaps depressing wage levels' (ibid.).

The importance of improving the attractiveness of research careers – through measures designed to improve contractual security and pay, for example – in order to improve recruitment, retention and transition are well-rehearsed at both European and national level. Indeed, the European Charter for Researchers (2005: paras 8/9) speaks explicitly about the need to improve working conditions in order to generate 'sustainable European labour markets and career development systems'. HEFCE (2006: 22) similarly acknowledges the importance of investing in order to ensure that positions are attractive and researchers feel valued: 'Enabling and nurturing truly excellent research remains the cornerstone of our research policy. We recognise that this can only be achieved in a research base that is properly funded, where there is critical mass, and with valued and well motivated researchers'.

Although many disciplines experience significant recruitment and retention difficulties at doctoral level, the transition from doctoral to postdoctoral research experiences the highest degree of attrition (Ackers et al., 2006). The situation in part reflects a combination of rising student debt, poor immediate and long-term financial prospects, favourable employment opportunities in alternative areas or sectors, contractual insecurity, pressures to move, long hours and stressful working environments.[23] At the present time, research suggests that recent policies at European and national level have yet to yield a significant improvement in perceptions of the viability and attractiveness of research careers in comparison to alternative forms of employment. Many of these issues were identified by our Bulgarian and Polish respondents as a partial explanation for the high level of internationalization in their host labs. Eugenia, a Bulgarian post-doc, observes the failure of many British doctorates to make the transition into post-doctoral research: 'I'm pretty much the only one in the three-year period – like when I was in the third year including the ones that were in the first year – that went on to do a post-doc, that went on to actually do what they're qualified for'.

Agata explains why she thinks it was relatively 'easy' for her to secure a doctoral position in Germany. According to her, doctoral positions are less attractive to home students and the lack of career prospects deters progression:

> I think it's because not many German students want to stay for a PhD, biological science is not something tempting for students here. Because it's quite difficult I guess to study, but maybe it's not the reason because law or medicine is also difficult but then when you finish it's not difficult to find work and you earn a lot of money. Here in science it's more difficult to get work because everything is very short term – like to work three years contract like two post-docs and if you don't find a permanent position at the university it's really tough.

Likewise Todor, a group leader in Bulgaria, describes the attrition that took place in the German system some years ago, resulting in a lack of progression of home-grown scientists to fill academic posts:

> German science has a problem with continuum of the generations, that means let's say 10, 15 or 20 years ago somebody . . . explained very successfully to the young people that doing science is not interesting, you have to open your mind and make money and they opened their minds, they started to make money . . . and now they have a big lack of people. That's why there are so many foreigners now in Germany at my age between 30 and 40, because the Germans have a lack of generation. That means that in the near future we will start to see how the Germans start to lose in the global competition because you cannot have an army which consists of soldiers and generals and not officers and now the officers are missing.

Todor's description of the situation in Germany is interesting and more or less exactly mirrors the descriptions that Bulgarian and Polish scientists have made in relation to the 'missing generations' in their own countries, as we discuss in Chapter 8. This would suggest that at least to some extent intersectoral losses witnessed in the receiving countries have contributed to the loss of a similar generation of researchers in the sending regions, thus emphasizing the relational quality of these processes.

Understanding career and migration decision-making, as we have seen, is highly complex. What is clear, however, is that two characteristics of early-career research positions emerge as particular deterrents to recruitment and retention: contractual insecurity and remuneration. These factors shape the decisions of both home and foreign researchers, and European and national laws prohibit direct discrimination on grounds of nationality so there is little evidence of universities paying foreigners a lower rate for the same job (as there is in the informal economy). However, it is clear that career decision-making is contextual and relational and different groups might respond in different ways to the same material circumstances. On the one hand, academic salaries in the UK remain competitive from a European perspective and the differentials, when compared with Poland and Bulgaria, are significant. The reference points of home and foreign researchers are therefore likely to vary. On the other hand, in some situations the relative importance of pay or contractual security, at a particular point in time, might shift as researchers weigh up the importance of gaining international experience or accessing a prestigious centre of excellence or joining a partner or children. This may be particularly evident when researchers are contemplating a finite period in that location before moving elsewhere or perhaps returning home with that experience under their belts. Provided these differentials are maintained – even if the supply countries shift – and some migrants are prepared to place a lower premium on those facets of science careers that deter home-grown researchers, then a recruitment crisis is avoided and the pressure on national research systems to restructure fundamentally is temporarily abated. One unintended but perhaps predictable consequence of this is the continued decline in home-grown transition – as we see at the present time – and an increasing reliance on foreign recruitment:

> Foreign researchers, at least at an early stage in their career, may be less sensitive to pay than UK nationals for a number of reasons. The incentives to come to the UK to 'boost their CV' through accessing UK centres of excellence, improve their English or simply to get a position at all might outweigh their immediate concerns about pay (although this will impact in the long term for those who decide to settle and form families here). In this context, the conventional wisdom that the UK pool is of declining quality might rather reflect the ability to retain the best UK researchers for the salaries on offer. The 'risk' is that the ability to recruit abroad might have a multiplier effect, depressing wage rates in the UK and eventually pushing out an increasing proportion of UK applicants. Put simply, it might not be that UK applicants are declining in quality per se, but that the pool of UK applicants prepared to accept the risks of an insecure and poorly paid research career is declining. (Ackers et al., 2006: 26)

Lucjan, a Polish post-doc, describes how he is willing to make temporary concessions to his lifestyle in order to manage on the salaries available in the UK:

> Coming from the Central European bloc it is definitely a much more attractive offer than back home but I'm prepared to live over a cheap supermarket and I don't find buying discounted stuff in an evening from the shop repulsive. So I can live half price and I enjoy what I do so it might be unfair comparison towards people who want to have 'normal' lives in a Western context. I do understand the concerns of English-born people who find the career not rewarding enough or not permanent enough as you are changing your job every two to three years . . . I'm quite happy with my salary but some of my colleagues are extremely unhappy. I'm looking up towards the Western level whereas people from the States or from other Western countries look down on the wages here especially in academia and they complain a lot. So for me it's okay but for them it's not enough.

Lucjan's account illustrates the importance of understanding the reference group. Whereas he compares his current situation with that in Poland, he suggests that people who have spent longer periods in the West are more likely to compare their situation, and compare it less favourably, with other sectors or with positions in the United States.

Kalina, a Bulgarian doctoral researcher, makes a similar point, suggesting that foreign labour is in Germany not so much because they are the brightest and the best but because Germans do not find the positions attractive:

> As foreigners we fill the empty positions here. I mean the people here finish their education and they think okay now this is a low paid job, so I think that we get the positions which none of the German people want. This is their benefit. The people think the PhD positions are in principle not that good pay so they think okay now I've got my degree and I would like to go to a company to work. They would like to take Germans but when nobody applies for the job they will take foreigners because somebody must do the job.

Munz and colleagues (2006: 5) have attempted to assess the impact of internationalization on wage levels and test the neo-classical economic prediction that 'when labour migrants enter a particular receiving country, the supply of labour increases and the average market wage falls'. According to this simple framework, they suggest that 'the migrants and the capital owners are the beneficiaries and the native workers in the receiving countries are net losers' (ibid.). In practice they conclude that the 'impact of migration on wages on average are small but tend to be slightly negative' (ibid.: ii). The limited effect on wages, they suggest, is due to the fact that highly skilled migrants 'filled vacancies that went unmet by the native labour supply and thus increased productivity' (ibid.). Whilst this analysis supports the work of Dustmann and Glitz (2005) who similarly note a minor effect on wages, it is perhaps important to consider the reasons why the vacancies are not filled by nationals and the extent to which remuneration is a factor.

It might not be that home-grown researchers are of lesser quality as such but rather that equivalently qualified home-grown researchers turn their backs on academic positions, enabling foreign scientists to fill those posts in increasing numbers. Our interviews with Polish and Bulgarian scientists suggest a further twist to this scenario, leading us to question whether employers are indeed faced with comparable situations. We have already emphasized the fact that employers in universities are unlikely to be offering positions to foreigners at lower wage levels. However, there is nothing to prevent them selecting more experienced people and effectively filling early-career positions with experienced, more senior, researchers. This kind of practice in other sectors is often referred to as de-skilling and was evident in some interviews where respondents or their partners had accepted inferior forms of employment on migration. The term suggests that people are being employed in contexts that do not fully utilize their skills. In the academic context it may not be that their skills are not utilized but rather that they are not always fully commensurate with their employment status and rewards.

Of course in some respects this is an immediate benefit to the receiving laboratory and country but raises critical issues about the progression of foreign scientists and also the effect of this competition on the prospects for home-grown early career researchers. Table 7.1 provides a breakdown of the ages of fixed-term researchers in the UK. It is interesting to note that whilst 23 per cent of UK nationals are aged over 40, only 8 per cent of other EU nationals fall into this group (so the population of mobile EU nationals is somewhat younger). However, 27 per cent of Bulgarian and 33 per cent of Polish fixed-term researchers in the UK are aged over 40.

Although the research we have conducted cannot claim to present statistical evidence of this process it did throw up a significant number of cases involving more experienced researchers appointed to what are generally seen as junior or early-career positions. Tzonka is a good example. She is a chemical engineer who did her first degree and the equivalent of a Masters at the University of Sofia, graduating in 1978. She then worked as a researcher in the same university but with close links to industry before doing her PhD by correspondence with Moscow. After many years of research she felt that opportunities for progression in Bulgaria were in marked decline. Initially she spent a few years in the same post but with short stays abroad before moving to the UK to take up a post-doc in her late 40s. This was followed by a second post-doc and at the time of

Table 7.1   The age of 'researchers'^{a} on fixed-term contracts in UK HEIs

Age group	Nationality		Selected Countries	
	UK	EU[b]	Bulgarian	Polish
≤25	11%	6%	2%	4%
26–30	30%	37%	17%	29%
31–35	23%	34%	37%	20%
36–40	14%	15%	16%	14%
41+	23%	8%	27%	33%
N=	18 156	5076	99	280

Notes:
a.   This table does not control for length of experience.
b.   NB EU figure includes Poles.

Source: HESA (2005).

interview – in her early 50s – she had moved to a two-year teaching fellow-ship position. Tzonka's case raises questions about the progression of foreign scientists: she had worked in a permanent and senior research-only position in Bulgaria for over 20 years and, although she was very pleased to have her current position, lamented the pressure it put on her ability to develop her research profile.

Vladimir, a Bulgarian physicist, is another example of someone who did his undergraduate degree and Masters in Russia before returning to Bulgaria to do his PhD. He then continued to work in Sofia with a period of time spent in the Czech Republic. Like Tzonka, Vladimir continued to work in Bulgaria in a permanent position until things became very difficult in the 1990s and he eventually secured a two-year post-doc in the UK in 1999. Since then he has been on a series of temporary contracts and is now 45, with less than a year to run on his current contract.

In this final example, Ivaylo's case illustrates the effect of dual science partnering on decision-making. Ivaylo had a permanent senior position in physics in Bulgaria and was reluctant to leave. However, his wife had been working as a scientist in the UK for nearly three years and they were under financial pressure to support their son through UK higher education (they were paying foreign student fees). He graduated with his Masters in St Petersburg in 1972, returning to Bulgaria to do his PhD and work in research for many years. He eventually came to the UK in 2003, taking up a temporary post-doc position in his early 50s.

These short cases raise many issues about the precariousness of employ-ment faced by many researchers. The point here, however, is to draw attention to the ability of universities in the receiving countries to attract very experienced people into positions that are essentially designed for early-career post-docs (that is, people in their mid-twenties) and to question whether a level playing field can exist for home-grown researchers in that context. Although recruitment processes might be described as meritocratic to the extent that they permit institutions to employ the best candidate for the post, it is clear that the ability to recruit highly experienced researchers from abroad into relatively poorly paid positions distorts national labour markets and fair recruitment. This may both discourage the progression of home applicants and also reduce the pressure to remunerate positions appropriately.

CONCLUSIONS

This chapter has examined various dimensions of the contribution that international, scientific migration makes to the host countries, with a focus on the British and German experience. It is clear from the material presented that international recruitment is playing a major role in mitigating the problems associated with the declining transition of home-grown young people into scientific research and sustaining scientific capacity, particularly at doctoral and post-doctoral level. Assessing the relationship between mobility and quality is highly problematic. Internationalization, in itself, is not and should not be taken as an indicator of quality. That said, Bulgaria and Poland present significant opportunities for the host countries in terms of scientific recruitment. The strong reputation in the natural sciences coupled with high transition rates and long and rigorous training programmes, generates an important pool of potential recruits. Respondents talked of a strong theoretical tradition arising out of resource-weak environments, which they felt stimulated innovation and problem-solving skills and enabled them to respond flexibly to the opportunities of working with high-tech equipment and resources. The challenges of working effectively in their home countries coupled with the opportunities available in Germany and the UK encouraged a powerful sense of commitment and drive, which often manifests itself in long and arduous working schedules in the host countries. Evidence suggests that recruitment processes in the UK and Germany enable the host countries to select from that pool on a relatively competitive basis. Interestingly, scientists felt that EU enlargement would make relatively little difference to recruitment at post-doctoral level and upwards although it is expected to increase undergraduate and postgraduate student flows significantly. The rules governing employment of foreign researchers prior to accession were believed to support a highly competitive situation in which non-EU nationals had to out-perform EU applicants. On that basis, respondents generally felt that the best scientists were already able to move and deregulation might, if anything, reduce quality.

There was little evidence of direct recruitment of established research stars from Bulgaria and Poland into the receiving countries although quite senior researchers are being recruited into early-career positions in many cases. Serious concerns were expressed about transition and progression into more senior positions in the host countries both from their own perspective – of achieving employment security – but also realizing their potential as scientists and maximizing scientific productivity. In some cases this was linked to a perception of employment discrimination. In practice it is likely to reflect the vagaries of the research systems in the host countries, which generate a large pool of highly skilled post-doctoral researchers in insecure and poorly remunerated positions. This situation stands in marked contrast to systems in Poland and Bulgaria, which generally deliver a much higher degree of security albeit at very low pay.

The evidence presented leads us to concur with Bekhradnia and Sastry's (2005: 12) conclusions that 'the growing significance of international mobility poses [both] opportunities and challenges for academic research in the UK'. The final section of the chapter considers some of the challenges. The awkwardness that we have witnessed in discussing some of these issues, around retention for example, stifles a more open and critical discussion about sustainability and risk-management in the context of human capital in the receiving countries. The fact that the UK and Germany continue to meet skills shortages through international recruitment does not mean policy-makers can afford to be complacent. As the UK Roberts Review (2002: 186) cautions, 'the flow of scientists and engineers from overseas is an elastic source of labour; migrant labour flows are highly sensitive to changes in demand'. HEFCE (2006), however, is one of the first to raise publicly the question of sustainability of overseas recruitment. Noting the marked increases in staff from Central and Eastern Europe, their report highlights the 'growing dependence on overseas recruitment' and concludes that 'the sector's increasing reliance on staff from overseas may not be sustainable in the longer term as this source of supply is not guaranteed – such staff may return home taking their skills with them' (ibid.: 44).

This takes us to another critical concern in relation to sustainability: whether a relationship exists between internationalization and the development of home-grown human capital. Research at national and European level raises serious concerns about the attractiveness of research careers, resulting in declining transition rates and even the closure of established academic departments. The preamble to the European Commission's

Recommendation on the European Charter for Researchers and Code of Conduct for the Recruitment of Researchers (2005), refers to the need for Europe to create the necessary conditions for 'more sustainable and appealing careers in R&D' (para. 4), to 'contribute to the development of attractive, open and sustainable European labour markets' (para. 8) and for Member States to 'offer researchers sustainable career development systems' (para. 9). The continued ability to recruit from abroad arguably reduces the urgency to respond to these fundamental policy shifts threatening the long-term sustainability of science. If careers are appealing to foreign researchers there is less need to ensure that they are appealing to home-grown researchers. If host countries can attract senior and experienced researchers from abroad into junior and early-career positions, can labour markets be said to be genuinely open and equitable with sustainable career progression?

NOTES

1. Data for Germany was provided by Jess Guth.
2. The term home-grown is used here in preference to nationals to encompass the broader group of scientists who have studied in the UK at undergraduate or school level. This will include the children of many of our respondents.
3. Immigrants in the UK are more likely to have experienced tertiary-level education compared with the general population. A recent report (Little, 2005: 58) contends that they 'are making a net contribution to the level of UK skills and are likely to be improving the UK's productivity and innovation performance'.
4. See Annex 3 for details of these studies, which included interviews designed to assess the perceptions of senior academic staff in the UK responsible for the recruitment of researchers.
5. These are complex issues that are discussed in more detail in Ackers and Gill (2005).
6. See Ackers et al. (2006).
7. The possibility of offering Bachelor and Masters courses was introduced in Germany in 1998 (Guth, 2006, 2007).
8. Thirteen per cent were domiciled elsewhere in the EU prior to their PhD and 28 per cent in third countries (HESA data). The figures for the UK include candidates who did their first degree in the UK irrespective of their nationality.
9. This raises complex definitional questions, which demand a detailed knowledge of career structures in UK universities. In the UK, doctoral candidates hold the status of students and not staff as they do in many other EU Member States (including Germany). According to HESA data, the category of 'researchers' includes all research grades that are not included as professors, senior lecturers and researchers, or lecturers. Although these groups of permanent academic staff also undertake research as part of their employment, in the UK the 'researcher' category generally includes those staff, mainly in early-career (post-doc or contract research) positions who hold research-only contracts, usually on a fixed-term basis.
10. Media attention to the brain drain issue often refers specifically to Nobel Prize winners or the heads of prestigious research groups.
11. Different trends could be seen some years ago when political events in the sending regions triggered the emigration of significant numbers of scientists at all levels.
12. The impact that partnering and parenting has on mobility was discussed in Chapters 4 and 5.

13. Chapter 8 considers the issue of quality in the context of the losses experienced by sending regions and identifies serious concerns around the 'youth drain'. Analysis of respondents' experiences of losses from the perspective of sending regions largely supports the idea that many of the scientists with the best potential did indeed leave Bulgaria and Poland.

14. Issues did arise in relation to return moves and the ability to work effectively and use the skills they had learnt in the West on return given the lack of modern equipment and resources. This is discussed in Chapter 8.

15. Many scientists with family responsibilities use short stays as a way of balancing the demands of their professional lives with the needs of their families and work intensively during their periods abroad. This is discussed in Chapters 4 and 5.

16. The European Commission's proposed scientific visa (CEC, 2004) to ease the entry of third country nationals into the European research area is designed to overcome this approach, introducing the non-discrimination principle to third country nationals. At the present time the UK has opted out of these provisions.

17. The role of tuition fees in shaping migration decisions is discussed in Chapter 3.

18. One key positive effect of accession discussed in Chapter 4 concerns the employment rights of spouses and also the fees status of their children. These factors played a significant role in shaping attitudes towards remaining in the host country.

19. Most respondents moved prior to accession so put themselves in this group.

20. Examples are discussed in Chapter 3.

21. In the case of the UK, as opposed to Germany, the concept of 'approach' implies an explicit policy rather than an evolutionary and, at times, complacent pragmatism.

22. It was recently reported that following the 11 September terrorist attacks US universities have noted the first decline in foreign enrolment in 30 years (Marcus, 2004: 11). Accordingly, the British Council are forecasting a dip in the number of overseas students, believing the recent growth rate of 20 per cent per year is unsustainable.

23. Concerns that research careers in the UK (and Europe) were unattractive led to a number of initiatives aimed at improving the conditions of research personnel. This can be charted from the introduction of the Researchers' Concordat (1996), which was implemented through the Research Careers Initiative (1997–2002). This was followed by implementation of Roberts Review recommendations to improve the training, conditions and career prospects of doctoral and contract researchers. The most recent developments are cross-EU initiatives such as the European Code of Conduct and Researchers Charter. In Germany, the BMBF has highlighted salary as a problem for retention in Germany and aims to introduce more 'merit-orientated' pay and better work-time flexibility (BMBF, 2005: XII).

8. Brain drain? The experiences of sending countries

INTRODUCTION

The previous chapter has demonstrated the importance of scientific mobility to scientific labour markets in receiving regions. In the process, it has attempted to expose both the opportunities and challenges that internationalization poses for scientific sustainability from the perspective of receiving countries. Sustainability is more commonly considered in the context of sending regions and features in many discussions around highly skilled migration and the phenomenon of brain drain. This chapter thus moves on to explore the effects of the kinds of mobility we have identified on scientific development and scientists from Bulgaria and Poland. As a result, this chapter is a lengthy one: but this detail is needed to understand fully the experiences of sending regions.

It focuses in more detail on the implications of the flows described in Chapter 2 and whether such flows, in themselves, can be considered as evidence of a negative brain or skills drain. The impact of scientific emigration is unclear and contested. Katseli and colleagues (2006a: 9) argue that whilst 'massive and unmanaged migration especially of highly skilled migrants can have deleterious effects on service delivery, inequality and labour depletion . . . [it can also] generate substantial direct and indirect gains for sending countries via employment generation, human capital accumulation, remittances, diaspora networks and return migration'. Recent work on the impact of highly skilled migration on Slovakia identifies a range of human capital outcomes, including brain gain, brain drain, brain waste, brain circulation and brain overflow (Baláž et al., 2004: 4). While the general view is that significant levels of outward mobility pose a serious threat to science infrastructures and competitiveness, other work indicates potential mitigating factors and positive returns.

I THE QUALITY OF FLOWS

Previous chapters have already discussed the relationship between mobility and quality and the problems of measuring this in any concrete and objective fashion. Chapters 4 and 5 talked about this in the context of the effect of partnering and parenting on selectivity and Chapter 7 in terms of the quality of scientific migrants from the perspective of receiving countries. Chapter 2 described our respondents' perceptions of the volume and characteristics of flows. Many respondents implicitly link the volume issue with the quality issue, suggesting that, as Stanislaw argues, the process is selective and results in a loss of 'really brilliant' young scientists.

The majority of our respondents made a link between migration and quality, suggesting that flows were generally selective and constituted a creaming off process, supporting the received wisdom of the brain drain debate. Of course, we need to remember in interpreting these views that the respondents were talking about themselves in this context and this might colour their perceptions of quality. However, in most cases, respondents were just as concerned about scientific *potential* as they were about levels of seniority and establishment.

Chompalov's (2000) assessment of the quality of Bulgarian emigration flows would support this perception. He suggests that it was mainly 'relatively young researchers who were familiar with modern methods and technology, knew foreign languages and were confident in their talents' (ibid.: 14) who left. The old 'elite' on the other hand, were more reluctant to leave and 'preferred to cling to their well-established positions especially in view of the tightening of the labour market' (ibid.). This presents a complex picture in terms of quality, suggesting that mobility was as much shaped by security of positions – where people had achieved an established and secure position – as it was by quality per se. Certainly the data on the age profile of migrant scientists in the UK, presented in Chapter 7, would suggest that many migrants are not young (in a chronological sense) but occupying early-career positions. As evidence of the relationship between mobility and quality, they refer both to the perceived decline in the quality of people applying for positions in the sending countries – and their perception that labour markets are becoming less competitive as a result – and to the role of the receiving countries in selecting people by ability and potential (particularly prior to accession).

Whilst it is relatively straightforward to show that mobility is dominated by graduates (Rangelova and Vladimirova, 2004; Haug, 2005), it is more difficult to demonstrate that a creaming-off process occurs. Many quickly jump to the conclusion that highly skilled migrants are 'the most talented' (Davenport, 2004: 618) and rarely if ever present any evidence to substantiate these assertions. Ghodsee is less convinced that a relationship exists between migration potential and 'quality' and cites Gächter's IOM report as evidence that 90 per cent of Bulgarian emigrants are not amongst the most highly skilled but returning ethnic Turks. She argues that it has been in the interest of Bulgarian government to portray émigrés as 'the brightest and the best' and also as young people in their 20s and 30s for political reasons. Nevertheless, this image, she argues, plays a powerful role in encouraging the public to believe that the 'best and brightest' Bulgarians go abroad. Unfortunately this image may play a role in shaping future migration flows as young people feel 'compelled to leave the country in search of validation' (2002: 6).

Certainly some of the respondents echo the language used in migration literature and popular press when talking about the quality of emigrants. Viktor, a post-doc in Germany is typical. He identifies the declining recruitment pool at doctoral level in Bulgaria as evidence of the selective quality of out-migration: 'The number of PhD students has degraded significantly and also [we are not retaining] the best PhD students. Only people who cannot find a PhD abroad or don't wish to for whatever reason; everybody is trying to escape at a very early stage'. Roumen, a senior scientist responsible for recruiting researchers in Bulgaria expresses similar concerns, alluding to a decline in the standard of recruits at doctoral and post-doctoral level:

> Yes, we do [have problems recruiting at doctoral and post-doctoral level]. It isn't difficult to find young people to do research here but the standards are so low – that is the Bulgarian problem. The good students are not here and those that want to stay here are not good with little exception. The good students are in some Western country, in some position abroad and we simply cannot compete. Mostly they are not in science – natural sciences are not popular anywhere.

It is interesting to note Roumen's assertion that many scientific emigrants are working outside of academic research in the receiving countries. This raises concerns about the validity of arguments (discussed below) that emigration is an effective means of storing and investing in expatriate scientists (to the ultimate benefit of sending countries).

Tzonka, a Bulgarian lecturer in the UK, describes the impact of scientific emigration as 'detrimental' because:

> The level in my university [in Bulgaria] goes down, the quality of lecturers and students also. The best people have left. I know some of my colleagues I respect as really good professionals and they are in the States and the UK. [Q: Do you mean more senior or the best potential?] Oh no, the best potential; the cleverest. Young people are usually also the best students.

Polish respondents made similar points. Fryderyk, a Polish physicist-turned-financier in the UK expresses his perception that out-migration is highly selective and damaging to home labour markets:

> The best people and all these colleagues of mine who are really good they are gone. Most of them have gone abroad but from the point of view of Poland and research there is a brain drain; all the good people they are somewhere else. The people who I've seen stay as researchers or started an academic career in Poland you wouldn't say they were the top people so basically the top people went somewhere else.

The discussion about the impact of migration on receiving countries (Chapter 7) referred to the association some respondents made between accession (and the relaxation of access conditions) and quality. This is clearly of relevance to the current debate (about the impact on sending countries). Rada argues that the opening of labour markets post-accession might actually reduce the competitive nature of recruitment into the West and pave the way for a less selective form of mobility:

> Bulgaria is losing the good people and especially now because for Poland everybody can come here [to the UK] and work so it's not very important that they are qualified, but for Bulgarians only the best qualified can move. [Q: So you think that whilst it's difficult for people to come in they're really selecting the best?] Yes.

Sylwia also refers to the importance of the nature of demand ('pull' factors) in shaping the quality of emigrants:

> I think that the best scientists are all going abroad because there are more positions abroad. [Q: Why do you think it's the best?] Well the demand is that most good scientists are going abroad because they are able to get a position abroad so I think all the best and most talented people are going abroad and staying.

Viktor and Agnieszka both identify a reduction in competition for positions in Bulgaria and Poland as evidence of the selective effect of outward migration: 'In the university in 1988 I needed to fight with five people for one place. However, nowadays there are two places for one applicant in physics – not in law or economics. [Q: So is your feeling that the cleverest and the best scientists are leaving Bulgaria?] Yes.' In response to a question about her ability to recruit doctoral researchers in Poland, Agnieszka replies:

> Some of them, yes. In general we have a selection system which is negative. The salaries are so small in comparison to others. If you take into account the qualification, languages, computer techniques, we are paid 10 or 20 per cent of

our ability. What I observe is the negative selection to the profession so the pro-portion between men and women is somehow disturbed. I'm not able to say in physics it should be more women or men but usually it should reflect the compo-sition of the population yes? Last year who applies for positions here are mostly women. So, that means there's some kind of conservative idea that men should earn money to keep the family at some level. The degradation of the profession starts when the majority of people who apply for the positions are women. As there is also some kind of conservative thinking in Poland around women's work. In my generation the number of women was not high. It doesn't mean the attrac-tion is bigger, it just means this profession is not financially attractive for men.

The link that Agnieszka makes between the growing feminization of aca-demic labour markets and quality is interesting. Similar trends were identified in relation to the representation of women in science in Southern Europe (Ackers, 2003). And, more recently, a report in the UK alluded to concerns that the increasing feminization becomes an indicator of the declining attractiveness of academic careers rather than the achievement of gender equality. It concludes: 'the report will fuel speculation that higher education is becoming feminised. It confirms that over the past decade women have come to dominate at every level, including in traditionally male courses such as law'.[1]

When scientists talk about quality it is not always clear what they are referring to. Certainly, as we have seen, many value potential as highly as credentialism. Tzonka and Kiril place less emphasis on the seniority issue. The following two respondents (Renata and Alina) add further nuance to this, suggesting that whilst migrants may not necessarily be the 'best' in purely scientific terms, the process is selective in other respects:

I think the most *active* people go, they are not necessarily the best but they have energy and they have will to do new things, they are open and to get jobs here they must certainly have something. I see how people are employed here so I see that it's not just anybody.

The one dangerous thing is that most people who leave are young people who want to change something in their life, so there's a possibility it's just going to drain even further the people who are actually *active, inspirational*, they want to do things basically.

Discussion

This first part of the chapter has summarized some of the literature con-cerning the volume and scale of highly skilled migration from Poland and Bulgaria into the UK and Germany. Available secondary data on levels of migration and the propensity to migrate is highly unreliable and, in many cases, misleading and contradictory.

On the basis of available data, the sending countries appear to have lost significant numbers of highly skilled citizens and scientists in particular, since the 1990s. However, much of this loss occurred during the initial transition period and losses appear to have levelled off since then. A significant proportion of these losses, however, were connected to the sudden and marked decline in scientific positions, with many scientists moving to other sectors as well as abroad.

The experiences of our respondents would tend to suggest that laboratories and departments in the sending countries have experienced a significant loss of scientific *potential* (as much as established scientists) and that the mid-career generation is often thin on the ground, with important implications for the training of researchers in future. There is also a sense that migration is selective in its effects, resulting in the losses of many high-quality and enthusiastic researchers, often in specific disciplines and sub-disciplines.

Just as 'losses' via migration need to be seen alongside within-country 'losses' to other sectors, it is also important to consider the demographic trends in the countries concerned. Both Poland and Bulgaria have ageing scientific labour forces and very low and declining levels of fertility. These demographic challenges pose serious problems for the countries concerned. Whilst the 'evidence' on scientific 'brain drain' is unclear and contentious, the loss of potential through increasing emigration of young people at or before undergraduate level is of grave concern.

The second part of this chapter moves on to consider in more detail what this all means in terms of the impact that scientific mobility has on the sending regions.

II   ASSESSING THE IMPACT OF MIGRATION ON THE SENDING COUNTRIES

The introduction to this book noted the complex range of factors that need to be taken into consideration when attempting to present a balanced and holistic appraisal of highly skilled mobility. The experiences of our respondents, both in the sending and receiving locations, provides general support for the view that scientific emigration from Poland and Bulgaria is both high in volume and quality. But this tells us little about the nature of causation or its consequences in terms of scientific capacity. A grounded analysis of responses supports a more insightful and nuanced perspective, drawing attention to some of the costs, causes and benefits of mobility. Respondents identify two key areas of 'negative' impact: namely the loss of investment in human capital and the effects of this in terms of regenerative potential. Furthermore, the interviews suggest that the alternative to migration is not necessarily flourishing scientific research but forms of 'brain waste' caused by serious deficiencies in national labour markets (as a result of declining funding and position-blocking), intersectoral losses and, for those who remain in science, the inability to work effectively and productively. In this context, respondents allude to the 'brain gain effect', citing the positive role that mobility can play in capacity-building, supporting investment in human capital, increasing access to resources, enhancing productivity, motivating young people to engage in science and supplementing income through remittances.

Assessing the Impact of Scientific Emigration: Loss of Investment

One of the strongest concerns raised by scientists in response to a question about the impact of migration on sending regions was the lack of return on the considerable investment they have made in educating their scientists. Davenport argues (in the New Zealand context) that, 'there is an undercurrent [in the moral panic over brain drain] that emigrants "owe" the taxpayer, in that they have not yet returned the investment in their education and skills' (2004: 628). This comment echoes the views expressed in the UK in the 1950s over the 'costs' of brain drain to the US. It is interesting to see the language used at the time to describe the impact of emigration on scientific capacity. Godwin, Balmer and Gregory's historical analysis of UK brain drain in the 1950s and 1960s includes reference to the then Prime Minister, Harold Wilson, who remarked in 1963, 'we are not even selling the seed corn; we are giving it away'. The UK Advisory Council on Scientific Policy pointed out that, 'some of the highest quality scientists whom we train at very substantial cost, are being exported to one of our industrial competitors' (cited in Godwin et al., 2006: 8). Echoing the language used in the 1950s, Katseli et al. identify the 'export of human capital in which the nation has invested' as one of three specific negative facets of international migration from the perspective of home country development (2006a: 34). Rangelova and Vladimirova go a step further, suggesting that not only does this represent a loss of investment to taxpayers in the home countries and a subsidization of human capital and productivity growth in the host countries but, furthermore, that these concerns might give rise to a 'difficulty in justifying an increase in such investment in subsequent years' effectively providing a rationale for limiting future investment in education and training 'to the detriment of young people who prefer to stay' (2004: 25). If that were the case this would certainly limit the opportunities for the 'brain gain effect' (see below).

Quite a number of MOBEX respondents referred to the costs of educating young scientists 'for export' and the extent to which emigration

implies a loss of the investment embodied in migrants, particularly in times
of economic crisis. As Yulian (a senior scientist in Bulgaria) puts it: 'It's a
problem for Bulgaria because the state at this moment gives money for
higher education. The level of this education is good and the state pays. The
UK or US is the dream of many many people; they use this money and take
their intellect abroad'. Monika makes a similar point:

> It's really awful because Poland – like my degree it's a five-year course and this
> is really expensive and there are a lot of people like myself . . . university courses
> are free of charge so the government is spending lots of money on our educa-
> tion and then off we go, so obviously the situation's not good.

Interestingly, Monika does not reflect in the same way on the costs of her
subsequent education in the UK. At the time of interview she had been registered with a fees waiver for five years for her PhD. Asked about her future
plans she was clear that she would not return to Poland due to the employment situation there but neither was she contemplating staying in the UK.
Some of her friends had told her that her earnings potential was much
higher in the States and she was considering this as an option. Ludwika also
argues that Poland gets little return on the investment it makes in undergraduates, which encourages selective out-migration and reduces the quality
of the labour force: 'Poland spends money on the education of these people
and it doesn't get anything back – it goes outside of Poland and only the
poor and non-educated people stay'. However, if we look more carefully at
Ludwika's own mobility and the investment in her training, it is apparent
that she did a Masters degree in Budapest before commencing a doctorate
in Poland. Although she left her PhD after only six months in order to take
up a doctoral position in Germany, she is confident that she will return to
Poland with her Dutch partner when he completes his PhD in a year's time.
They both work in an emerging field in environmental science, which, she
suggests, presents strong employment opportunities in Poland.

Ania expresses similar concerns but does acknowledge the fact that the
investment process continues over the academic life-course in the receiving
country/ies: 'The government [in Poland] gave me the education and I've
arrived here. I'm finishing here on another level'. Ania came to the UK at
the end of her first degree and at the time of interview was just about to
submit her PhD thesis after a three-year scholarship. Asked about her
future plans, she said that she would like to return to Poland within five
years and feels that, by maintaining close contacts with her Polish supervisor, she will be able to do so.

Although Yulian's perception of loss is understandable (as a scientist
working in Bulgaria and training undergraduates there) if we place the

other three respondents' comments about the loss of investment in the context of their own trajectories, it is more difficult to argue in any straight-forward way that this represents a net loss of investment on the part of the sending countries, although it may indeed represent a hemorrhaging of potential. The investment in all of the cases has continued for a number of years in the host country and it is by no means clear that the current host country will reap the benefits of the accumulated training.

It is also perhaps important to point out that the higher education systems are changing rapidly in both of these countries. Although many of our respondents will have experienced 'free education' as Ania indicates, recent years have witnessed a massive growth in private institutions that charge tuition fees. Interestingly, Dabrowa-Szefler, argues that, 'the situation in higher education [in Poland] looks more favourable [than in industry] because 62% of students pay tuition fees, which make up 31.6% of universities' revenue', including 18.6 per cent of total income earned by public HE establishments (2004: 42). Kwiek also observes an 'explosion' in private HE institutions in Poland during the 1990s, supporting a massive increase in student numbers (2003: 455).[2]

The Impact of Emigration on Regenerative Capacity

In addition to these specific fiscal concerns, other authors indicate a relationship between highly skilled migration and regenerative capacity. Velev expresses specific concerns about losses in the fields of science, technology and engineering on the grounds that 'these sectors are indeed considered as the new major source of wealth and development and their magnitude characterizes the stage of the knowledge society' (2002: 5). Chompalov echoes these concerns: 'from the point of view of the future development of Bulgaria as a modern European nation it is of great, if not vital, importance to preserve the creative research and development *manpower* potential. Limiting this capacity could have tragic consequences' (2000: 3). Chompalov goes on to suggest that scientific emigration is a critical factor affecting capacity, although he attributes this predominantly to 'push' factors, including the marked decline in funding of science, the 'tightening of the labour market', the slow pace of reform and political instability. Vizi argues that scientific emigration has a multiplying effect that damages regenerative capacity and, in particular, the ability to reproduce the next generation of young researchers: 'When the best scientists leave their laboratories, they take with them not only their scientific knowledge, but also their reputations, which are a valuable force for recruiting younger scientists' (1993: 103).

Certainly many of our respondents echoed these concerns about the impact of emigration on the potential of their home countries to recover and regenerate. Rada left Bulgaria to start her PhD in the UK three years ago. She expresses concern at the loss of scientists through migration and the impact this has on the country's ability to rebuild its science base: 'It's getting worse and worse – a lot of people are moving and there are not very good chances for Bulgaria. They go back eventually sometimes but it's hard to regenerate this science and research'. Irina, also now based in the UK, describes the effects of selective out-migration on the staff that remain behind as a 'struggle': 'They have no highly qualified staff and that is what is happening in Bulgaria. Most active research people go abroad. Yes, it is affecting seriously, most active researchers are now away and the people who are there they struggle'.

Valentina (a senior scientist in Bulgaria) suggests that the loss of scientists is having a major impact on the supply and quality of teaching, restricting Bulgaria's ability to educate the next generation. Although she identifies this as a problem in terms of the country's ability to continue to export high-quality labour to the West, it is clearly an issue for Bulgarian regenerative capacity also:

> Of course what's happened now there are no more good students because there are no more good teachers and my colleagues from Europe and the US complain to me, 'Oh Valentina, since 2001 we cannot find any more people from Eastern countries. What happened, you don't have people willing to study science?' I told them we don't have professors any more. It was this brain movement almost finished.

Both Marta and Beata argue that losses via emigration will ultimately affect the quality of teaching and restrict industrial development:

> The effect is that most of these people stay and you have to create some new persons to lead new researchers. To teach them you have to be a good teacher. When you are not a good teacher you couldn't do this so this is the reason I think that in future the society will be on a poor level in Poland when all these people go abroad.

> First you do less good science and finally the studies for the undergraduate students will also [deteriorate]. It's much harder to start without the scientists and it's also much harder to do any corporate advanced research – with high-technology companies – because there are not so many people who would think about starting their own company or being employed there or lobby for that and in the future this is quite a big problem.

Ivan makes a similar link between research and industrial development more generally:

> I thought it was very bad because all clever, no not clever, well-educated, people went abroad and there were no people to work in Bulgaria and if you want to

make some production and if you want to develop some industry and have investment and research you need some people. You need this intellectual potential in Bulgaria and because all the people, especially young people, are leaving and they are well educated it's really difficult to find these kinds of people.

Vladimir raises a more specific issue in relation to mobility and regenerative capacity, namely the effect of retained, unpaid, positions. The practice, in both Poland and Bulgaria, of allowing scientists to retain positions, often for many years whilst abroad and either not replacing them or replacing them at lower level, Vladimir feels contributes to a decline in the quality of teaching and research:

> The time you are away they can hire somebody on temporary contracts on the lower grade, which is not very good, but the thing is that even if they want to substitute you with somebody on the same level it's very difficult because in countries like Bulgaria it's very small and you have only one lab specialized in a certain area so it's virtually impossible.

Kiril is also concerned about the impact of migration on capacity-building. For him though, the losses are not just in the area of scientific know-how but also political skill and motivation to make wider systemic changes (as Beata indicates above). In the absence of fresh blood and new approaches he fears that any increase in resources might not reach the science base at all:

> People who have the best capacity are gone; it may be the politicians or the people who could be politicians are gone then there isn't that much left in the country and that is a problem. While there's no motivation to get the resources there's no one to use them and there's no one to get the resources. If in the end any resources come they just get corrupted away and appear in people's pockets.

Kiril's comments about the wider ramifications of losing highly skilled scientists are echoed in Katseli et al.'s work. It is not only the immediate effects on science that are at stake, but the 'spillover' effects of losing an 'enlightened elite that has the potential to improve governance and civic performance' more generally (2006a: 34). Both Georgieva (2004) and Bobeva (1997) make a similar point, emphasizing the contribution that scientists and teachers make to the 'driving forces of systemic transformation' (Georgieva, 2004: 363).

Godwin et al.'s historical analysis indicates a relationship between attitudes towards perceived brain drain in the 1950s–1960s in the UK and what they term 'declinism' (2006). According to the authors, fears around brain drain were, 'seemingly connected with wider feelings of British decline in the post-war period', which conveyed important psychological messages about the state of the economy at the time. They refer to this historical period as the 'Stagnant Society'. Interesting parallels could be drawn with the situation in Bulgaria and to a lesser extent, Poland, at the present time. At the very least, Godwin et al.'s work reminds us of the need to understand the impact, both symbolic and material, of scientific emigration from these sending countries in their economic and political context. Jalowiecki and Gorzelak, for example, talk about the frustration that highly educated people experience by 'stagnation, inertia and anti-innovation attitudes' as a motivational factor encouraging emigration (2004: 301). The 'push' effect of decline must also be seen in the context of the 'pull' associated with newly acquired freedoms to live and work abroad following accession to the EU (Chompalov, 2000: 13; Jalowiecki and Gorzelak, 2004: 302).

Not all respondents presented the same perspective, however. Magdalena is less convinced that migration is exhausting potential. For her, the continuing ability to export Poles to prestigious institutions abroad is evidence of the Polish system's ability to continue to produce high-quality scientists both for home and abroad:

> I think it has [damaged training] to a certain degree because there are several people that I know from university who are really quite good – they're abroad now but I don't know. People are still coming out and the students that my supervisor has had after me have all . . . like one has gone to Stanford.

Magdalena's 'optimism' is to some extent justified by figures suggesting an explosive increase in both undergraduate and doctoral registrations in Poland. According to Dabrowa-Szefler, the number of doctoral students in Poland increased from 2695 in 1991 to 28 345 in 2001 – a tenfold increase in only a decade (2004: 17). Okólski stresses that highly skilled emigration from Poland needs to be seen in the context of the 'educational breakthrough' that has taken place in recent years, resulting in an increase in the share of university graduates in the Polish population from 2 per cent in 1970 to 12 per cent in 2001. By 2003, 46.4 per cent of 19–24-year-olds had enrolled in HE – a figure reaching the standards of the developed countries (Okólski, 2006: 49). Kicinger also notes both the 'explosion of third level HE' (doctoral registrations) and the marked growth in the number of undergraduates in Poland from 410 000 in 1991 to 1 800 500 in 2003 with a 3.2 per cent increase in 2003 alone (2005: 22). One of the Polish key informants refers to the uniqueness of this growth in doctoral research in Poland (compared with other EU Member States), identifying it both as a potential benefit for Europe, as a whole, but a serious problem for Poland, which risks 'misusing this potential resulting in a great loss for society in general' (cited in Kicinger, 2005: 31).

Brain 'Waste': The Alternative to Brain Drain?

It is clear from the discussion above that a significant number of respondents both in the sending and receiving locations believed migration to be taking place on a large scale and with a specific 'skew' in favour of younger and mid-career researchers. Many also expressed concern about this process and its potential impact on the countries concerned. It is important to remember, however, that the corollary of international migration, in the context of the new Member States and accession countries, may not be flourishing scientific research but forms of 'internal brain drain', 'brain freeze', 'brain waste' or 'brain stagnation' (Iredale, 1999; Mahroum, 2001; Kofman, 2002; Sretenova, 2003; Okólski, 2006). This raises the question of whether higher levels of retention (or lower levels of mobility) might be of benefit to scientific capacity-building and regeneration in the sending regions or whether it might simply result in under-employment and de-skilling. Katseli et al. argue that, 'the issue of how effectively highly skilled workers are employed in the home country is quite central to the whole question of the brain drain; in contexts of over-supply or "brain overflow" the costs imposed by emigration may be quite minimal' (2006a: 36).

The perspectives of respondents can be broadly grouped into a number of concerns reflecting the volume and quality of employment opportunities in science. First, many respondents talked of a general dearth of positions and a problem of 'over-supply'. Second, serious concerns were expressed about the nature of recruitment and progression systems and their ability to access positions. Third, scientists referred to the *quality* of employment both in terms of personal income (and their ability to sustain themselves and their families at an acceptable level) and whether the scientific resources and infrastructure existed to support effective functioning and productivity. In sum, many respondents felt that the underlying conditions in their home country, at the present time, were not adequate to foster effective regeneration even if scientists remained or returned.

Employment Opportunity in Poland and Bulgaria

One factor shaping the impact of emigration on capacity concerns the existence of surpluses and over-supply in domestic labour markets, resulting in un- and under-employment (Georgieva, 2004; Haug, 2005; Katseli et al., 2006a). Davenport uses the language of 'brain overflow' to describe the over-supply of educated professionals in some sending regions (2004: 618). An extensive survey of Polish scientific institutions in the period 1980–96 reported a 25 per cent decrease in staffing due to 'termination'. Of this group, emigration constituted 9.5 per cent of staff in 1991 compared with

15.1 per cent, resulting from 'internal brain drain' as scientists 'took up jobs across Poland that were bringing higher profit or better career opportunities' (Hryniewicz et al., 1997: 51).[3] More recently, Okólski's review of the data and literature on the impact of migration concludes that, 'no detrimental impacts of the loss of personnel could be observed as far as research output of Polish R&D . . . mainly because of the need to reduce over-employment in the sector' (2006: 17). Furthermore, the losses via emigration, he suggests, have remained 'rather low'. According to Okólski, this 'proves that the migration stream originated mostly from no alternative effective application of human resources in Poland . . . as researchers gave up their scientific activities to work in other industries' (ibid.: 51).

Dabrowa-Szefler further substantiates this assertion, suggesting that the progressive decline in R&D investment has resulted in a 'lack of demand for young researchers' and a serious decline in employment opportunity in scientific research, especially in the industrial sector (2004: 39). A recent external review of the Bulgarian higher education system conducted by the UK's Higher Education Policy Institute concluded that although lack of resources was a major problem, 'there appears to be a large degree of over-staffing' (Bekhradnia, 2004: 3). This perspective is echoed by many other authors (Chataway, 1999; Chompalov, 2000; Slantcheva, 2003; Kicinger, 2005). Data from the Bulgarian National Statistical Office indicates a massive decline (50 per cent) in research personnel in the government R&D sector from 12 842 in 1993 to 6387 in 2001 (Sretenova, 2004: 5).[4]

Many MOBEX respondents emphasized these 'push' factors in determining their out-migration and restricting their potential return and ability to achieve professional reintegration. In some fields, such as computer science in Bulgaria, for example, the effects of post-Communist transition were still being felt. Roumen talks of the massive cuts in the area of computer science, which had been so strong in Communist times, resulting in a surplus of researchers:[5]

> After the democratization in 1989 all those people were thrown out of work overnight because the military complex didn't exist any more. Computers were a by-product of the military regime. Moreover, Bulgarian computers were less highly developed than the best American computers. So all these huge plants and thousands of people had nothing to do and lost their jobs.

In addition to the specific effects of transition, other respondents referred more generally to the declining level of investment in science, resulting in a lack of positions. Boris, a senior scientist in Bulgaria, identifies the lack of employment opportunity as a key factor shaping out-migration: 'because of the situation at the moment and [the lack of] money for science there are not many possibilities here'. Monika did her first degree and an MBA in Poland before moving to the UK for her PhD. The main factor shaping her decision was the lack of employment opportunity. It is clear from her comments that she had hoped to stay in Poland and would return if opportunities improved but many of her peers had not managed to secure employment in their field of expertise:

> Why I came here? I mean when you look at the economic situation in Poland it's difficult in terms of getting a decent job after graduation so many of my friends who graduated from the materials department have either switched to completely different work or they were downgraded doing basic office work because they simply couldn't find work within this qualification. When I applied for this Masters degree I was hoping that within five years the situation in the market would change and then I would be able to work but it didn't change very much. There was no work.

Monica, in common with many other respondents, expressed a clear interest in return and we had little evidence to suggest as some authors have postulated, that return is linked in any direct way to quality or 'failed' migration.[6] More concretely, it reflects perceptions about their prospects of securing effective and sustainable employment, ideally but not always in their area of expertise. As Saxenian (1999) concludes, in the context of returns from the States to South Korea and China, return appears to have been instigated largely by improving economic conditions at home.

Stanislaw accepts the value of scientific circulation, especially at the post-doctoral stage, but argues that return in itself is of little relevance unless sufficient attractive positions exist:

> It's not only because people always will like to go to new places to see but I think that if there would be more job positions in Poland with a higher salary than now and with much better funding of research that people at first would go to do post-docs but the majority would return. [Now] they go and they know okay I will return but probably I will not find work.

According to Stanislaw, the problems in finding work relate not simply to the lack of positions but also to the nature of recruitment processes, the dominance of hierarchy and the importance of connections to securing positions in Poland: 'When you finish your PhD here it is very hard to find a job in an institute, because we are very tight and it's very hard to stay in science in Poland. You have to have very good connections, not your results from your work but the connections and the politics'.

Slantcheva (2003) identifies the continued importance of personal connections to career progression in Bulgaria. Although positions are 'theoretically open on a competitive basis . . . it is most likely that former graduate students of the Chair will be given preference. Institutions have tended to reproduce themselves with people drawn from the same institution' (ibid. 2003: 440). This situation reduces staff mobility, which is 'the exception', favours 'insiders' and forms of 'internal reproduction [which] hinder the development of competition' and 'represents a potential threat to the establishment of a system based on merit' (ibid.).

Other authors make a similar point, referring to the dominance of local elites restricting access to positions and the 'pull' effect of meritocratic recruitment in the West (Dabrowa-Szefler, 2004; Georgieva, 2004; Jalowiecki and Gorzelak, 2004). In more dramatic language, Gächter suggests that emigration is not *the* major problem for Bulgarian science. Many people remain and many would return but the conditions awaiting returnees are not conducive to retention. Many Bulgarians who have graduated abroad find it hard to find employment in Bulgaria both because positions do not exist and:

> at least as grave an obstacle is the uncertainty over being able to get fair treatment. Return migrants do not usually have a dense network of personal relationships. High rates of corruption . . . and continued government control of significant sectors of the economic impede competition and equality of opportunity. (Gächter, 2002: 46)

Other MOBEX respondents echoed these concerns, expressing the view that many positions were effectively 'blocked' and systems of recruitment (based on contacts, patronage and corruption) made it very difficult for them to access those positions that do exist. In practice, if we accept that migrants are a selective group of high-quality researchers, then this process is of serious concern. Valentina describes the 'risk' associated with mobility in terms of being able to access positions on return. She suggests that this rather depends on who you are working with and how you negotiate your move:

> It depends on the people with whom you work. If you work with someone here and go abroad you ask your boss if there is a position and then he should organize a free position for you. But it can be difficult because people prefer to work with people that they know.

We have already discussed (in Chapter 6) the value of networks and also the importance of having connections with senior people in the home country who have the authority necessary to generate the kind of 'free' positions Valentina is referring to.

Vanya is trying to establish a career in Bulgaria, as a post-doc, but she is concerned that systems there do not support open and fair recruitment. In practice, most appointments do not take place via formal advertisement of positions and objective selection processes (although some respondents suggested that interviews were becoming more common). Vanya describes the approach as 'insular' with 'most positions obtained through contacts'.

Whilst the emphasis on connections might constitute a form of indirect discrimination against people who have spent years working outside of their home country, in some cases respondents suggested a more direct form of discrimination against 'outsiders'. Piotr, an established senior scientist in the UK, expressed real interest in returning to Poland with his family after spending over 20 years abroad. The problem, as Piotr describes it, is of being able to re-enter the Polish labour market and secure an acceptable position after so many years away. After the interview he asked whether any EU schemes existed to support returns for a five-year period, as this, he felt, would enable him to be eased back in at no cost to the Polish institutions. As it stood, he suggested that Polish institutions would not fund this type of scheme as they favoured 'insiders'; only 'new money' would work.

Roumen describes how his colleagues responded to him when he returned to Bulgaria after a period abroad: 'Differently – everything between admiration and support and envy. I am afraid that many people were envious and jealous'. Asked whether he felt that this 'envy' might restrict his future career progression he replies, 'It might. Not decisively though. I am a lucky person. Other people would tell you different things; that they were undermined by colleagues and prevented from achieving the standing they deserve'.

Respondents were not simply concerned about securing employment in science but also about the quality of positions and their ability to achieve progression. A recent report on the Polish 'brain drain' by the BBC (BBC Newsnight, 2006) refers to fact that Poles who left initially for short periods are, 'staying longer because it's easier to get promoted on the basis of ability' in the West. Okólski refers to the problems that many Polish scientists have 'in terms of their acceptance' by Polish scientific and research institutions should they attempt to return. Furthermore, 'feudal' structures, 'hinder promotion and the development of young scientific staff thus pushing them abroad' (2006: 57).

Certainly, evidence of this emerged in our interviews. In some cases, respondents adopted a specific 'strategy' of moving abroad and working intensively during the early career phase in order to secure accelerated promotion in the host country, which would enable them to 'leap-frog' what they perceived to be arduous and corrupt local promotions system by moving directly into a senior position. Krzysztof, a Polish post-doc, was planning to remain in the UK for five years or so, which he felt would give him time to 'acquire as much experience and research papers' that would enable him to complete his habilitation and access a higher professorial position on his return. For him such a position was important as it would provide the kind of autonomy and independence that he felt was essential in scientific research.

These experiences are not restricted to Poland and Bulgaria of course. A recent survey of Marie Curie Fellows conducted by the authors (Van de Sande et al., 2005) reported similar concerns amongst the nationals of many other Member States over the nature of recruitment and progression systems and highlighted the attraction of what were perceived to be more objective and transparent systems. The UK emerged as one of the most attractive from this perspective. Tzonka explained that one of the main reasons for seeking work in the UK related to the existence of explicit and direct age discrimination. Although she had worked for 20 years in research in Bulgaria she had not been able to achieve promotion and referred to a 'law' preventing her applying in future:

> I expected to be promoted but I knew when I became 40 there was a law that I was not able to apply so I had two or three chances before I became 40 years old. It was a very restrictive law. When I came [to the UK] I was 45 so yes, it was my second reason.

Slantcheva (2003) explains that access to positions of 'assistants' (that is, all positions that do not require the habilitation) involve a maximum age limit of 35 or 40 for people with a doctorate. Once such a position is achieved, however, they can remain on that level for the rest of their career. Tzonka felt that accession to the European Union would mean that this law (and practice) will have to change, resulting in the introduction of more meritocratic systems.[7] Dessislava, a Bulgarian returnee, also had high hopes that accession to the European Union will make important changes to both the law and culture and result in a more open form of recruitment, which would enable quality researchers to remain or return and re-integrate:

> I hope [accession] will make a difference. At least it will put some working rules. Not just the rules written on the web pages but working rules. I mean if you have referees of the project they should be referees from all over Europe not a referee to say 'Oh I know this fellow so I give him money, nevertheless he wrote rubbish on the paper but I give him money or I don't know this fellow so I don't give him anything', this is the way it works now. [Q: You hope that Europe will influence the way that the Bulgarian system works?] Yes, and now there are interviews and companies like to take the best applicants and not just if somebody recommends somebody.

It is important to acknowledge changes that are currently taking place in both Poland and Bulgaria with the aim of modernizing and democratizing employment in the academic sector (Slantcheva, 2003; Dabrowa-Szefler, 2004). The success of these programmes is, however, very much limited by the decline in investment, for as Kwiek notes, 'the positive changes were accompanied by the chronic under funding of public higher education' leaving Polish academics in a 'permanent state of uncertainty' (2003: 455).

In other cases, scientists spoke of forms of position-blocking that were not so much about patronage and recruitment processes as the simple ageing of a substantial existing workforce and 'fluid' practices in relation to retirement. During the fieldwork we were aware of a large number of professors continuing to hold academic positions in both Poland and Bulgaria who were over the age of 65. Jerzy feels that it is easier to access positions in the UK because of the higher level of circulation and turnover: 'When you have a position [in Poland] you stay there forever, we have very old scientists in Poland'.[8]

Dessislava reports that the lack of a formal retirement policy in Bulgaria means that 'most of my colleagues are above 60'. She goes on to suggest that the majority of this group are relatively inactive: 'Unfortunately the biggest part are people who are just taking their salaries because we do not have official retirement so you can be 70 and you work'.

According to Slantcheva, 'academia in Bulgaria is still winning battles with respect to retirement age. Although the formal retirement age of habilitated staff is now 65 years . . . institutions have been authorised . . . to retire those who have reached retirement age only if they wish to' (2003: 449).

Intersectoral Moves: Internal Brain Drain or Effective Knowledge Transfer?

Georgieva refers to what she calls the 'meltdown of scientific capital leaving traditional sectors of innovation paralysed' (2004: 365) but argues that this is increasingly a result of internal rather than external brain drain; the 'brain drain country profile has shifted. Of those academics that left their institutions, the majority now remain within the country . . . having left science altogether' (ibid.: 367). Chataway makes a similar point in relation to the Polish context (1999: 355).

Chompalov concludes his overview of the literature on brain drain with the following comment: 'what most empirical studies seem to converge on is the stronger effect of "push" factors, the main of which is the internal structural imbalance in the donor country – which educates more professionals than the economy or job market can absorb' (2000: 7). He also argues forcefully for carefully contextualized studies that are capable of grasping the specificity of situations and, in the case of Poland and Bulgaria, the effect that major political transformations (which he describes as 'explosive push forces') have in reshaping labour markets (ibid.: 32).

Recent figures indicate growing rates of graduate unemployment in both Poland and Bulgaria (Slantcheva, 2003: 451). Haug and Diehl talk of unemployment rates in Bulgaria in the year 2000 of 19.6 per cent, rising to 39.5 per cent for persons aged under 25 (2004a: 26). Bobeva (1996) presents figures showing a massive decline in employment in the Bulgarian science sector from 86 310 in 1990 to 46 880 at the end of 1992 and infers that emigration (brain drain) played a major part in this. However, Gächter criticizes this inference as unfounded and indicates that other studies run contrary to this proposition – suggesting that 'only 10 per cent of the personnel reduction was connected to emigration' (2002: 11). According to Gächter:

> Bulgaria enjoys a large and rising supply of highly educated personnel; this supply is far in excess of the requirements of the economy and cannot be absorbed productively . . . the reductions represent an adjustment of numbers to a sustainable level of science employment. Emigration played only a minor role in the reductions. (Gächter, 2002: 53)

Haug and Diehl's analysis of Bulgarian Census data also leads them to conclude that 'the problems of the specialists in the Bulgarian labour market can be seen in the fact that most of them are not occupied in the field of their specialisation', placing the emphasis on involuntary intersectoral moves rather than emigration (2004a: 18).

As we have seen, many respondents talked of the lack of positions in science in the sending countries and the effects of major resource cutbacks on the over-supply of scientists as well as problems in re-entering domestic labour markets. Others emphasized the relative impact of 'internal brain drain' or intersectoral moves. In some cases, these forms of mobility should not be conceptualized as losses particularly where scientists are using their skills and knowledge, albeit in different ways, to support economic growth more generally. Certainly in the West and at EU level this is a major policy objective. On the other hand, where intersectoral moves take people into completely new areas of work and away from scientific research and development altogether, there is a net loss in *scientific* capacity. This raises interesting questions about the respective impact of international moves (where people continue to develop *as scientists*) and domestic intersectoral moves (where they cease to develop as scientists but may use their skills in other ways). In practice it is rather hard to assess the quality of knowledge transfer processes in many of the cases below. The first group of cases concern 'horizontal' mobility into the business sector or industry, and the second, resort to less skilled forms of employment.[9] Dessislava and Dimitar are senior scientists in Bulgaria. They both refer to colleagues who have remained in Bulgaria but have left science, moving to entirely new forms of work:

> Most of them needed to leave science because it's not simple to find a job . . . some of them went to private companies; I have friends who were very good physicists and they opened a private insurance company. It's a question of surviving okay?

> [After transition] few of my colleagues – maybe no one – joined science . . . some of them were selling engineering products, marketing mainly, but staying in Bulgaria.

Alina, a Polish post-doc in the UK, makes a similar observation: 'Quite a lot of people left science. Programmers, networking people, finance – there just weren't opportunities to do science outside universities and there aren't that many positions in universities'.

Ironically, increased losses to science through intersectoral mobility might have been exacerbated by the build up to EU enlargement as an unintended consequence of economic development. A number of respondents referred to the growth in IT companies and opportunities in business although not in R&D capacity. Beata, a doctoral researcher in the UK, for example, talks of the growth in non-research positions in informatics in Poland: 'We have brilliant computer companies and if you're studying informatics it's very easy to get a job but in many areas like biology and pure science it's really bad'. The tone of Yulian's reference to opportunities in computing companies in Bulgaria reflects his concerns about the public sector's ability to compete: 'At the moment many young people go to the computer firms because they pay too much'.

Teresa makes the interesting observation that Poland's accession not only makes it easier for people to leave but also to return. She goes on to refer to growing opportunities in the business sector:

> Some people will argue that enlargement will actually make it easier for Polish people to go back home. I think people are coming back who want to set up businesses because this is a growing economy, which is maybe good but in science actually I don't know anyone who goes away for a few years and then comes back.

Both Tzonka and Rumiana talk of the attraction of business opportunities in Bulgaria. It is clear that in most cases these 'opportunities' are not in science-related fields, however. Tzonka has observed some return amongst Bulgarian business people but not among scientists: 'Some people who are involved in business, they go back to Bulgaria because they already have contacts and they can develop their business from Bulgaria. Yes [there is growth] mainly in the business sector, not research, not science and not edu-cation'. Rumiana, a post-doc in the UK, spoke at length during her inter-view about leaving science to return and set up a property development business aimed at British expats: 'I don't know if we stayed in Bulgaria I don't think the institutes I used to work for exist any more. [If I had stayed] I was going to find the possibility to run a business or to do something different'.

Interestingly, Boyko and his wife were also talking about potentially returning to Bulgaria to develop a business supporting British people inter-ested in buying property in their home town. Whilst this kind of move implies a permanent loss to scientific capacity, other forms of intersectoral mobility could be viewed positively as forms of knowledge transfer sup-porting industrial growth. In practice, however, the kinds of industrial development currently taking place in the sending regions are not generat-ing positions in research and development as such.

Dabrowa-Szefler laments the 'serious decline' in industrial R&D, arguing that, 'neither Polish nor foreign businesses are interested in con-ducting R&D work in Poland' (2004: 40). This assertion is echoed in an external review of the Bulgarian HE system, which found that the rate of decline in business R&D over the past decade has been more sharp than in the academic sector (Bekhradnia, 2004: 81). Jalowiecki and Gorzelak refer to the growth in 'executive' recruitment in the ex-Communist countries, especially in areas such as banking, finance and information technology. Whilst welcome in many respects, they suggest that this devel-opment is responsible for the 'sucking out' of intellectual workers from the 'quasi-markets' in the academic sector where the price of labour con-tinues to be dominated by state bureaucracies with total disregard for the level of qualifications, effectively accelerating internal brain drain (2004: 303).

Viktor remembers the close, indeed obligatory, relationships that existed between industry and universities in the former Communist times and con-trasts this with the kind of companies developing in Bulgaria at the present time:

> Foreign IT companies are offering reasonable salaries to very young scientists; they are not scientists but young clever people and they have drained some of the young Masters students which they have considered for PhD . . . I remem-ber in the beginning we had a number of companies – okay some of them related to the military production – producing things strongly associated with our uni-versity and for many people it was essential to go to work there if you don't like to make an academic research career. They need people and there was some kind of contribution of the university towards the economy, however nowadays there are no companies producing hi-tech in my country so there is no need for these people staying there.

Viktor's account is repeated many times by respondents who feel that the losses of human capital abroad are at least matched by losses within the country through forms of 'internal brain drain'. In such situations it might be more effective to export human capital and 'keep it hot' rather than allowing it to stagnate in the home country. On the other hand, returns to non-scientific positions and perhaps in order to set up businesses might also make an important contribution to the economy and society. Katseli et al. suggest that 'a common goal of migrants is to start a small business of their own' contributing more generally to a more entrepreneurial and well-functioning society (2006a: 41).

Magdalena presents a more optimistic picture of the development of employment opportunities in Sofia in the computer software sector. She feels that she could quite easily return and secure an attractive and well-paid position as a software engineer in one of these companies and was only prevented from doing so by her personal circumstances. However, it was clear that this work would not involve research and development. Although some of Ivaylo's ex-colleagues in Bulgaria have managed to secure positions in industry, he suggests that such companies 'do not give money for investigation or research and the foreign companies which came just hire people – they don't want to do their R&D stuff there [in Bulgaria]'. A recent interview with the Major of Wroclaw for the BBC suggested that Poland is currently experiencing serious skills shortages, as a result of emigration, in areas such as skilled construction and IT, which are 'threatening plans to bring dozens of high-tech foreign companies to the region' (BBC Newsnight, 2006). It remains to be seen whether such developments will involve an increase in industrial R&D capacity.

Although most of the scenarios identified above involve intersectoral moves and associated losses to scientific potential, they cannot be described as de-skilling as such. In other cases, however, respondents talked about people having to take casual or unskilled work either in addition to or instead of research. Lucjan, a Bulgarian post-doc explains the choices he faced:

> A lot of people with degrees they work in a pub or something – it's very common. [Q: So if you hadn't come to the UK do you think you would have had an equivalent position in science in Bulgaria?] I don't really; I'd like to find something but if not I would go for a less qualified job. What else would I do?

In many cases people talked optimistically about return but at the point of retirement rather than during their professional lives. Rumiana and her husband, who moved to the UK in their 40s and have worked here for 15 years, potentially fall into this category due to the lack of employment opportunity:

We are always saying me and my husband that when we retire we will go back. [Q: I guess that's too late for you to transfer the science isn't it?] Yes, but if an opportunity comes to go back and do research when my project finishes in a year . . . I'm looking for work everywhere, applying everywhere but there are no positions in Bulgaria.

The impact of return in such situations is limited. As Cerase explains, many returnees 'look upon their return as the last stage of their life'. At this point, 'Ultimately, they are of little consequence in the society' (1974: 258).

Working Effectively in Science

Whilst 'de-skilling' can occur in such cases – where scientists are forced to find less skilled work in other areas – it may also occur *within* scientific positions. Although, of course, many scientists continue to work in science in Bulgaria and Poland, the research suggested that in many situations these people are working less effectively and productively than they might in other contexts due to severe resource constraints affecting the quality of positions. Sretenova suggests that Bulgarian scientists face two stark options:

> frozen brains at home or brain drain to a foreign country. It is not a big surprise then that the most brilliant and skilful scientists prefer the mobility option and a nomadic life style in order to practise their profession in an effective and productive way instead of being frozen at home and waiting for better times. (2004: 8)

We have seen (in Chapter 3) that this experience is a major factor encouraging out-migration. These constraints manifest themselves in two respects. First, very low levels of remuneration often require scientists to take on additional supplementary employment limiting the time they can devote to their research. Second, limited access to basic office and research facilities restricts scientific productivity.

During the interviews we became aware of many people who either personally held, or had colleagues who held, second or third jobs. Prior to the fieldwork, we had become aware of the practice of researchers taking second positions in lecturing in order to augment their salaries. The phenomenon of 'flying professors' is identified by Georgieva (2004: 366) both as a response to increased demand due to the rapid expansion of higher education and to earn additional money. Slantcheva expresses concern at the growing number of 'travelling professors' in Bulgaria who are forced to engage in 'faculty moonlighting', holding jobs both outside and within academia in order to augment their meagre salaries. This situation, she suggests is 'most often at the expense of teaching and research' (2003: 453).

Notwithstanding the benefits of what Velev (2002) calls 'double employ-ment' in terms of the researcher's financial status, the costs of this are identified by these authors in terms of the loss of research time and pro-ductivity. Dabrowa-Szefler points to the massive increases in the numbers of undergraduate and postgraduate students in Poland as a key factor increasing both the teaching hours of university staff within their own insti-tutions and encouraging them to take additional remunerated positions in the fast-emerging private institutions. This, she suggests, overloads them with teaching responsibilities with the result that 'they devote increasingly less time to research' (2004: 42; see also Chataway, 1999 and Kwiek, 2003).

The interviews corroborated this trend but also identified more worrying practices, involving the taking of second and third jobs in unskilled areas of employment. We were told, for example, of researchers selling news-papers or cleaning and working in shops before or after work and at week-ends so that they can continue to work in science. Violeta explains the specific pressures facing dual science career couples in Bulgaria where both partners are living on subsistence wages and having to augment these through unskilled work: 'Yes [I have to take casual work] otherwise it was difficult to pay for my house. And of course my husband is having the same so for us it is really difficult. If at least one of us had another job'. Tomasz speaks optimistically, arguing that the pace of change in Poland is sufficient to begin to attract return moves. However, the financial situation has not improved sufficiently to avoid the 'two job' problem: '[Poland] has changed enough to encourage people. I predict many will probably be back. They would think with one exception of salaries. I am forced to get a second part-time job'.

Of course, staying put and not moving does not necessarily mean that scientists are working effectively. Georgi, a doctoral researcher in Germany, questions the contribution he could make should he return given the lack of resources: 'It's difficult to say what's my contribution if I [returned]. I probably wouldn't have much scientific impact on Bulgaria due to lack of opportunities and resources'.

Todorka and Vanya have both returned to Bulgaria but express serious concerns about the lack of resources to support their research and enable them to work effectively. Todorka says that if she was younger she would go abroad again, 'if there was a chance to work effectively. I am motivated all my life to work as a scientist but I want to be able to buy chemicals and to use modern equipment but it is not possible here'. Although Vanya has returned to join her partner she laments that the lack of resources limits her ability to produce high-quality research: 'Here it's not possible to do what I wanted to do on plant metabolism. The essay I was able to do here was really poor. I didn't have the equipment to measure things'.

Valentina also refers to the problems of being able to achieve an acceptable level of productivity in the Bulgarian scientific environment. His experience of working in Germany made him aware of marked differences in efficiency:

> They have lots of computers and I make computer simulation. If I want to make a test I can run jobs on different computers and it will take two days and here on our computers I need to run it for a month. This is a very good advantage and I had not thought about this before I went to Germany but when I came back I saw the difference. Before that it's difficult to understand the difference to work here or to work there.

Elzbieta, a Polish returnee, sums up the importance of matching human capital with physical resources: 'The brain alone is not enough these days and you cannot make an excellent publication if you don't have a fair amount of money because biology is extremely money consuming'. Velev also emphasizes the fact that 'the return option' is not realistic for Bulgaria in the near future because the necessary conditions do not exist to utilize fully the very high qualifications of returnees. In the absence of significant infrastructural investment, returning scientists will be 'entirely disconnected from the environment they are used to' (2002: 7).

Lazarova and Tarique's research on knowledge transfer following repatriation in multinational enterprises resonates with the experiences of our interviewees. According to these authors, 'Accumulating knowledge abroad is necessary but not sufficient for knowledge transfer to take place . . . repatriates' motivation to contribute to collective organizational learning is primarily driven by the fit between their individual career objectives and the career development opportunities upon return' (2005: 366). In many cases, Lazarova and Tarique found that repatriation was associated with 'loss of status and autonomy, non-challenging jobs, lack of promotion opportunities' (ibid.: 366).

Capacity-building through Mobility?

We have already noted respondents' concerns that emigration might fundamentally damage the regenerative potential of sending regions. This argument rests on a critical assumption that those who do not move remain within science and are able to work effectively, develop their research and attract and train the next generation of scientists. Subsequent discussions around science labour markets and 'internal brain drain' suggest that the losses of scientists through emigration may be a by-product of a more fundamental decline in scientific investment, both in human capital and physical resources.

Emigration then may be as much a consequence of wider resourcing decisions than a primary cause of decline (Rangelova and Vladimirova, 2004: 23). Furthermore, scientists have indicated that mobility plays a critical role in maintaining the sustainability of science in the sending regions in three key respects. First, in 'allowing' receiving countries to encourage their scientists to remain in high-level productive scientific research in the hopes that at least a proportion of these may return or use their knowledge to the benefit of their home country in the future, perhaps when conditions improve. Second, in providing incentives and opportunities for existing scientists currently based in the home countries to remain within and work effectively, at the present time, through short-stay mobility and international connections. And finally, to provide incentives for school leavers to consider embarking on scientific study at a time when employment prospects in science at home are particularly unattractive.

Suter and Jandl suggest that the rapid internationalization of undergraduate education and the settlement of students in host countries has given rise to a new and more nuanced debate. They note a 'discernable tendency towards a greater differentiation of the possible effects on sending countries'. Whilst commentators recognize concerns around the net loss of human capital they also point to the compensating effects as 'sending countries benefit from highly skilled nationals educated abroad; either upon their return or when they remain abroad' (2006: 8). Gent and Skeldon's briefing on policy options for skilled migration similarly notes the relational dynamics of international mobility. Whilst, 'the developed world clearly benefits from importing skilled people, much greater consideration needs to be given to where people are trained and who funds their training . . . [the receiving countries] often provide advanced training for these workers' (2006: 3). This then is the flip side of regeneration. Rather than simply sapping a country of its human capital, mobility may play a critical role in maintaining a pool of highly qualified and motivated scientists that may then enable the 'sending' countries to retain scientific capacity and the potential for regeneration.

'Storing' and Investing in Expatriate Scientists

Assessing the relative impact of compensatory factors, such as return and reverse knowledge transfer, requires not only that we address the existence of these processes but also the quality of the knowledge. This raises the question of whether and to what extent migration 'adds value' to expatriate scientists in ways that could not be achieved in its absence. The discussion around brain 'stagnation' and 'internal brain drain' above highlights the complex relationship between mobility and scientific capacity in

sending regions. In very many situations, scientists reported that the alternative to emigration was leaving science altogether or juggling scientific
employment with other forms of work to achieve a sustainable income.
Migration, on the other hand, might retain key researchers in science and,
moreover, enable the sending regions to reap the benefits of external investment in their expatriates. In this context, even if only a small proportion of
'enriched' scientists return, this may represent critical potential for the
sending regions. Certainly a number of our respondents expressed the view
that they were of greater value to their home country as a result of their
mobility. One of the Polish key informants, for example, said that:
'[Returnees] bring new techniques, new visions and new contacts . . . They
bring inspirations, then based on these inspirations build grant proposals
and try to find money for it' (cited in Kicinger, 2005: 34). However, Kicinger
goes on to suggest that these 'new skills and attitudes of returnees are not
necessarily always thought to suit the Polish conditions, the returnees may
be accused of being too funding-oriented' (ibid.). Two other Polish key
informants expressed concern about the relevance or applicability of skills:
'The business attitude is great but doesn't necessarily work here' and
returnees often have inflated expectations: 'They come back and think they
can jump at managerial positions right away . . . [they are] extremely
ambitious'.

Viktor believes that the opportunities associated with mobility have
enabled him to continue working at a high level in science research.
Reflecting on his situation he suggests that the alternative (of staying in
Bulgaria) would have meant that his scientific knowledge and potential was
'lost forever':

> If [scientists] had stayed there it will not help so much. If I'd stayed in Bulgaria
> I would not stay in university. Right now I would care for the network of a small
> company being paid reasonably to live and installing Windows and their print-
> ers when they don't work to people who can't do it themselves and such stuff and
> I would be forever lost to science. Being [in the UK] however is giving the country
> some second chance in case things improve significantly – there is a huge number
> of good scientists [abroad].

Bogdan, a Bulgarian returnee, similarly recognizes the relationship that
exists between sending and receiving countries. Although he feels the
balance at the present time is tipped in favour of the receiving countries he
nevertheless argues that mobility is essential to maintaining scientific
know-how in Bulgaria:

> [Scientific mobility] is a must for Bulgaria. As a country we have to keep a
> scientific level and the scientific community, otherwise we will become just a

servicing country in the European Union; it's not possible to keep this level by staying here. My feeling is that now we feed more Europe and the States than they give back just because education is quite expensive.

Ivan shares Bogdan's perspective that not only is mobility good for him as an individual scientist but also, in the longer term, for his country, which has the opportunity to benefit from the investment made in him in Germany:

> Maybe later I will be back in Bulgaria but I need a very good development in my studies first. I think it will be more useful for me and for the country also if I get some knowledge abroad and then come back and if I have the possibility to do that. I was born there so I love that country so if I have the possibility to do some international work from Bulgaria I will do it but I need to go somewhere to get some idea what the level is or what is going on in my scientific field and after to come back. If Bulgaria can keep some people and send some people to study for five years and after to bring back it will be better.

In a Polish context, Elzbieta, a returnee, believes that her home department has gained from her time abroad in terms of both know-who and know-how:

> Of course it benefits because at first if you have like on the intellectual level a problem to solve and so it's easier from the point of contacts from different labs and lots of people who can help you to solve the problem and answer your questions. People are sending me things and it's much easier if you have this network of people you know. Then me and my friends are coming back from the post-docs with new techniques and it's not only for us but for our students; you can then teach them more.

Irina said she was reluctant to leave Bulgaria in the first instance as she felt this would be letting her country down. She refers to the influence of a particular Bulgarian professor who persuaded her of the contribution that she could make to Bulgarian science as an expatriate. It is clear that she is talking here not only about substantive scientific skills but approaches to work more generally:

> I really wanted to stay in Bulgaria and help. This professor told me something which actually made me think and I now believe it strongly. That the only way for Bulgaria to change is for the capable people to go abroad and to see the difference and then to go back. He said the country will not change from within because the people are like clones and they are afraid. You need to see a difference in order to prepare and then to go back and change something. So I think that if this happens then in the future it will be better. If [the state increases funding for science] many people will go back and the country will benefit from people who have degrees from abroad or worked abroad.

The final comment underlines the importance of improving scientific investment in order to reap the benefits of the expatriate scientific community. Like Irina, Krzysztof also talks of the benefits of his mobility to Polish science in terms of the development of both scientific and transferable skills: '[Q: So people moving like yourself could actually be a positive benefit to Poland?] Yes I think so . . . Yes, how to research and how to work efficiently. If you think about organizational skills and university I think I have learnt a lot from [the UK]'.

Of course this belief in the ability to reap the benefits of foreign investment in expatriate human capital is closely linked to the issue of return. Dessislava identifies the high level of scientific emigration as a factor inhibiting the pace of progress in the short term but firmly believes that this pool of highly trained expatriate scientists will underpin scientific development in Bulgaria: 'So, the modernization here is slowed down because there are not many young scientists left but I would expect that if one day they come back as specialists in their field then a new intense scientific era will start'.

Return in itself may not be critical; attention needs to be paid to both the propensity to return but also the conditions under which return takes place and whether the environment supports effective integration and achievement. Some authors have expressed concern about the relational quality of skills and the transferability of skills developed in the host country to the home context as the key informants indicated above (Davenport, 2004; Gamlen, 2005). Certainly, in the case of medical migration, for example, it has been argued that doctors and nurses trained in more developed environments may be unable to function effectively on return (Katseli et al., 2006a: 38). Our experience of working with Bulgarian and Polish scientists would suggest that, although some concerns did exist about access to equipment and resources conducive to effective research, in many cases scientists were able to apply the knowledge they had acquired. This is often achieved through continued contact with the networks and institutions of the host country and through short stays and remote forms of data transfer (see below).

Much of the more general literature around brain waste and stagnation is concerned primarily with the post-migration employment experiences of highly skilled migrants (their professional activities in the host country). Although the discussion above, reflecting the concerns of our respondents, placed greater emphasis on the ability of scientists to use and develop their human capital in the home country, it is important to recognize that migration does not imply retention and further investment in a scientific capacity in all cases. Many authors point to evidence of 'brain waste' in the receiving countries as migrants find it difficult to resume equivalent positions and are de-skilled as a result (Munz et al., 2006: iv). The sampling strategy of the MOBEX project, which was aimed at locating people who *were* in science in the UK and Germany, is unlikely to identify cases in which scientists have migrated into other employment sectors (although evidence of this arose in relation to their partners and is discussed in Chapter 4). Okólski's study suggests that only about half of Polish emigrants continued working in science in the host country. He concludes that, in such cases, 'human resources should not be considered transferred but partially lost, similarly to the scientists who left for other jobs in Poland' (2006: 51).

The above discussion tends to give an impression of migration as a two-stage process involving an outward and potentially return move. The patterns of mobility identified in Chapter 2 emphasize the prevalence of more complex trajectories and high levels of circulation, including forms of 'shuttle' or 'pendular' migration. Many scientists in our sample use repeated short-stay mobility as a means of increasing the viability of their home positions, both in terms of scientific productivity and personal income.

Increasing Scientific Productivity Through Mobility

The importance of repeated short stays abroad to the ability to function effectively and achieve a high level of productivity in a competitive global context embraces a range of issues. At the most basic level, some respondents argued that they could not function in scientific research without this kind of contact and collaboration. The resources and facilities necessary to conduct their experimental work often do not exist in the domestic context (Chataway, 1999; Velev, 2002). Okólski refers to the importance of 'fellowship-type short trips whose major effect was upgrading of migrant skills and social capital, evidently to the benefit of the home country' (2006: 17).

Agnieszka, a returning Polish scientist, talks of the importance of accessing specific high-level research infrastructures. As she says, this situation is common across Europe and not peculiar to Poland or Bulgaria:

> A lot of people who are working for this institute are abroad because nuclear and high-energy physics practically there is no experiment done in Poland. We don't have such big accelerators that are necessary nowadays and since at least 15 years the tendency in Europe is to create just some communities working around one or two accelerators in Europe. So in most countries their experiments are done abroad – there is one in Switzerland, one in Italy and one in Germany. All nuclear physicists in Europe are working around these centres in big collaborations.

In other situations it is clear that much more basic resources are required. Bronislaw, another returning Polish scientist, talks of how she finds it

necessary to travel abroad in order to work with her international colleagues as the basic facilities do not exist to support such collaboration in
her home institute: 'We haven't an opportunity to invite [people to Poland]
and create working conditions to do some parts of experiments here; so we
rather travel abroad'. Bronislaw had established a strong collaboration with
a Norwegian research group that included a variety of different kinds of
stays:

> From my team it was in total six persons in Norway working for shorter or
> longer time periods. I was in Norway the first time for two years then almost each
> year I spent one or two months in Norway and then I had a five-year position
> of professor too and during my stay I took one of my students who preferred
> full PhD in Norway so she was five years in total. The others spent shorter or
> longer times, say from three weeks to half a year so they prepared a large part
> of their experiments in Norway.

Although the stays in this case appear to be organized to meet the specific
needs of the individual scientist there is clearly a collective effect too,
strengthening the ongoing collaboration between the two research groups
and supporting opportunities for future researchers. Yulian, an experienced
scientist in Bulgaria, suggests that international placements are critical to
his ability to provide adequate research opportunities for his doctoral
researchers who could not otherwise conduct their experimental work
effectively:

> At this moment scientific equipment is old. We have no possibilities to make
> science on a higher level and we use our contacts abroad for our PhD students
> spending some months or years abroad to make experiments. [Q: What do these
> labs give them?] Equipment is first, second the money of course and time for this
> scientific work for students to spend three or six months. The level of our life
> here in Bulgaria is low. Our students usually go abroad for work not for high
> salary or money, only for the idea to work with high-level equipment. It is very
> important.

As this case suggests, short stays are an important means of making doctoral research viable in the home country. Other respondents make similar
points about the value of short stays in terms of accessing vital equipment
and resources. Although Andrey had been in the UK since 2004 on a two-
year fellowship, he had visited a number of times previously: 'My visits here
were the most efficient periods because there were better microscopes, col-
lections and libraries. In fact I did a lot of my research here just for that
period of one, two or three months and after that finishing the papers in
Bulgaria'. According to Andrey these successive short stays significantly
increased his efficiency as a scientist to the benefit of his home country.

In common with Andrey, Stefan describes the value of a number of quite short (one-month) stays as follows:

> It was very useful to see the place and to be able to discuss with them directly what we were trying to achieve. We managed to publish several papers together. It was a very useful experience. [Later on] I started needing several commercial programmes which were expensive and difficult to get in the BAS. So these were the main reasons I started looking for temporary positions abroad.

Although he acknowledges that such 'strategies come with a certain risk', Stefan argues quite forcefully that short stays (of up to two years), 'are viewed from Bulgaria as opportunities to learn new methods, do some research and then come back and use the knowledge gained in this way to improve the research in the [home] institute'.

Whilst accessing equipment is of critical importance, other scientists spoke more generally of the importance of short stays to international collaboration and connections.[10] These examples evidence the contribution that ongoing mobility can make to scientific research in Poland and Bulgaria. Although most of the stays referred to are quite short, these are often interspersed with longer stays of one or two years' duration. This form of mobility plays an important role in supporting both the viability of doctoral research but also the motivation to take early career positions. A number of respondents argued that the opportunities for mobility associated with science careers have increased the incentives for young people to enter and remain in science in recent years. Roumen, a senior scientist in Bulgaria, talked about the importance of mobility to his early career researchers: 'I have a young PhD student and she has undergone a miraculous change to be honest and I have been trying to help her by sending her abroad to various places through my acquaintances and this made a major impact on her – suddenly she got motivated and interested and suddenly it was not just killing time'.

In this case the student did not actually wish to leave Bulgaria in the longer term. The point her supervisor is making here is that mobility plays a critical role in maintaining an active interest and satisfaction in scientific research *in Bulgaria*. According to several respondents, the opportunities associated with mobility are responsible for increasing the incentives and interest in science amongst early career researchers in the home country. One of the professors in the Bulgarian Academy of Sciences put it quite simply:

> Neither the level of the necessary scientific equipment, nor the available library information make it possible to carry out any meaningful research, if one relies on national sources in Bulgaria. The salaries of young scientists in higher

education and research cannot attract any gifted and bright students. The only motivation to stay in science is mobility, the contacts with researchers from abroad and with modern equipment as well as the prospect of some better payment in terms of fellowships during scientific visits.

Another BAS professor (Bogdan) explains how short-stay mobility helps his doctoral researchers:

> It's not a secret that we are very poor here. It depends on the place where they are; I would say that in our department they have possibilities to do research . . . just because we have very close relations with quite a number of scientific centres abroad and so we do our research in collaboration with those centres and send our PhDs and young people there for short periods and they do research on very good I would say European level, but just because we have these relations. The funding we have here cannot support research of high quality.

Asked whether it might be possible for early career researchers to remain in Bulgaria and develop research in his field (particle physics) he replied:

> No. So you can stay at our department for example as a teacher, as assistant professor and continue research or develop new research . . . just find a group to join that has relations with abroad or if you already have a relation during your PhD and so to travel for time to time there and back and do research, it is possible.

Bogdan's experience of the difficulties in supervising doctorates in Bulgaria are echoed in Georgieva's survey findings, which suggest that, although the number of doctoral registrations has doubled since 1989 in Bulgaria, the completion rate is causing concern and limiting the potential of this group to replace retiring scientists. According to her, less than 10 per cent of BAS PhDs complete on time, perhaps reflecting their ability to work effectively in the current resourcing context (2004: 366).

On a more personal note, the following respondent talks of how the alternative to short-stay mobility, in her situation, was to leave science altogether: 'I personally found it very important especially for my career; it had quite a high impact the fact that I started travelling and visiting laboratories'. Asked why she had decided to make the various moves she replied:

> Okay at that time the working conditions here in two or three years really dropped drastically, we even didn't have money to pay electricity one year . . . the main point I can answer for quite a big group of scientists who are also now abroad – was the fact that the working conditions and the salaries dropped drastically so I didn't do science here so you go somewhere to find a better place or you just leave it and do something else. At the same time according to the rule at the Academy of Sciences I was obliged to come every day here just to spend eight hours to do nothing . . . without equipment you cannot do anything so let's be honest there

is nothing. I realized I was learning much faster things [abroad] compared to what I learned here. The second point is that you are far from your family and your friends and you have enough time to work and you simply enjoy it.

The 'practice' referred to above, of requiring attendance at the institution for specific hours irrespective of whether the basic equipment exists to work effectively, can mean that scientists can only work effectively after normal office hours at home (on their personal computers). Although the respondent is talking about the situation several years earlier it was evident from our research visit to Bulgaria that these problems remain. During a visit to one of the respondent's laboratories, the whole building was plunged into darkness due to a not infrequent power cut, which, she informed us, would have destroyed her experiment (involving plant cells). This example reiterates the importance of remembering that the alternative to mobility is often not successful integration in scientific research but forms of 'internal brain drain'.

This final point about the ability to work faster and more efficiently during short stays, particularly if you are able to leave children with family back home, is echoed by many other respondents. Short-stay mobility often implies intensive periods of research activity using equipment they do not possess in the home country and often exhaustive working schedules during stays abroad. They can then spend time analysing data and writing papers on their return. Boris explains how he uses short stays abroad to conduct his experiments:

If the work needs one month . . . The problem is in Bulgaria we haven't good apparatus and systems to do complicated experiments so we make these experiments abroad and the next time here in Bulgaria we write papers and analyse, calculate. I usually work 24 hours per day [when I am abroad].[11]

Lazarova and Tarique's work on mobility within multinational companies points to the importance of repeated moves to sustaining the knowledge transfer process following return: 'Although expatriates participate in knowledge transfer, they act as knowledge sources and, as a result, acquire little new knowledge themselves. Indeed, over time their own level of competence may decrease, as they are neither optimally utilizing their skills nor are they developing any new expertise' (2005: 366). Williams (2006) makes a similar point but talks more optimistically of a two-way process of 'knowledge transformation', which occurs as the knowledge a migrant returns with is integrated effectively with local knowledge to generate new forms of knowledge relevant to the local context.

Mobility is not only a means to access the resources necessary for scientific research. It also enables scientists to achieve an acceptable standard of living. We have already noted (in Chapter 3) the role that financial considerations play in migration decision-making. Whilst marked salary differentials (or more simply low income) remain a central factor encouraging out-migration, opportunities for salary augmentation via repeated short stays were also cited as a critical factor, enabling many scientists in the sending regions to remain there and continue working in science. Regular short-stay mobility is an important means of supplementing a subsistence or inadequate salary. This places researchers under less pressure to take second (non-scientific) jobs in the home country as many of their non-mobile colleagues do. Furthermore, 'shuttle' movers are often able to retain a permanent position, and sometimes their remuneration, during the periods spent abroad (although this varies in practice). The following researcher describes her situation and how it enables her to remain in science in Bulgaria: 'I'm happy with that because you can be paid quite well going for one month somewhere. I can always go to Spain for one month to teach . . . so somehow you manage and you try to stay in science. One of the reasons (for making short stays) is that you can raise your salary.[12] Haug's analysis of Bulgarian Census data on migration intentions emphasizes the importance of short stays to 'solving material problems' with 41.6 per cent of people planning short stays abroad citing financial imperatives (2005: 14). Interestingly, short-term migrants are more motivated by the need to 'solve material problems than achieve higher living standards . . . Short-term circulation . . . might therefore be a transitional solution to economic problems' (ibid.: 17, 21). Katseli et al. (2006a) use the term 'target saving' to describe planned moves, often of a short-term nature, specifically designed to augment family income. In all of the cases identified as part of the MOBEX research, however, the income generation motive was closely linked to specific research objectives. Through short stays, respondents were accessing both personal and scientific resources.

Bagatelas and Kubicova place significant emphasis on the importance of recognizing remuneration as the driver of Bulgaria's problems and not emigration as such:

> those who perceive a 'brain drain' as the root cause regarding the lack of development in Bulgaria simply miss the point. Perhaps we should say they choose to miss the point. . . A democratic debate regarding emigration is really about wages, not skills. The term 'brain drain' is highly misleading because the image created is one of lack of opportunity as opposed to remuneration. (2003: 35)

The authors point to the 'high turnover rate' for Bulgarians going to Greece as evidence of the use of short stays for salary augmentation. Chompalov also hints at the 'politics' of the debate, referring to figures released by the Bulgarian government on the extent of the brain drain as inflated and 'undoubtedly false' (2000: 3).

Increasing Incentives to Study Science: The 'Beneficial Brain Drain Effect'

The cases discussed above focus both on the personal mobility of more senior scientists and their doctoral researchers. Georgieva concludes her survey of Bulgarian research institutions with the finding that, 'almost every higher education institution is experiencing difficulty in recruiting doctoral students and bringing them through to the conclusion of the degree' (2004: 365). This does not seem to be the case in Poland, which, as we have seen, has experienced a marked increase in doctoral registrations (Dabrowa-Szefler, 2004).

Interviews with academics in the university sector in Poland and Bulgaria also indicated that the opportunities associated with mobility had a motivational impact on younger students, encouraging a greater take up of undergraduate science courses and progression into postgraduate research. The general decline in recent years in the transition from school into science degrees in both Poland and Bulgaria reflects the declining attractiveness of science careers in general across Europe (Gotzfried, 2005). Stark argues that developing countries gain more from migration than they lose via brain drain as migration increases the incentive of individuals to invest in their education. He concludes that:

> migration is conducive to the formation of human capital. Thus, we cast migra-
> tion as a harbinger of human capital gain, not as the culprit of human capital
> drain. . . The gains from migration to the home country accrue neither from
> migrant's remittances nor from migrant's return home with amplified skills . . .
> but from this effect on incentives to human capital formation. (Stark, 2004: 16)

Although Gamlen finds little evidence of the 'beneficial brain drain effect' in his work in the New Zealand context (2005: 18) our fieldwork in Poland and Bulgaria would lend some support to the idea suggesting a further positive, if unintended, impact of mobility on scientific potential in the sending countries. Many respondents talked of how the opportunities for mobility associated with science careers, were beginning to increase the attractiveness of science to students at undergraduate and doctoral level. Although, of course, some of these students will ultimately realize their ambitions and emigrate, this process generates the potential for scientific renaissance and the future generation of scientists. Dimitar sums up the thoughts of many scientists not only in relation to their own careers but also the incentives for younger undergraduates: 'If I couldn't see the opportunity to travel I wouldn't go for a science career because it is not changing at all'. Kicinger (2005) notes increasing trend for undergraduates in Poland to study social sciences rather than natural sciences – a pattern also evident in Bulgaria

(Slantcheva, 2003). To the extent that natural sciences might be associated with increased opportunities for mobility and career advancement, this might go some way to reverse this trend.

Katseli et al. refer to the potential for significant 'productivity increases' to be associated with moderate levels of emigration, 'if the improved prospects associated with migration induce non-migrants to invest in education and skills accumulation in expectation of better future prospects abroad'. They predict that such positive outcomes are possible 'under the presumption that not all skilled migrants will actually migrate and that access to education and training is feasible' (2006a: 26). Arguably such a situation exists in both Bulgaria and Poland (Gächter, 2002). Evidence of the recent 'educational breakthrough' referred to above to some extent reflects the kind of 'beneficial brain gain' effect partly stimulated by perceived opportunities for migration.[13]

Remittances and Development

In the context of scientific migration from the third world, Abella argues that concerns about the effects of highly skilled migration have been 'overblown' in that they neglect 'the substantial impact of migrants' incomes and investments in their home countries' (2004). The findings of a recent UK government report would support this assertion to some extent. According to this study, about 50 per cent of respondents were sending money home and many were remitting 'a sizeable proportion' of their salary. The scientific group in their sample were, however, found to be sending the lowest amounts partly due to their lower wages and relatively young age (DTI, 2002: 63). The specific issue of remittances and the extent to which this form of mobility (of financial capital) can mitigate the losses of human capital associated with scientific emigration was not specifically addressed in our previous studies and did not emerge as a salient factor in the interviews. Arguably, these issues are more significant in the context of the new Member States. While evidence of remittances may indicate an important financial return to the economies of the sending regions (and families) this is unlikely to have a direct impact on science in those regions, however, and in that sense does not dampen concerns about balanced growth in the European research area. While Williams et al. argue that this is the only measurable dimension of mobility and acknowledge the significant value of remittances and their contribution to 'well-being' they suggest that 'financial capital has limited impact on uneven development' because it is 'returned to conspicuous consumption' and is rarely used as venture capital or as a means of transforming production structures (2004: 38). Sretenova makes a similar point in the Bulgarian context, arguing that flows of remittances are largely unrecorded (many will

not go through the formal banking system so to that extent they defy measurement) and, even if large in financial terms, will have 'no strategic
significance for the home country as the individuals who return home do not
become agents of modernisation, their goal is to guarantee themselves a relatively safe well-being and material situation'. The money is not used in the
science sector partly because of the 'lack of conditions for their implementation in the homeland; inadequate facilities often do not allow further research
investigations in the same field' (2003: 3). Rangelova and Vladimirova similarly argue that any such money transfers are directed primarily at consumption with little direct effect on economic growth. If anything, they may have
an inflationary effect (2004: 26).

Korys, on the other hand, points to the 'significance' of financial remittances that not only mitigate the negative effects of systemic transformation at the level of individual households but also play an important role in
economies through stimulating real estate and start-up businesses (2003:
50). Research in other contexts also showed how such remittances, from
Philippino domestic workers in the UK, were used primarily to support the
education of children in the home country (Phizacklea, 2000). Okólski also
draws attention to the use of remittances to support children's education in
Poland (2006: 32). The interviews with migrant scientists suggest that the
education of children is an important factor shaping the migration decisions of scientists (an issue discussed in Chapter 5). These financial flows
may have an indirect but important impact on the future science base of the
countries concerned, either supporting and channelling forms of 'youth
drain' and/or the training of the next generation. It may be interesting to
consider the ways in which such resources are used by migrant scientists,
not least in terms of underwriting the costs of their children's education
and perhaps encouraging their subsequent mobility and career progression.

The interviews with Bulgarian and Polish scientists included some questions about remittances. In practice, few scientists answered these questions
in any detail and many were slightly awkward or embarrassed about this
shift in the discussion. The overall impression gained was that very few of
the scientists based in the receiving countries were remitting significant or
regular payments. In the few cases where respondents did talk about
sending money back home this was generally fairly small amounts, usually
in response to specific needs. Several scientists referred to the very meagre
pensions received in Bulgaria (with one stating that his mother received
only £40 per month) and said that they on occasion supplemented this. The
only person who spoke of regular remittances said these were for her
mother who was retired as 'medically unfit' to work; she sent £50 a month
home. Another spoke of the costs of medicines and health care and said
they occasionally covered these costs.

Quite a few respondents said there was no need to send money back as their families were managing adequately. Several added to this that remittances were much more of an issue for less skilled (or working class) families or, conversely, for the very rich who had more surplus income. Vladimir's comment is typical:

> Mostly the people who work abroad send money back. A large part of the Bulgarian national product comes from abroad now. There is some truth in that but it depends who you are and what background you come from. Most of the people I know as a scientist come from a middle-class background where their relatives will never be in a very desperate position. They had a profession and savings so they are not in that desperation level. It's more about the people in lower classes who don't have much skills and when they emigrate to Spain they go there picking olives or cleaning dishes or in the building industry or whatever so their relatives need money for survival. My relatives, although they don't live a very comfortable life, they don't want any money but that doesn't exclude the option that I'm ready to do it and I have this provision made if I need to do it.

Asked about whether remittances are usual among scientists, Piotr replies that this is more true of 'lower-income families' not scientists. He then goes on to talk about the continued practice in some occupational groups to work intensively abroad for a number of years in order to save money, return and 'set themselves up': 'I think there is still a big market, a big number of people who go especially to America despite Poland joining the EC. They go for one year or two working as construction workers and bring back $100 000 and have their future fixed'.

Although income differentials were high in relative terms, many of our sample were not earning high salaries and were living in some of the most expensive areas (especially in the UK) and admitted that, as Jerzy put it, 'I don't have any money!' Rumiana echoes his comments: 'Yes, I read some Bulgarian articles that say that the investment from that sort of people back to Bulgaria is [a substantial proportion of GDP] but I don't think that's with the scientific community. Our wages are not enough to do a big investment. No, living in Cambridgeshire is expensive enough!'

Our findings would tend to support other research that suggests an inverse relationship between educational levels and the size of remittance flows (Gamlen, 2005; Séguin et al., 2006a; Fajnzylber and Lopez, 2007). Although some individuals were remitting funds to meet specific health care needs or to invest in property, there was little if any evidence that these flows were of any significance in terms of economic development or scientific capacity-building. That said, it was apparent that many of the shorter-term 'shuttle' moves were motivated primarily by the need to supplement local income in order to support families, although these flows of income are not remittances as such. This supports Katseli et al.'s assertion that, 'temporary migration tends to be more conducive to higher remittance flows, although once again they suggest that lower-income groups exhibit a greater propensity to remit (2006a: 4).

CONCLUSIONS

This chapter has discussed a wide range of factors shaping the impact of highly skilled, scientific mobility. All of these need to be taken into account and 'balanced' in order to support an holistic and contextualized appraisal. Large flows of people who have been educated in the home country do represent a significant loss in investment. However, most of our respondents were the beneficiaries of continued, often more specialized, investment abroad. Whilst investment in R&D is critical to the emergence of a competitive knowledge economy, it is less clear that migration, in itself, restricts regeneration. Evidence suggest that losses of scientists may damage the stock of human capital (both in a strictly scientific sense but also in terms of their wider role as 'change agents'). However, it is also clear that the alternative to migration is often not conducive to effective deployment of human capital. A far greater number of skilled scientists exit the sector to remain in their home countries but work in another capacity and are often de-skilled in the process. Others attempt to combine scientific research with other employment, restricting their ability to work productively and achieve an acceptable balance in their lives. Migration, in many cases, offers an opportunity for the country to 'store' its brains abroad and benefit, eventually, from the investment made in them there. The opportunities associated with international mobility are often the primary means of attracting young people into and retaining more senior people in science research in the sending countries; mobility in many ways is the life-blood of science in Poland and Bulgaria. Short stays are often a means of providing scientists with access to critical resources, enabling them to both lift themselves and their families into an acceptable standard of living and work effectively and productively.

We have alluded to the importance of understanding the political context within which debates about brain drain are situated. Various authors have hinted that the brain drain debate, in the sending countries, might be distorted by political objectives operating as a form of 'smoke screen', concealing the true causes of scientific decline. Gächter concludes that:

> Bulgaria has not been suffering a decline in national development potential from emigration . . . 'brain drain' is far too big a word to describe what is happening. There has been a trickle of highly qualified emigrants, no more and even cumulatively it is not big enough to make any difference at all. If there is a science

problem for the nation, it is excessively low wages necessitating non-science work on the side which eats into time devoted to research, and, second, the totally inadequate funding of research facilities. (2002: 53)

Ghodsee goes a step further. On the basis of extensive discourse analysis, she argues that political and economic interests have led Bulgarians to 'construct a truth about "brain drain" both in terms of the characterisation of émigrés and the impact of their emigration' (2002: 2).[14] The lack of adequate data has played an important role in allowing 'the government and media considerable leeway in telling their stories about brain drain' (ibid.: 2). Echoing the sentiments of Gächter, Ghodsee suggests that, 'constant attention to the brain drain and the emigration of the young allows the media and politicians to externalise the blame for a deteriorating standard of living' (ibid.: 3). It is interesting to note that Georgieva's summary of the eight principal factors relating to brain drain in Bulgaria are all connected with the quality of the research environment, its resource base, infrastructure, salaries and the lack of controls on 'academic honesty', which together render research careers unattractive and 'intolerable' and result in a haemorrhaging of human capital into other sectors. There is no reference here to the 'pull' of receiving countries. Jalowiecki and Gorzelak advocate the use of the term brain 'escape' in preference to 'drain' as this 'refers more precisely to migrant individuals who leave their country due to difficult living conditions or unsatisfactory professional prospects frequently quoted by scientists as the crucial motivating factor' (2004: 299). We leave the final word to one of our respondents (Eugenia):

> I frankly get so annoyed at the state in Bulgaria – not the country. I'm so not in love with the state as a state. I don't think it really cares in the slightest or not in any way that I can understand or feel. You only get what you ask for and if the state doesn't do anything then it's down to the individual to sort out their personal goals.

NOTES

1. *The Times* 15 September 2006 'Britons spurning postgrad research' reports on a new report by Universities UK, *The Patterns of Higher Education Institutions in the UK.*
2. The sustainability of this growth is questioned in a recent news article in the *Times Higher Education Supplement* (30 March 2007, 10), which reports that 'a third of Poland's 300 private higher education institutions face closure as young Poles choose to study outside Poland'.
3. Of the total complement of 28 500 academic and research workers, some 2706 emigrated mainly in technical sciences (791), medical sciences (441), biological sciences (292) and physics (224).

4. Slantcheva notes the 'significant decrease' in the number of people engaged in research in Bulgaria since 1989, reflecting a marked decline in the proportion of the national budget allocated to higher education from 3.2 per cent in 1992 to 0.9 per cent in 1997 (2003: 427).

5. Ghodsee explains how the 'over-production of IT specialists in Bulgaria reflects the country's role as a COMECON country profiled to design the computer systems for the Soviet space and defence programmes' (2002: 3).

6. Gamlen, for example, contends that an element of negative selection takes place resulting in 'failed' migrants returning home (2005: 18).

7. In principle it lies in contravention of EU law in relation to age discrimination (Article 13 EC implemented via Council Directive 2000/78 establishing a general framework for equal treatment in employment and occupation). The European Commission has recently removed reference to age criteria in its own fellowship schemes.

8. The Polish Academy of Sciences (PAN) describes itself as a 'learned society acting through an elected corporation of top scholars and research organisations' and a 'major scientific advisory body'. Members are elected by a general assembly and membership 'is held for life'. In practice this results in an ageing complement of senior scientists. (http://www.pan.pl cited in Kicinger, 2005: 10).

9. Our sample was confined to those who were in research positions. This meant that we did not sample people who had left research.

10. The role of networks is discussed in Chapter 6.

11. The tendency of migrant scientists to work extensive hours in the host country is discussed in Chapter 7.

12. Respondent pseudonyms are not stated in cases where preservation of anonymity is critical. Other examples are given in the discussion on financial determinants of migration decisions in Chapter 3.

13. The article referred to in note 2 above claims that the recent general decline in student enrolments in Poland is less evident in courses that offer 'extensive opportunities for study abroad within existing programmes'. This supports the arguments underpinning the beneficial brain gain effect.

14. The authors also argue that governments in the receiving countries have constructed parallel truths characterizing Bulgarian migrants as unskilled and often undesirable.

9. Summary, conclusions and policy implications

The MOBEX research has sought to understand the processes shaping highly skilled, scientific, mobility. It has considered three related dimensions of 'impact'; first on scientists as individuals or members of families; second, on the countries concerned and finally, on what it means for Europe and the success of the European Research Area. This concluding chapter summarizes some of the key findings before considering some policy implications.

PATTERNS OF SCIENTIFIC MOBILITY

Analysis of patterns of mobility in the MOBEX sample indicate an increase in the level of short-term circulation both prior to longer mobility episodes and following returns. The majority of respondents in our return sample (those based in Poland and Bulgaria) were using the mechanism of repeated short stays to achieve a kind of work–life balance and sustain their scientific productivity and well-being. Even the most apparently 'settled' respondents in the host countries often exhibited a form of 'shuttle return mobility' spending repeated short stays in their home country. This circulation indicates a strong potential for return and associated collaboration and knowledge transfer should the conditions exist to support the effective reintegration and retention of scientists.

The short-term nature of mobility to some extent reflects the nature of employment positions available in the host countries. 'Foreign' researchers typically occupy temporary, early-career, positions even when they held more senior positions prior to moving. There was little evidence of direct recruitment of established 'research stars' from Bulgaria and Poland into the receiving countries although quite senior researchers are being recruited into early-career positions.

Undergraduate and doctoral mobility amongst Polish and Bulgarian researchers was somewhat restricted, prior to accession, mainly due to financial issues. However, there are signs that this will increase in the near future, with the UK emerging as an increasingly popular destination.

MIGRATION PROCESSES: MOTIVATIONS AND TRIGGERS – PROFESSIONAL FACTORS

Mobility is rarely, if ever, the result of a single 'decision' but rather an ongoing reflexive and adaptive negotiation responding to a wide range of shifting stimuli over time and place. Although many scientists do make conscious and planned 'decisions', it is important to recognize the role that serendipity or 'chance' plays in influencing moves and careers. Mobility is often triggered by unplanned, often fortuitous, events. Equally, where a strong migration motivation and careful plans exist, the 'trigger' actioning these may be absent.

The 'expectation of mobility' in science careers is supported by a perception that 'international experience' is inherently valuable. Moreover, mobility is often seen as a tool for selecting the most 'able' candidates. Mobility increases exposure to new skills, ideas and ways of working and, as such, forms a critical means of facilitating the transfer of knowledge. The importance of the 'expectation of mobility' and international experience to career progression in scientific research has led to the characterization of scientists as 'knowledge' rather than 'economic' migrants.

In practical terms this manifests itself in the 'pulling power' of established and resource-rich centres of excellence, which contain both the know-how and, critically, the know-who that will enhance scientific productivity and individual career progression. These kinds of stimuli were certainly evident amongst our sample of scientists. Some individuals developed a conscious strategy focused on building up their human and social capital through mobility in order to increase their scientific productivity and long-term employability security.

Economic factors played a critical role in the majority of cases, however, with moves shaped by concerns around absolute or relative economic circumstances. In some situations scientists faced the prospect of no wages (or employment in other sectors), were struggling with wages that were incapable of sustaining adequate basic living standards (in the absence of 'moonlighting') or wage differentials that supported a significantly higher quality of life.

In addition to these concerns around personal income and well-being, mobility was often the only means of accessing the physical resources that enabled scientists to function effectively in experimental research. It was not so much the desire to access optimal facilities but to have access to basic chemicals and equipment and funding for travel. These concerns do not always lead to longer-term moves. Many scientists in Poland and Bulgaria were using short-stay mobility as a transnational strategy, enabling them to work effectively in situ.

The volume of 'early-career' entry positions in the UK and Germany coupled with a powerful perception of transparent and meritocratic recruitment, at least in comparison with the situation in Poland and Bulgaria, is a major factor motivating and directing moves. Scientists are both attracted by evidence of objective employment and repelled by experiences of patronage and corruption. This is an important factor facilitating outward moves and also restricting return as opportunities are often seen to 'close' behind them.

Notions of *employability* security are becoming increasingly popular in discussions about highly skilled mobility. However, the stimulus of *employment* security (having a permanent contract) remains evident. Its effect can be seen most acutely in relation to the impact of retained positions in Poland and Bulgaria. The ability to move for quite long periods without relinquishing a secure and high status, albeit low paid, position in the sending country has an important 'anchoring' effect, increasing return potential and connectedness.

As scientists move they accrue 'migration capital'. Moves made early in a career and in relatively protected, 'risk-delimited' contexts, increase the appetite for and confidence to move again. They also generate networks and contacts. This increases the probability of re-migration following return often to the same location.

The characterization of scientists as 'knowledge migrants', at least in the context of Bulgaria and Poland, amounts to an inaccurate and misleading over-simplification. These scientists are generally more 'pushed' by economic necessity than 'pulled' by the 'lure' of knowledge per se.

FAMILY MATTERS: PARTNERING AND PARENTING

Our findings emphasize the impact that personal and family relationships and obligations have on migration behaviour. Personal relationships both generate resistance to the 'pull' of economic considerations or, in other contexts, lubricate mobility.

Although single, young, people show a higher propensity to be mobile, most of our sample were partnered even at early-career stage. The overwhelming majority of partnered mobile scientists will be in dual career situations and most of these will have partners who are also trying to develop a career in scientific research.

The presence of a partner can dampen mobility; both in the initial stages, preventing people becoming mobile at all and, at later stages, in their life-course and career. This is especially true for women. Where partnering dampens mobility, it is likely to have a negative effect on career development, limiting scientists' ability to work effectively and productively and, in some cases encouraging 'brain freeze' or 'stagnation'. This situation may be to the detriment of the sending regions to the extent that they are unable to profit from the foreign investment arising as a result of mobility.

On the other hand, the presence of partners in the home country may have an 'anchoring effect', either discouraging mobility or shaping the form that it takes. In other cases, migrant scientists either move with, are joined by or form new relationships in the host country. The effect of post-migration partnering depends on a complex array of factors. Where partnerships form with host nationals there is a greater likelihood that the couple will eventually 'settle' in that location. The prospects of return decline markedly where both partners manage to secure proximate and acceptable employment in the host country and, in particular, where children are present.

The pressure on same-national couples to return or move elsewhere is high where one member of the dual career partnership experiences significant difficulties in achieving professional reintegration in the host state. This situation manifests itself in a level of initial 'de-skilling' amongst partners. In the majority of cases, however, this experience was often connected to language skills and was relatively short-lived and partners did manage to re-establish themselves in the host state, increasing the propensity to 'settle' at least for a critical part of their productive working lives. The findings emphasize the importance of recognizing the value of the human capital that is embodied in the partners of highly skilled migrants both in terms of the gains to receiving regions and the losses to the sending countries.

The presence of children has an important effect on scientific mobility. Three key concerns emerged: the challenges of organizing child care in a migration context; the influence of children's educational opportunity on decision-making and the effect of children's social integration on subsequent mobility.

Child care responsibilities generally dampen mobility, effectively 'locking people into spaces' either in the home or receiving country. Academic scientists moving on relatively low wages and with little corporate support often express serious concerns around the provision and cost of child care in the host countries. The culture of long and unpredictable working hours coupled with ongoing work-related travel (often abroad) make this a particularly difficult problem for scientists to manage.

Strategies included the tolerance of separation (involving both parents or of siblings) perhaps using grandparents to provide care and 'fertility' solutions (postponing parenthood, reducing the number of children or deciding not to have children at all).

Younger, pre-school or primary-aged children, are 'easier' to move and parents often felt that their children benefited from mobility at this stage. Concerned about the economic and political situation at home and recognizing the value of educational opportunities, reputational capital and language skills, respondents often placed a premium on mobility for their children, increasing the incentives to move.

Children's educational circumstances in the post-migration period frequently trigger a re-evaluation process, which often reconfigures family relationships and location decisions quite significantly. Having older (teenage) children in the family increases the propensity to remain for a longer period and restricts return. In such circumstances parents often become 'tied stayers.'

For the reasons given above, it is not clear to us that scientific mobility is as selective a process as conventional wisdom/popular perceptions infer. The ability to respond to the existence of opportunities abroad is shaped by a wide range of factors and only partially reflects scientific talent or potential. Personal circumstances, including partners and family ties, a commitment to the home country or simply a desire not to be mobile, mediate any direct relationship between mobility and scientific excellence. Respondents who exhibited the highest level of circulation often had no partners or children.

THE ROLE OF NETWORKS AND CONNECTIONS IN SHAPING MIGRATION PROCESSES AND EFFECTS

The research examined the kinds of contacts that exist within 'traditional diasporic', 'scientific diasporic' and 'international scientific' communities and examined the factors shaping the growth and effectiveness of these connections.

Whilst 'traditional diasporic' connections linking expatriates together in geographical proximity in the host countries do exist in some cases, and may be important to settlement and personal lives, these kinds of contacts are not particularly strong or significant to the professional lives of mobile scientists.

Links with other scientists from their home country through the 'scientific diaspora' are more prevalent and influential. It is useful to distinguish links formed with expatriates in the host countries from those retained or established with scientists in the sending countries. The former are less developed and less 'active' than the latter, often playing more of a social role. There was some evidence of a renewed interest in establishing and reinvigorating links with the scientific diaspora but it was not clear that these networks currently played a major role in shaping migration patterns or 'reverse' knowledge transfer.

Connections with scientists in their home country shape the propensity to return. Without established and carefully nurtured 'anchors' with scientists in the sending regions, scientific labour markets can become more or less impenetrable to potential returnees. Where such networks exist, and particularly where the contact point in the sending country is highly established and active, they have strong potential to shape both return moves and support reverse knowledge transfer (flows of knowledge in the absence of physical moves or between physical moves). These contacts are primarily individual or informal and do not link up 'communities' as such.

Expatriate networks play a major role in stimulating and channelling initial *outward* migrations. They work most effectively when linked into broader 'international scientific' networks. Connections achieved through the social capital of supervisors play a particularly influential role. The interface of these connections between the scientific diaspora and the wider international scientific community has the greatest impact on migration and represents the greatest potential for effective knowledge transfer.

For the majority of scientists, networks based on the science of what they do and not their national ties are perceived as both more legitimate and more effective. Moving through these 'international scientific' networks does facilitate mobility but in a less spatially defined way, with scientists moving across international space.

The opportunity exists for a more positive 'back-flow' of knowledge and expertise. Nevertheless, serious barriers restrict its effective transmission. The dislocation of networks through continued emigration, retirement and scientific decline restricts the potential to retain active links.

For connections to function as an effective conduit for knowledge there must be an active and willing agent in the sending country. In many cases this agent will be someone who has 'opted' to move on a shuttle basis rather than for longer periods as this form of mobility enables them to function at an international level.

The practice of permitting scientists to retain unpaid positions in the home country during their stays abroad has an important networking effect in some cases, encouraging them to maintain live connections with their home country and institution.

Analysis of the findings on networks has encouraged us to reconsider the relationship between seniority and brain drain. Although 'losses' of more senior and established scientists, on the face of it, might be predicted to have a more serious impact, not least because of the level of investment that the sending country has made in these individuals, the potential for reverse knowledge transfer in such cases is much higher. Early-career scientists generally have fewer or less effective networks. Their migration may, in some respects, imply a more permanent and unilateral loss of knowledge and expertise. More established and senior expatriates are more likely to have active links with scientists in their home country.

In the *European context*, Bulgarian and Polish scientists are increasingly able to communicate and, importantly, conduct research at a distance. Ultimately, harnessing the potential of the scientific diaspora and inter-national research community demands the existence of a critical mass of powerful and willing anchors in the form of human and physical resources in the home country.

ASSESSING IMPACT: THE EXPERIENCES OF 'RECEIVING' COUNTRIES

The received wisdom, implicit in the 'brain drain' debate, suggests that host countries are the net beneficiaries of highly skilled migration, capable of 'skimming' the cream of employees in competitive global markets. It is clear from the findings that international recruitment is playing a major role in mitigating the problems associated with the declining transition of 'home-grown' young people into scientific study and research and sustaining scientific capacity particularly at doctoral and post-doctoral level.

Assessing the relationship between mobility and quality is highly prob-lematic. Internationalization in itself is not and should not be taken as an indicator of quality. That said, Bulgaria and Poland present significant opportunities for the host countries in terms of scientific recruitment. The strong reputation in the natural sciences coupled with high transition rates and long and rigorous training programmes generates a valuable pool of potential recruits.

Most respondents felt that EU enlargement would make relatively little difference to recruitment at post-doctoral level and upwards although it is expected to increase undergraduate and postgraduate student flows significantly. The rules governing employment of 'foreign' researchers prior to accession were believed to support a highly competitive situation in which non-EU nationals had to out-perform EU applicants. On that basis, respondents felt that the 'best' scientists were already able to move and deregulation might, if anything, reduce quality.

Respondents expressed serious concerns about transition and progres-sion into more senior positions in the host countries from the perspective of achieving employment security and realizing their potential as scientists. In some cases this was linked to a perception of employment discrimina-tion. In practice it is likely to reflect the vagaries of the research systems in the host countries, which generate a large pool of highly skilled post-doctoral researchers in insecure and poorly remunerated, 'cinderella' positions. This situation stands in marked contrast to systems in Poland and Bulgaria, which generally deliver a much higher degree of security albeit at very low pay.

Foreign researchers often have little awareness of scientific labour markets and career progression systems in the host countries. The association of the UK and Germany with open labour markets and 'fair' recruitment (penetrability) is arguably as much linked to the growth of insecure, contract research, positions as the quality of recruitment processes per se. Progression into established academic positions is governed by more complex rules and often a wider range of skills. This situation is subtly different from progression systems in their home countries and especially in the academies of science.

Our research has brought to light the need for a more open and critical discussion about sustainability and risk management in the context of human capital in the receiving countries. A critical question is whether a relationship exists between internationalization and the development of 'home-grown' human capital. Research at national and European level raises serious concerns about the attractiveness of research careers, resulting in declining transition rates. The continued ability to recruit from abroad arguably reduces the urgency to respond to these fundamental concerns threatening the sustainability of science. If early-career positions are 'appealing' to foreign researchers there is less need to ensure that they are appealing to home-grown researchers. If host countries can attract senior and experienced researchers from abroad into such positions, can labour markets be said to be genuinely 'open' and equitable with sustainable career progression?

Where reliance on international recruitment reaches the levels witnessed in the UK and elsewhere, it is important to begin to plan more strategically for a sustainable workforce. In the words of Hatakenaka, 'The future of internationalism is too important to be shaped as a series of unintended consequences of miscellaneous policies or market forces' (2004: 6).

THE EXPERIENCES OF 'SENDING' COUNTRIES

Sustainability is more commonly considered in the context of sending regions and features in many discussions around highly skilled migration and the phenomenon of 'brain drain'. The sending countries have lost significant numbers of scientists since the 1990s. However, much of this loss occurred during the initial post-Communist 'transition period' and appears to have levelled off. A significant proportion of losses were connected to the sudden and marked decline in scientific positions, with many scientists moving to other sectors as well as abroad.

The accounts of our respondents suggest that the sending countries have experienced a significant decline in scientific *potential* as a result of international and intersectoral 'losses' (as much as established scientists) and that the mid-career generation is often thin on the ground, with important implications for the training of researchers in future. There is also a sense that migration is selective in its effects, resulting in the losses of many high-quality and enthusiastic researchers often in specific disciplines and sub-disciplines. Demographic trends including marked declines in fertility and increasing emigration of young people at or before undergraduate level (the 'youth drain') are of growing concern. The research supports Meyer et al.'s conclusion that flows are largely unidirectional and go from 'haemophiliac' regions to more competitive places (2001: 309). Although Bulgarian and Polish scientists choose a range of destinations, very few nationals of the host countries spend time working in labs in Poland and Bulgaria. To the (still limited) extent that foreign scientists are beginning to study and work in Poland and Bulgaria they are likely to come from 'weaker' regions.

While the general view is that significant levels of outward mobility pose a serious threat to science infrastructures and competitiveness, the research also indicates potential mitigating factors and positive returns.

Large flows of people who have been educated in the home country do represent a significant loss in investment. However, most respondents were the beneficiaries of continued, often more specialized, investment abroad.

Whilst investment in R&D is critical to the emergence of a competitive knowledge economy, it is less clear that migration, in itself, restricts regeneration. The alternative to migration is often not the effective deployment of human capital. A far greater number of skilled scientists exit the sector to remain in their home countries but work in another capacity and are often de-skilled in the process. Others attempt to combine scientific research with other employment, restricting their ability to work productively and achieve an acceptable balance in their lives.

Mobility, in many respects, is the lifeblood of science in Poland and Bulgaria. Mobility and international connections offer opportunities for the sending country to enrich their 'brains' abroad and benefit, eventually, from the investment made in them there. The opportunities associated with international mobility are often the primary means of attracting young people into and retaining more senior people in science research. Short-term moves provide a means of increasing scientists' access to critical resources, enabling them to both lift themselves and their families into an acceptable standard of living and work effectively and productively.

The book opened with a discussion of the tensions inherent in European Union research policy. On the one hand, the commitment to the freedom of movement of European citizens and individual equity in employment opportunity lies at the heart of European integration. On the other, concerns around the consequences of free and open labour markets, in the context of significant persistent diversity in economic capacity between the Member States, raise questions about balanced growth and regional equality.

Historically the 'brain drain' debate has tended to focus on movements of highly skilled people either from Europe to the United States or, more recently, from developing countries into Europe (and the developed world more generally). In recent years, greater attention has been paid to East–West flows in the European context and the impact of these on sending nations. The accession of some of these countries into the European Union implies a more complex analysis. Indeed, it has been argued that analysis of these flows must now be considered as a dimension of 'internal' or 'interregional' migration within the European Union rather than international migration between individual nation states. Processes, such as scientific clustering and specialization and the mobility that goes with these, which may appear to be detrimental to individual nation states may augment the competitiveness of the EU as a whole. Nevertheless, the persistence and arguably the exacerbation of regional equalities that form the necessary 'exhaust' of these policies raises difficult political questions for the European Union. One 'approach' developed in the context of highly skilled migration from developing countries is to attempt to restrict mobility or at least active recruitment campaigns on the part of host countries through the introduction of 'ethical' recruitment policies.

These policies are not appropriate within the EU and would generate new forms of opposition particularly in the political climate of the new Member States in Central and Eastern Europe. Any measures that could be interpreted as restricting the access of European Citizens from opportunities to move and work in other Member States – or restricting the right of employers to advertise positions and seek to recruit from the wider European labour market, would be seen as fundamentally discriminatory. This view was expressed unequivocally by the respondents in our study.

The research presents evidence of a high degree of circulation and connectedness and, importantly, an even greater propensity for this pattern of behaviour should conditions exist to support it. Very many respondents expressed a willingness and desire to increase their connections with their home country and spend more time working in or working with scientists there. In many respects the significance of place of residence is declining, at least in terms of scientific productivity, as new opportunities emerge, supporting distance-working, circulation and international collaboration.

Short stays provide opportunities for networking, experimental work, collaboration and project-building. They also increase the opportunity for people who, for personal reasons, are unable or unwilling to make longer-term moves. This includes both scientists 'stuck' in the sending regions unable to work, as productively as they might, and scientists in the receiving countries who might profit from short stays in Poland and Bulgaria.

Scientists in the sending countries would also benefit substantially from an increase in the level of funding provided to support foreign visits, enabling them to attend conferences abroad and also to organize seminars and conferences in their home institutions. Increasing this kind of activity is relatively inexpensive and has the potential to increase the attractiveness of positions and scientific productivity.

Funding bodies at national and European level might usefully consider the value of shifting the emphasis from longer fellowships in order to increase the availability of funding for shorter stays and shuttle moves.

An important factor emerging from the study concerned the 'quality' and penetrability of national labour markets. Scientists are attracted by objective recruitment systems. The continued influence of patronage and 'closed' forms of recruitment and progression constitute a powerful factor motivating people to leave (and restricting entry and return).

Sending countries need to address their approaches to recruitment and employment opportunity and develop more transparent and merit-based systems in compliance with European Union employment law. In so doing they need to encourage both their own expatriates and foreign researchers to spend time in their institutions.

Despite the massive decline in positions post-transition, significant over-supply continues to exist in some institutions in Poland and Bulgaria, reducing efficiency and restricting the availability of new opportunities for early-career researchers. In particular, attention needs to be paid to perfor-mance management and to the ageing of academic staff and effective retire-ment policies brought into play (in compliance with recent EU legislation designed to prevent discrimination on the grounds of age).

The role and value of retained positions in the home countries raises a number of interesting questions. On the one hand, it is clear that they provide important 'anchors' to the home country, increasing the potential for physical return, collaboration and knowledge transfer. However, they also contribute to the phenomenon of 'position-blocking' especially when positions are retained for many years and home institutions are either unprepared or unable to replace staff at the appropriate level (generating new opportunities and safeguarding the quality of teaching and research).

The importance of retained positions to Bulgarian and Polish scientists is increased by the dominance of insecure, fixed-term, employment in the host countries. The experience of contractual insecurity and uncertainty over the prospects of securing permanent positions in the host countries increases circulation. In one respect this could be considered a positive factor, increasing the propensity to return. On the other hand, it also generates retention problems in the host countries and raises questions about whether the scientific potential that host countries invest in is utilized optimally.

The effect of recent European legislation designed to regulate the abuse of fixed-term contracts remains to be seen. Although the legislation only came into effect in the UK in July 2006, it appears to be having a fairly marked impact on the proportion of fixed-term employment in the university sector although its full effect on externally funded research-only posts remain unclear.

Our research supports the conclusion that the concepts of 'brain drain' or 'brain gain' are far too simplistic to capture the dynamics of highly skilled, scientific, mobility. There is not a 'migration' as such but an ongoing flux and circulation, with scientists engaging in dynamic and diverse ways with other individuals and institutions on an international basis. In some cases or for certain periods of time, the opportunities available might restrict this activity to forms of electronic or 'virtual' connections or occasional conference attendances, whilst in others, scientists may work in close collaboration with a particular lab abroad or spend their whole lives relocating across geographical space. Internationalization is a continuum and its specific manifestation reflects a range of factors. Life-course considerations and personal concerns may modify the level of engagement over time, perhaps moving from a lengthy period abroad at early-career level, followed by return and limited travel coupled with remote forms of communication and collaboration, and eventually a resumption of more active mobility before retiring in the home country. The nature of their scientific project and the importance of mobility and collaboration to its success is also a critical factor. In some fields or for certain periods of activity, scientists can work well on a remote basis. In others, they need to access equipment and know-how critical to their research.

One of the most important factors remains the issue of resources, including personal financial well-being (an acceptable salary and standard of living) and the resources necessary to support scientific productivity and excellence. The economic situation in the sending countries, and Bulgaria in particular, and the serious lack of resources lies at the heart of the 'problem'. This is not simply a matter of economics, however, but also of politics and the specific priority attached to scientific investment. Both Poland and Bulgaria have experienced a marked and continued decline in the proportion of GDP allocated to science.

The positioning of individual scientists on the continuum of internationalization at any point in time reflects the interplay of these diverse factors and determines the potential gains and losses both to themselves and to the countries concerned. If the resource framework fosters engagement with the home country it will take place in one form or another. In some cases scientists will be motivated to remain resident and employed in their home country through opportunities to travel and collaborate with researchers abroad. In others, for various reasons, they may decide to locate their families abroad and take residence there, for a time at least but use the resources available to engage actively with colleagues in their home countries, enriching scientific exchange and output in both locations.

The research emphasizes the importance of understanding the political context within which debates about brain drain are situated. Various authors have hinted that the brain drain debate, in the sending countries, might be distorted by political objectives operating as a form of 'smoke screen' concealing the underlying causes of scientific decline. As Eugenia, a Polish post-doc in the UK, puts it: 'The problem is not for the individual but for the politicians. They simply have to create a labour market for scientists in Poland otherwise all the scientists will go abroad'.

The European Research Area has increased the opportunities to move to and fro for the purposes of scientific research and access employment opportunities in other Member States. It has also played an important role in funding scientific mobility and fostering the growth of centres of excellence. These activities, in themselves, do not exacerbate forms of 'brain drain': rather they generate new and more fluid resource frameworks and critical opportunities for investment in scientists in the new Member States. The onus lies on the Member States to respond to these developments and develop policies designed to harness this investment and stimulate opportunities for connections and collaboration.

Annex 1 Summary of MOBEX2 methods

PHASE 1: ENLARGEMENT – ANALYSIS OF EU LAW AND POLICY IN RELATION TO TRANSITION

The first phase analysed EU regional policy associated with scientific mobility. This involved a desk-based literature and policy review. Existing measures shaping mobility, such as the Free Person Provisions, the European Research Area and the European Area of Higher Education were re-examined in the context of EU enlargement; in particular, questioning whether the imposition of transitional measures by 'old' Member States would limit mobility from 'new' and 'accession' states.

PHASE 2: NATIONAL-LEVEL LEGAL AND POLICY ANALYSIS

This second stage was conceived to provide context on the socioeconomic and scientific conditions in two existing EU Member States, a new EU Member State and an accession country. Poland and Bulgaria were selected as case studies to highlight some of the differences between science labour markets in Central and Eastern European countries. Both countries had a strong tradition of higher education and scientific research during Communist times. In terms of 'host' countries, the UK and Germany were selected as two of the most popular countries in Europe for mobile researchers to visit (Van de Sande et al., 2005). A full justification for the countries selected is provided in the introductory chapter.

Key informant interviews were completed that focused on science strategy, mobility schemes and policies in relation to the attraction, support, retention and legal status of 'migrant' scientists. This included consultations with representatives from the Wellcome Trust, the Royal Society, Research Councils UK, Department of Strategy and the Development of Science, Ministry of Scientific Research and Information Technology (Poland), a member of the State Committee for Scientific Research (Poland), Conference of Rectors of Academic Schools in Poland,

Chairman of the II Faculty of Biological Sciences (PAN), the German Academic Exchange Service, the Deutsche Forschungs Gemeinschaft (German Research Foundation, DFG), a German regional Ministry for Science and Research, Hochschul-Informations-System GmbH (HIS) and the Centre for Advanced Study (Bulgaria).

PHASE 3: AN E-MAIL/POSTAL QUESTIONNAIRE TO SCIENTISTS IN SENDING AND RECEIVING REGIONS

Using electronic methodologies to conduct surveys has caused some debate in research. Its main advantage is providing an inexpensive, fast channel to contact respondents, particularly useful in comparative work as a way to access people worldwide. This was less of a concern in the MOBEX2 study as the population of highly skilled workers in the scientific and technological labour market routinely have access to e-mail for work purposes. Taking into account differences by country, hard copies of questionnaires were also distributed in scientific departments in Bulgaria. In total, 284 questionnaire responses were received.

PHASE 4: QUALITATIVE INTERVIEWS WITH MOBILE SCIENTISTS, POTENTIAL LEAVERS AND RETURNEES

The final stage of the research was designed to gather a more nuanced picture of mobility processes and decision-making as experienced by individual researchers. In total, 89 semi-structured interviews were made with migrant scientists. After transcription the interviews were analysed using a qualitative software package, N6. Effectively this means that the text is 'indexed' to 'nodes' to thematically group or 'code' concepts.

Annex 2   Respondents' pseudonyms

Prefix P = Interviewees in Poland
Prefix B = Interviewees in Bulgaria
Prefix UK = Interviewees in the UK
Prefix D = Interviewees in Germany

ID	Pseudonym	ID	Pseudonym	ID	Pseudonym
P01	Pawel	UK06	Svetlana	D05	Beata
P02	Ewa	UK07	Andrey	D06	Lech
P03	Sylwia	UK08	Ivanka	D07	Vasil
P04	Dorota	UK09	Fryderyk	D08	Nikolina
P05	Marta	UK10	Krzysztof	D09	Margarita
P06	Stanislaw	UK11	Lucjan	D10	Stanislav
P07	Tomasz	UK12	Eugenia	D11	Agata
P08	Maria	UK13	Magdalena	D12	Alicja
P09	Elzbieta	UK14	Boyko	D13	Ivan
P10	Bronislaw	UK15	Rumiana	D14	Jan
P11	Jacek	UK16	Vladimir	D15	Alexander
P12	Zofia	UK17	Ivaylo	D16	Radka
P13	Agnieszka	UK18	Michal	D17	Božena
P14	Barbara	UK19	Marek	D18	Mariusz
B01	Pepka	UK20	Renata	D19	Violeta
B02	Todorka	UK21	Justyna	D20	Radoslava
B03	Vanya	UK22	Krystyna	D21	Todor
B04	Boris	UK23	Monika	D22	Leszek
B05	Dessislava	UK24	Ania	D23	Maciej
B06	Valentina	UK25	Alina	D24	Viktor
B07	Roumen	UK26	Stefan	D25	Ludwika
B08	Dimitar	UK27	Irina	D26	Wanda
B09	Bogdan	UK28	Andrzej	D27	Adam
B10	Yulian	UK29	Roman	D28	Antoni
B11	Elena	UK30	Piotr	D29	Marcin
UK01	Rada	UK31	Jaroslaw	D30	Jaroslaw
UK02	Jerzy	D01	Kalina	D31	Bartosz
UK03	Teresa	D02	Georgi	D32	Sylwia
UK04	Tzonka	D03	Martyna	D33	Hanna
UK05	Kiril	D04	Janina		

Annex 3   Summaries of further CSLPE[1] projects that have informed the study

MOBEX: MOBILITY AND EXCELLENCE IN THE EUROPEAN RESEARCH AREA

Funder: Economic and Social Research Council, UK (ESRC)
October 2002–October 2003 The 'MOBEX' project funded under the ESRC Science and Society Programme – small grant for work on the mobility of Italian scientists (the MOBEX project)

At EU level, science mobility is seen as essential for the promotion of scientific growth and competitiveness and, more specifically, in promoting its strategy of regional specialization and scientific clustering and the kinds of 'knowledge transfer' this demands. Nevertheless, the EU is also concerned about the issue of inequality both in terms of individual opportunity and also in a regional context. Unchecked these European Research Area (ERA) policies lie in tension with the commitment to 'balanced growth' to the extent that they encourage the relocation of scientists to centres of excellence (typically located in the economically stronger regions), potentially reducing the ability of weaker regions to regenerate. The 'circulation' of scientific talent, in itself, is not constitutive of 'brain drain'. The 'problems' arise when the rates of return are very low and also when the country or region in question fails to attract scientific talent from outside. On an individual level, the emphasis on mobility potentially generates differential opportunity as more 'footloose' scientists are able to respond to these challenges whilst others, perhaps with family or caring commitments, are less able to do so. Increasing emphasis upon the 'expectation of mobility' in science careers – the corollary of clustering policy – may thus disadvantage certain groups of scientists, restricting their ability to progress.

MOBEX examined these issues, focusing on the flows of scientists between Italy and the UK. The decision to focus on Italy was taken for a number of reasons. First, because we knew from our previous research (Ackers, 2003) and other studies of global 'brain drain' that Italy was a major 'donor' country within the EU and the UK, a key 'recipient'. We also knew from our links with Italian scientists that the issue of 'brain drain' had moved onto the Italian political agenda in recent years and that various policy initiatives were being taken to mitigate its effects. Italy was thus selected as a case study, enabling us to study, in an in-depth, contextualized fashion, the factors shaping scientific mobility and migration decision-making.

MOBISC: EQUAL PAY, CAREER PROGRESSION AND THE SOCIO-LEGAL VALUATION OF CARE

Funder: European Commission, DG Research
January 2003–March 2004

MOBISC – funded by the Employment and Social Affairs Directorate of the Commission under a programme relating to the Community Framework Strategy on Gender Equality (2001–05) – aimed to develop a better understanding of the factors shaping the career progression and representation of women in highly skilled, scientific labour markets. Within this broad aim, the project also wanted to consider the impact of time committed to care and unpaid work on the progression of men and women in science. Put simply, the research sought to examine the determinative effect of 'mobility' as a variable explaining the leakage of women from science and their failure to achieve equivalent levels of status and pay to their male counterparts. The study was completed in June 2004. It involved work in the UK, Portugal, Italy, Austria and Greece and took a socio-legal approach, combining legal and policy analysis at EU and national level; analysis of statistical data on the representation and progression of women in science; key informant interviews with policy-makers and employers; and questionnaires and life-history interviews with mobile male and female scientists.

The tendency of research and policy to focus on female participation rates has, to some extent, distracted attention from the issue of women progressing in science. An inverse relationship exists between the level of feminization and seniority as women fail to progress in science careers at an equivalent rate to their male peers. The reasons for this are complex. The 'expectation of mobility' reflects both the valuation of international and diverse experience but also the prevalence of fixed-term positions and, in some countries, the lack of positions. Women are as mobile as men in the early stages of research but their ability or willingness to continue to move decreases over the life-course as other responsibilities emerge. Dual science career situations are highly prevalent in science careers. These situations place additional pressures on scientists, and female partners in particular, seeking to combine the demands of a mobile research career with their personal lives. In many cases women fall behind in this process as male careers gain priority.

IMPAFEL: IMPACT ASSESSMENT OF THE MARIE CURIE FELLOWSHIP SCHEME

Funder: European Commission, DG Research
May 2003–June 2005

The European Union has invested considerable efforts to promote the training and mobility of researchers in Europe. The Marie Curie Fellowship Scheme of the 'Training and Mobility Programme' of the 4th Framework Programme (1994–98) and the 'Improving Human Resources and Mobility Programme' of the 5th Framework Programme (1998–2002) have jointly funded almost 12 000 researchers to undertake a period of research activity in a different European country. The European Commission decided to launch a large-scale impact assessment study of the Marie Curie Fellowship's activity. Three independent organizations (APRE,[2] CSLPE and HSTF[3]) were awarded the tender to carry out the independent assessment. The study made use of an online questionnaire, interviews and analysis of background documentation, adopting a combination of objective and subjective measures of impact – 2918 Marie Curie Fellows (75 per cent former Fellows, 25 per cent current Fellows) completed questionnaires; a further 1389 supervisors completed questionnaires. According to the Fellows who answered the questionnaire, the perceived impact of the Marie Curie Fellowship was most significant in relation to three factors: their international research experience; the development of research skills; the opportunity to have dedicated time to carry out research. Supervisors identified the strongest impacts in the areas of: research competence; time/workforce to do research; the ability to attract excellent researchers.

The scheme was perceived as meritocratic and a successful means to 'match' researchers and supervisors, helping to build research groups and retain researchers in Europe. Flows within Europe were unbalanced, with Mediterranean countries supplying more researchers than they received and Western European countries, most notably the UK, being the most popular 'host' countries. Yet, the scheme could not be accused of creating a 'drain'. Not only did it provide a means for some scientists to stay in research, many of the researchers surveyed had subsequently returned to their country of origin after their Fellowship and most surveyed had continued in research careers. There were many ongoing collaborations established during the

Fellowship that had led to further projects and publications, although limited interaction had been made between academia and industry.

ASSESSING THE IMPACT OF THE ROBERTS' REVIEW ENHANCED STIPENDS AND SALARIES ON POSTGRADUATE AND POST-DOCTORAL POSITIONS

Funder: Research Councils UK (RCUK)
September 2005–January 2006

One of the key findings of Sir Gareth Roberts' 2002 review *SET for Success* was that the supply of researchers for the UK academic base was hampered by the level of PhD stipend and post-doctoral salaries. Following the government's acceptance of the review's recommendations, funding for a raft of reforms was channelled through the Research Councils. Research Council doctoral maintenance awards were generally increased to £12 000 per annum (tax-free) and funding was also ring-fenced for Enhanced Salaries and Stipends (ESS) in areas experiencing particular recruitment difficulties.

In October 2005 the CSLPE was commissioned by RCUK to assess the initial impact of ESS on post-doctoral and postgraduate positions in key shortage areas. The study focused on BBSRC,[4] ESRC and EPSRC[5] areas (which were all at different stages in implementing the policy) and conducted 11 site visits (81 interviews), three online questionnaires (1433 responses) and key informant interviews.

In short, the main findings were:

- Where post-doctoral pay has been enhanced, there is evidence to suggest that it made a significant difference in rendering a position viable or in shaping the post-doc's decision of which academic post to take.
- Those responsible for recruitment remarked that enhanced salaries increased the attractiveness of the post and the volume of applicants – this made them more competitive in comparison with other universities and not so much with other sectors.
- The level of enhancement required to match salaries in some sectors was considerable – at least double existing levels. Here, enhancements were seen as a 'drop in the ocean'.
- Concerns around the 'pay ceiling' limit the ability of this scheme to support retention of more experienced and expensive researchers.

E-MEP-LAB: EXPLORING THE HUMAN CAPITAL DIMENSION OF A EUROPEAN CELL BIOLOGY CONSORTIUM

Funder: European Commission FP6
2005–2010

The European Membrane Protein Consortium – E-MeP – is a group of European researchers funded under the European Commission's 6th Framework Programme to explore membrane proteins found in all types of cells from bacteria to human tissues. E-MeP is committed to the development of a 'sustainable European membrane protein structural genomics research area' through the generation and transfer of knowledge. Its sister project – E-MeP-Lab – is a specific response to perceived skills shortages in this area of research and includes measures to support a series of training events for early-career researchers. It seeks to improve the quality of, and access to, training as a means of encouraging the recruitment and retention of researchers and ensuring that opportunities are genuinely open to all.

E-MeP-Lab has a particular interest in encouraging the involvement of researchers from the new EU Member States and Accession countries and promoting a balanced representation of both men and women. In order to achieve these twin objectives, the European Law and Policy Research Group at Liverpool University (ELP) is conducting research with E-MeP scientists. The focus of this project is on the retention and progression of early career researchers (ECRs) within E-MeP specifically, and in this discipline of biological science more widely, and how gender and life-course impacts upon these issues. The objectives are two-fold: (1) to provide an analysis of the presence of Eastern European scientists within E-MeP-Lab; and (2) to reveal and understand the work–life balance issues raised by ECRs in E-MeP more broadly.

NOTES

1. Centre for the Study of Law & Policy in Europe, Leeds University, UK.
2. Agency for the Promotion of European Research, based in Rome.
3. Hungarian Science and Technology Foundation.
4. Biotechnology and Biological Sciences Research Council.
5. Engineering and Physical Sciences Research Council.

References

Abella, M.I. (2004), 'Labour migration in East Asian economies', Annual World Bank Conference on Development Economics, Brussels, 10–11 May.

Ackers, H.L. (1998), *Shifting Spaces: Gender, Citizenship and Migration in the EU*, Bristol, UK: Policy Press.

Ackers, H.L. (2003), *The Participation of Women Researchers in the TMR Marie Curie Fellowships 1994–1998*, vol. 2, Brussels: Court of Justice of the European Communities.

Ackers, H.L. (2004a), 'Managing relationships in peripatetic careers: scientific mobility in the European Union', *Women's Studies International Forum*, **27** (3), 188–201.

Ackers, H.L. (2004b), 'Citizenship, migration and the valuation of care in the European Union', *Journal of Ethnic and Migration Studies*, **30** (2), 373–96.

Ackers, H.L. (2005a), 'Moving people and knowledge: the mobility of scientists within the European Union', *International Migration*, **43** (5), 99–131.

Ackers, H.L. (2005b), 'Promoting scientific mobility and balanced growth in the European Research Area', *Innovation: the European Journal of Social Science Research*, **18** (3), 301–17.

Ackers, H.L. (2005c), 'Academic career trajectories: identifying the "early stage" in research careers', *CSLPE Working Paper 2005-1*, Leeds, UK: University of Leeds.

Ackers, H.L. (2005d), *Gender, Mobility and Progression in Science Careers: MOBISC Summary Report*, Leeds, UK: University of Leeds.

Ackers, H.L. (2007), 'Legislating for equality? Working hours and progression in science careers', *European Law Journal*, **13** (2), 169–85.

Ackers, H.L. and P. Dwyer (2002), *Senior Citizenship? Retirement, Migration and Welfare in the European Union*, Bristol, UK: Policy Press.

Ackers, H.L. and B. Gill (2005), 'Attracting and retaining junior researchers in English HEIs: is there a problem?', *Innovation: the European Journal of Social Science Research*, **18** (3), 277–300.

Ackers, H.L. and E.A. Oliver (2007), 'From flexicurity to flexsecquality? The impact of the fixed-term contract provisions on employment in science research', *International Studies of Management and Organization*, **37** (1), 53–79.

Ackers, H.L. and H.E. Stalford (2004), *A Community for Children? Children, Citizenship and Internal Migration in the EU*, London, UK: Ashgate.

Ackers, H.L. and H.E. Stalford (2007), 'Managing multiple life-courses: the influence of children on migration processes in the European Union', in K. Clarke, T. Maltby, and P. Kennett (eds), *Social Policy Review 19: Analysis and Debate in Social Policy*, Bristol, UK: Policy Press, pp. 317–18.

Ackers H.L., B. Gill, K.A. Coldron and E.A. Oliver (2006), 'Assessing the impact of the Roberts' Review Enhanced Stipends and Salaries on Postgraduate and Postdoctoral Positions', Swindon, UK: Research Councils UK (RCUK). Available at: www.rcuk.ac.uk/rescareer/rcdu/enhanced.htm. Accessed: 22 April 2008.

Adams, J., D. Mount, D. Smith, H.L. Ackers, B. Gill, E.A. Oliver and S. Hazlehurst (2005), 'Researchers in HEIs: a scoping study of career development and human resource management', Bristol, UK: Higher Education Funding Council for England (HEFCE). Available at: www.hefce.ac.uk/pubs/rdreports/2005/rd16_05/. Accessed: 22 April 2008.

Altbach, P. and U. Teichler (2001), 'Internationalization and exchanges in a globalized university', *Journal of Studies in International Education*, **5** (1), 5–25.

Amin, A. (2000), 'Organizational learning through communities of practice', paper presented at the Millennium Schumpeter Conference, University of Manchester, 28 June–1 July.

Amin, A. (2002), 'Spatialities of globalization', *Environmental and Planning A*, **34**, 385–99.

Aston, L. (2004), 'Projecting demand for UK higher education from the accession countries', Oxford, UK: Higher Education Policy Institute (HEPI). Available at: http://www.hepi.ac.uk/pubdetail.asp?ID=122& DOC=Reports. Accessed: 21 April 2008.

Avveduto, S. (2001), 'International mobility of PhDs', in S. Avveduto (ed.), *Innovative People: Mobility of Skilled Personnel in National Innovation Systems*, Paris, OECD, pp. 229–43.

Bagatelas, W. and J. Kubicova (2003), 'Bulgarian emigration: a closer look', *South-East Europe Review for Labour and Social Affairs*, **6** (4), 27–35.

Bailey, A. and P. Boyle (2004), 'Untying and retying family migration in the new Europe', *Journal of Ethnic and Migration Studies*, **30** (2), 229–41.

Bailey, A.J., M.K. Blake and T.J. Cooke (2004), 'Migration, care, and the linked lives of dual-earner households', *Environment and Planning A*, **36** (9), 1617–32.

Baláž, V. and A. Williams (2004), 'Been there, done that: international student migration and human capital transfers from the UK to Slovakia', *Population, Place and Space*, **10** (3), 217–37.

Baláž, V., A.M. Williams and D. Kollar (2004), 'Temporary versus permanent youth brain drain: economic implications', *International Migration*, **42** (4), 4–34.

Balter, M. (1999), 'Foreign exchanges: Europeans who do post-docs abroad face re-entry problems', *Science Magazine*, **285** (3 September), 1524–6.

BBC Newsnight (2006), 'Can Poland woo back its emigrants?' 6 July 2006, www.news.bbc.co.uk/1/hi/programmes/newsnight/5154002.stm.

Bekhradnia, B. (2004), 'Higher education in Bulgaria: a review for the Ministry of Education and Science', Oxford, UK: Higher Education Policy Institute. Available at: www.hepi.ac.uk/pubdetail.asp?ID=166& DOC=misc. Accessed: 28 July 2008.

Bekhradnia, B. and T. Sastry (2005), 'Brain drain: migration of academic staff to and from the UK', Oxford, UK: Higher Education Policy Institute. Available at: www.hepi.ac.uk/pubdetail.asp?ID=180&DOC= Reports. Accessed: 28 April 2008.

Biggin, S. and V. Kouzminov (eds) (1993), *Proceedings of the International Seminar on Brain Drain Issues in Europe*, Venice: UNESCO–ROSTE.

Blair, A. (2006) 'British talent deserting universities', *The Times*, 7 November 2006.

BMBF (2005), 'Report of the Federal Government on Research 2004', Berlin: Federal Ministry of Education and Research. Available at: www.bmbf.de/pub/bufo_2004_eng_full_version.pdf. Accessed: 28 April 2008.

Bobeva, D. (1996), 'Bulgaria', in T. Frejka (ed.), *International Migration in Central and Eastern Europe and the Commonwealth of Independent States*, New York and Geneva: United Nations Population Fund Staff, pp. 37–47.

Bobeva, D. (1997), 'Migration, European integration and the labour force brain drain: a synthesis report', in D. Bobeva (ed.) (1997), *Brain Drain from Central and Eastern Europe: A Study Undertaken on Scientific and Technical Staff in Ten Countries of Central and Eastern Europe*, Sofia, Bulgaria: Centre for the Study of Democracy. Available at: www.csd.bg/ fileSrc.php?id=10685. Accessed: 21 April 2008.

Bonney, N. and J. Love (1991), 'Gender and migration: geographical mobility and the wife's sacrifice', *The Sociological Review*, **39** (2), 335–48.

Boswell, C. (2005), *Migration in Europe*, Switzerland: Global Commission on International Migration. Available at: www.gcim.org/attachements/ RS4.pdf. Accessed: 5 May 2008.

Boyd, M. (1989), 'Family and personal networks in international migration: recent developments and new agendas', *International Migration Review*, **23** (3), 638–70.

Bryson, C. (2004), 'What about the workers? The expansion of higher education and the transformation of academic work', *Industrial Relations Journal*, **35** (1), 138–57.

Buchinger, B., D. Gödl and U. Gschwandtner (2002), *Berufskarrieren von Frauen und Männern an österreichs Universitäten. Eine sozialwissenshcaftliche Studie über die Verienbarkeit von Beruf und Privatem. Materialien zur Förderung von Frauen in der Wissenschaft*, Wien: Bundesministerium für Bildung, Wissenschaft und Kultur.

Casey, T., S. Mahroum, K. Ducatel and R. Barré (eds) (2001), 'The mobility of academic researchers: academic careers and recruitment in ICT and biotechnology – a joint JRC/IPTS-ESTO study', Brussels: European Communities. Available at: ftp://ftp.jrc.es/pub/EURdoc/eur19905en. pdf. Accessed: 22 April 2008.

CEC (2004), 'Communication from the Commission to the Council and the European Parliament on the presentation of a proposal for a Directive and two proposals for Recommendations on the admission of third-country nationals to carry out scientific research in the European Community, Brussels, 16.3.2004, Com(2004) 178 final.

Cerase, F.P (1974), 'Expectations and reality: a case study of return migration from the US to Southern Italy', *International Migration Review*, **8**, 245–62.

Chataway, J. (1999), 'Technology transfer and the restructuring of science and technology in Central and Eastern Europe', *Technovation*, **19** (6–7), 355–64.

Chompalov, I. (2000), 'Brain drain from Bulgaria before and after the transition to democracy', paper to the *Bulgarian Research Symposium and Network Meeting*, Atlanta, USA, April.

Cismas, C. (2004), 'Young researchers in Romania: survival and hope', paper presented at a workshop on 'The Special Situation of Young Researchers in Central and Eastern Europe' at the *European Science Open Forum*, Stockholm, 25–28 August.

Coldron, K.A. and Ackers, H.L. (2007), '(Ab)using European citizenship? Retirement migrants and the management of healthcare rights', *Maastricht Journal of European and Comparative Law*, **14** (3), 287–302.

Cooke, T.J. (2001), ' "Trailing wife" or "trailing mother"? The effect of parental status on the relationship between family migration and the labour-market participation of married women', *Environment and Planning A*, **33** (3), 419–30.

Cooke, T.J. (2003), 'Family migration and the relative earnings of husbands and wives', *Annals of the Association of American Geographers*, **93** (2), 338–49.

Court, S. (2004), *The Unequal Academy*, London, UK: Association of University Teachers.

Crosier, D., L. Purser and H. Smidt (2007), 'Trends V: universities shaping the European higher education area – a EUA report', Brussels: European University Association. Available at: www.eua.be/fileadmin/user_upload/files/Publications/Trends_V_universities_shaping_the_european_higher_education_area.pdf. Accessed: 24 April 2008.

Dabrowa-Szefler, M. (2004), 'Basic demand and supply problems concerning research personnel in Poland', *Higher Education Policy*, **17**, 39–48.

Davenport, S. (2004), 'Panic and panacea: brain drain and science and technology human capital policy', *Research Policy*, **33** (4), 617–30.

Department for Education and Skills (DFES) (2003), *The Future of Higher Education*, London, UK: The Stationary Office (TSO).

Department of Trade and Industry (DTI) (2002), *Knowledge Migrants: The Motivations and Experiences of Professionals in the UK on Work Permits*, London: DTI.

Deutscher Akademischer Austauschdienst (DAAD) (2006), '*Wissenschaft weltoffen*', Bielefeld: Bertelsmann. Available at http://www.wissenschaftweltoffer.de. Accessed: 24 April 2008.

Dickmann, M., N. Doherty and C. Brewster (2006), 'Why do they go? Individual and corporate perspectives on the factors influencing the decision to accept an international assignment', paper to the Academy of Management Annual Meeting, Atlanta, USA: 11–16 August.

Dickson, D. (2003), 'Mitigating the brain drain is a moral necessity', *SciDevNet*, 29 May 2003. Available at: www.scidev.net/Editorials/index.cfm?fuseaction=readEditorials&itemid=76&language=1. Accessed: 19 April 2008.

Docquier, F. and A. Marfouk (2004), 'Measuring the international mobility of skilled workers (1990–2000): Release 1.0', *World Bank Policy Research Working Paper*, No. 3381, Washington, USA: World Bank.

Dustmann, C. and A. Glitz (2005), *Immigration, Jobs and Wages: Theory, Evidence and Opinion*, London, UK: Centre for Economic Policy Research (CEPR).

European Commission (EC) (2001), 'Communication from the Commision to the Council and the European Parliament: a mobility strategy for the European Research Area', Com(2001) 331 final of 20.6.2001.

European Commission (EC) (2007), 'Key figures 2007: towards a European research area – science, technology and innovation', Brussels: European Communities. Available at: http://cordis.europa.eu/documents/documentlibrary/97946551EN6.pdf. Accessed: 21 April 2008.

European Universities Association (EUA) (2005), *Doctoral Programmes for the European Knowledge Society: Report on EUA Doctoral Programmes Project 2004–2005*, Brussels: European Universities Association (EUA).

Fajnzylber, P. and J.H. Lopez (2007), *Close to Home: The Development Impact of Remittances in Latin America*, Washington DC, USA: The World Bank.

Falagas, M.E., E. Fabritsi, F.C. Chelvatzoglov and K. Rellos (2005), 'Penetration of the English Language in Science: the case of a German national interdisciplinary critical care conference', *Critical Care*, **9** (6), 655–6.

Ferro, A. (2006), 'Desired mobility or satisfied immobility? Migratory aspirations among knowledge workers', *Journal of Education and Work*, **19** (2), 171–200.

Gächter, A. (2002), 'The ambiguities of emigration: Bulgaria since 1988', *International Migration Papers*, IMP 39, Geneva: International Labour Organization (ILO).

Gaillard, J. and A.M. Gaillard (2003), 'Can Scientific Diaspora Save African Science?', *SciDevNet*, 22 May 2003. Available at: http://www.scidev.net/en/opinions/can_the_scientific_diaspora_save_african_science.html. Accessed: 19 April 2008.

Gamlen, A. (2005), 'The brain drain is dead, long live the New Zealand diaspora', *COMPAS Working Paper*, No. 10, Oxford, UK: Centre on Migration, Policy and Society (COMPAS).

Gent, S. and R. Skeldon (2006), 'Skilled migration: new policy options', *Briefing* No. 5 (March), Sussex, UK: Development Research Centre on Migration, Globalisation and Poverty (DRC). Available at: www.migrationdrc.org/publications/briefing_papers/BP5.pdf. Accessed: 1 May 2008.

Georgieva, P. (2002), *Higher Education in Bulgaria: Monographs on Higher Education*, Bucharest, Romania: UNESCO-CEPES.

Georgieva, P. (2004), 'Bulgaria: the double edge of economy and demography', *Higher Education in Europe*, **XXIV** (3), 364–72.

Ghodsee, K. (2002), 'Mobility in Bulgaria and the European Union: brain drain, bogus asylum seekers, replacement migration and fertility', *East European Studies Occasional Paper*, No. 70 (November), Washington DC, USA: Woodrow Wilson International Center for Scholars.

Gill, B. (2003), 'Science in Central and Eastern Europe – higher education, labour markets and highly skilled migration – an overview', Conference paper, Symposium on Science Policy, Mobility and Brain Drain in the EU and Candidate Countries, University of Leeds, 27–28 July.

Gill, B. (2004), 'Reversing the gaze of migration studies: scientific return mobility', *CSLPE Research Report 20*, Leeds, UK: University of Leeds.

Gill, B. (2005), 'Homeward bound? The experience of return mobility for Italian scientists', *Innovation: The European Journal of Social Science Research*, **18** (3), 319–42.

Godwin, M., B. Balmer and J. Gregory (2006), 'The anatomy of the "brain drain" debate in the UK: full ESRC research report'. Available at: www.esrcsocietytoday.ac.uk/ESRCInfoCentre/ViewAwardPage.aspx? AwardId=4133. Accessed: 30 April 2008.

Gotzfried, A. (2005), 'Science, technology and innovation in Europe', *Statistics in Focus: Science and Technology 8/2005*, Luxembourg: Eurostat.

Gotzfried, A. (2007), 'R&D expenditure and personnel', *Statistics in Focus: Science and Technology 23/2007*, Luxembourg: Eurostat.

Guth, J. (2006), 'The Bologna process: the impact of higher education reform on the structure and organisation of doctoral programmes in Germany', *Higher Education in Europe*, **31** (3), 327–38.

Guth, J. (2007) 'Destination Germany: early career scientific mobility, the Bologna process and choosing whether and where to move', unpublished report to the T.H. Marshall Fellowship Programme, London, UK.

Hadler, M. (2006), 'Intentions to migrate within the European Union: a challenge for simple economic macro-level explanations', *European Societies*, **8** (1), 111–40.

Hansen, W. (2003), *Brain Drain: Emigration Flows for Qualified Scientists*, Brussels: European Commission/MERIT.

Harris, E. (2004), 'Building scientific capacity in developing countries', *European Molecular Biology Organization (EMBO) Reports*, **5** (1), 7–11.

Hasluck, C., J. Pitcher and C. Simm (2001), *Academic Research Careers in Scotland: A Longitudinal Study of Academic Contract Research Staff, their Jobs and Career Patterns*, Edinburgh/Coventry, UK: Scottish Higher Education Funding Council and Institute for Employment Research.

Hatakenaka, S. (2004), 'Internationalism in higher education: a review', Oxford, UK: Higher Education Policy Institute (HEPI). Available at: www.hepi.ac.uk/downloads/12InternationalismReport-ExdcutiveSummary.pdf. Accessed: 28 April 2008.

Haug, S. (2005), 'Migration and migration potential in Bulgaria and Romania', paper at the International Conference on New Patterns of East–West Migration in Europe, Hamburg, Germany: 18 November.

Haug, S. and C. Diehl (2004a), *External Migration in Bulgaria: External Migration and Emigration Potential in Bulgaria and Its Consequences for Demography and Economy*, Wiesbaden, Germany: Federal Institute for Population Research.

Haug, S. and C. Diehl (2004b), *Migration between Germany and the Central and Eastern Europe EC Accession Countries*, May, Warsaw, Poland: Federal Institute for Population Reasearch.

Hellemans, A. (2001), 'Beating the European brain drain', *Nature*, **414** (4–5), 22 November.

HESA (2005), 'HESA Student Records, 2003/04'. Available at: http://www.hesa.ac.uk/index.php?option=com_datatables&Itemid=121&task=show_category&catdex=3. Accessed: 24 July 2008.

Higher Education Funding Council for England (HEFCE) (2006), 'The higher education workforce in England: a framework for the future – Issue Paper 2006/21', Bristol, UK: HEFCE.

Hilgendorf, S. (2005), 'Brain gain statt (instead of) brain drain: the role of English in German education', *World Englishes*, **24** (1), 53–67.

Home Office (2005), *Controlling Our Borders: Making Migration Work for Britain – Five-year Strategy for Asylum and Immigration*, Norwich, UK: TSO.

Hryniewicz, J., B. Jalowiecki and A. Mync (1997), *The Mobility of Science Workers in 1994–1997*, Warsaw, Poland: European Institute for Regional and Local Development.

Iglicka, K. (2000), 'Mechanisms of migration from Poland before and during the transition period', *Journal of Ethnic and Migration Studies*, **26** (1), 61–73.

Iglicka, K. (2003), 'Priorities and developmental directions of Polish migration policy', *Analyses and Opinions 13*, Warsaw, Poland: Institute of Public Affairs. Available at: www.isp.org.pl/files/564046626047328 1001117524431.pdf. Accessed: 21 April 2008.

Iredale, R. (1999), 'The need to import skilled personnel: factors favouring and hindering its international mobility', *International Migration*, **37** (1), 89–111.

Iredale, R. (2001), 'The migration of professionals: theories and typologies', *International Migration*, **39** (5), 7–24.

Iredale, R. and R. Appleyard (2001), 'International migration of the highly skilled: introduction', *International Migration*, **39** (5), 3–6.

Jalowiecki, B. and G.J. Gorzelak (2004), 'Brain drain, brain gain and mobility: theories and prospective methods', *Higher Education in Europe*, **29** (3), 299–308.

Johnston, R., A. Trlin, A. Henderson and N. North (2006), 'Sustaining and creating migration chains among skilled immigrant groups: Chinese, Indians and South Africans in New Zealand', *Journal of Ethnic and Migration Studies*, **32** (7), 1227–50.

Katseli, L.T., R.E.B. Lucas and T. Xenogiani (2006a), 'Effects of migration on sending countries: what do we know?', *Development Centre Working Paper No. 250*, Paris, France: OECD. Available at: http://www.un.org/esa/population/migration/turin/Symposium_Turin_files/P11_Katseli.pdf. Accessed: 26 April 2008.

Katseli, L.T., R.E.B. Lucas and T. Xenogiani (2006b), 'Policies for migration and development: a European perspective', *Development Centre Policy Brief No. 30*, Paris, France: OECD. Available at: www.oecd.org/dataoecd/55/37/37862315.pdf. Accessed: 21 April 2008.

Kelo, M., U. Teichler and B. Wachter (2006), 'Toward improved data on student mobility in Europe: findings and concepts of the Eurodata Study', *Journal of Studies in International Education*, **10** (3), 194–223.

Kicinger, A. (2005), 'National Context Paper for Poland', unpublished report prepared for MOBEX2 team.

King, R. (2002), 'Towards a new map of European migration', *International Journal of Population Geography*, **8** (2), 89–106.

King, R. and E. Ruiz-Gelices (2003), 'International student migration and the European "year abroad": effects on European identity and subsequent migration behaviour', *International Journal of Population Geography*, **9** (3), 229–52.

King, R., A.M. Warnes and A.M. Williams (eds) (2000), *Sunset Lives: British Retirement Migration to the Mediterranean*, Oxford, UK: Berg.

Kinnaird, B. (2006) 'Sorry vacancy filled. . .' *Times Higher Education Supplement*, 24 November, 21. Available at: www.timeshighereducation. co.uk/story.asp?storyCode=206937&sectioncode=26. Accessed: 28 April 2008.

Kofman, E. (2002), 'The invisibility of skilled female migrants and gender relations in studies of skilled migration in Europe', *International Journal of Population Geography*, **6** (1), 45–59.

Kofman, E. (2004), 'Family-related migration: a critical review of European studies', *Journal of Ethnic and Migration Studies*, **30** (2), 243–62.

Korys, I. (2003), 'Migration trends in selected EU applicant countries: Poland', *CEFMR Working Paper 5/2003*, Warsaw, Poland: CEFMR. Available at: www.cefmr.pan.pl/docs/cefmr_wp_2003-05.pdf. Accessed: 19 April 2008.

Krieger, H. (2004), *Migration Trends in an Enlarged Europe*, Dublin: European Foundation for the Improvement of Living and Working Conditions.

Kupiszewski, M. (2002), 'How trustworthy are forecasts of international migration between Poland and the European Union?', *Journal of Ethnic and Migration Studies*, **28** (4), 627–45.

Kwiek, M. (2003), 'Academe in transition: transformations in the Polish academic profession', *Higher Education*, **45** (4), 455–76.

La Madeleine, B.L. (2007), 'Lost in translation', *Nature*, **445** (January) 454–5, 24 January. Available at: www.nature.com/naturejobs/2007/070125/full/nj7126-454a.html. Accessed: 5 May 2008.

Langer, J. (2004), 'The special situation of young researchers in Central and Eastern Europe', paper presented at a workshop on 'The Special Situation of Young Researchers in Central and Eastern Europe' at the European Science Open Forum, Stockholm, 25–28 August.

Lazarova, M. and I. Tarique (2005), 'Knowledge transfer upon repatriation' *Journal of World Business*, **40** (4), 361–73.

Ley, D. and A. Kobayashi (2005), 'Back to Hong Kong: return migration or transnational sojourn?', *Global Networks*, **5** (2), 111–27.

Little, A.D. with R. Veugelers (2005), 'Internationalisation of R&D in the UK: a review of the evidence – report to the Office of Science and Technology', Cambridge, UK: Arthur D. Little Ltd. Available at: www.berr.gov.uk/files/file30063.pdf. Accessed: 28 April 2008.

Lowell, B.L. (2003), 'The need for policies that meet the needs of all', *SciDevNet: Policy Brief*, May 2003. Available at: http://unpan1.un. org/intradoc/groups/public/documents/APCITY/UNPAN022371.pdf. Accessed: 5 May 2008.

Lowell, B.L. and A.M. Findlay (2001), *Migration of Highly Skilled Persons from Developing Countries: Impact and Policy Responses*, Synthesis Report, Geneva: International Labour Organisation.

Lowell, B.L., A.M. Findlay and E. Stewart (2004), 'Brain strain: optimising highly skilled migration from developing countries', *Asylum and Migration Working Paper No.3*, London, UK: Institute for Public Policy Research (IPPR).

Lungescu, O. (2004), 'EU newcomers "risk brain drain"', *BBC News*, 27 February. Available at: http://news.bbc.co.uk/1/hi/world/europe/ 3492668.stm. Accessed: 19 April 2008.

Mahroum, S. (1998), 'Europe and the Challenge of Brain Drain', *IPTS Report* 29, Seville, Spain: IPTS. Available at: www.jrc.es/home/report/ english/articles/vol29/SAT1E296.htm. Accessed: 19 April 2008.

Mahroum, S. (2000a), 'Scientists and global spaces', *Technology in Society*, **22** (4), 513–22.

Mahroum, S. (2000b), 'Highly skilled globetrotters: the international migration of human capital', *R&D Management*, **30** (1), 23–32.

Mahroum, S. (2001), 'Europe and the immigration of highly skilled labour', *International Migration*, **39** (5), 27–42.

Mahroum, S. (2003), 'Brain gain, brain drain: an international overview', background paper for the Austrian Ministry for Transport, Innovation and Technology Alpbach Technology Dialogue, 22–23 August.

Mahroum, S. (2005), 'The international policies of brain gain: a review', *Technology Analysis and Strategic Management*, **17** (2), 219–30.

Marcus, J. (2004), 'Harvard foots bill to ease visa clearance', *Times Higher Educational Supplement*, 26 November, 11. Available at: www.times highereducation.co.uk/story.asp?storyCode=192677&sectioncode=26. Accessed: 29 April 2008.

Martin-Rovet, D. (2003), 'Opportunities for outstanding young scientists in Europe to create an independent research team', Strasbourg, France:

European Science Foundation. Available at: www.astro.sk/~choc/VT/ABROAD/EU/OpportunitiesFinal.pdf. Accessed: 19 April 2008.

McNeil, L. and M. Sher (1999), 'Dual science career couples: survey results'. Available at: www.physics.wm.edu/~sher/survey.pdf. Accessed: 24 April 2008.

Metcalf, H., H. Rolfe, P. Stevens and M. Weale (2005), 'Recruitment and retention of academic staff in higher education', Research Report RR658, Nottingham, UK: Department for Education and Skills (DfES).

Meyer, J-B. (2001), 'Network approach versus brain drain: lessons from the diaspora', *International Migration*, **39** (5), 91–110.

Meyer, J.-B. (2003), 'Policy implications of the brain drain's changing face', *SciDevNet: Policy Brief*, May 2003. Available at: http://unpan1.un.org/intradoc/groups/public/documents/APCITY/UNPAN022374.pdf. Accessed: 18 April 2008.

Meyer, J-B. and M. Brown (1999), 'Scientific diasporas: a new approach to the brain drain', *UNESCO Management of Social Transformation (MOST) Discussion Paper 41*, Paris, France: UNESCO. Available at: http://www.unesco.org/most/meyer.htm. Accessed: 28 April 2008.

Meyer, J-B., D. Kaplan and J. Charum (2001), 'Scientific nomadism and the new geopolitics of knowledge', *International Social Science Journal*, **53** (168), 309–21.

Millard, D. (2005), 'The impact of clustering on scientific mobility', *Innovation: The European Journal of Social Science Research*, **18** (3), 343–60.

Morano-Foadi, S. (2006), 'Key issues and causes of the Italian brain drain', *Innovation: The European Journal of Social Science Reasearch*, **19** (3), 209–23.

Morano-Foadi, S. and J. Foadi (2003), 'Italian scientific migration: from brain exchange to brain drain', *CSLPE Research Report 7*, Leeds, UK: University of Leeds.

Munz, R., T. Straubhaar, F. Vadean and N. Vadean (2006), 'The costs and benefits of European immigration', *HWWI Policy Report No. 3*, Hamburg, Germany: Hamburg Institute of International Economics. Available at: www.hwwi.org/uploads/tx_wilpubdb/HWWI_Policy_Report_Nr__3_01.pdf. Accessed: 29 April 2008.

National Science Foundation (2006), *Science and Engineering Indicators*, Arlington, VA: National Science Foundation.

Okólski, M. (2000), 'Recent trends and major issues in international migration: Central and East European perspectives', *International Social Science Journal*, **52** (165), 329–41.

Okólski, M. (2001), 'Incomplete Migration: A New Form of Mobility in Central and Eastern Europe – the case of Polish and Ukrainian migrants', in C. Wallace and D. Stola (eds) (2001), *Patterns of Migration in Central Europe*, Basingstoke, UK: Palgrave, pp. 105–28.

Okólski, M. (2004), 'New Migration Movement in Central and Eastern Europe', in D. Joly (ed.), International Migration in the New Millenium, Aldershot, UK: Ashgate, pp. 36–56.

Okólski, M. (2006), 'Costs and benefits of migration for Central European countries', *CMR Working Papers No. 7/65*, Warsaw, Poland: Centre of Migration Research (CMR), University of Warsaw. Available at: www.migracje.uw.edu.pl/obm/pix/007_65.pdf. Accessed: 21 April 2008.

Opengart, R. and D.C. Short (2002), 'Free agent learners: the new career model and its impact on human resource development', *International Journal of Lifelong Learning*, **21** (3), 220–33.

O'Reilly, K. (2000), *The British on the Costa del Sol: Transnational Identities and Local Communities*, London, UK: Routledge.

Ouellette, J. (2007), 'Scientists in love: when two worlds collide', *Nature*, **445** (14 February), 700–702.

Peixoto, J. (2001), 'The international mobility of highly skilled workers in transitional corporations: the macro and micro factors of the organizational migration cadres', *International Migration Review*, **35** (4), 1030–53.

Pelizon, C. (2002), 'Is the Italian brain drain becoming a flood?', *Science Careers*, 10 May. Available at: http://sciencecareers.sciencemag.org/career_development/previous_issues/articles/1470/is_the_italian_brain_drain_becoming_a_flood. Accessed: 19 April 2008.

Peridy, N. (2006), 'Welfare magnets, border effects or policy regulations: what determinants drive migration flows into the EU?', *GEP Research Paper 2006/06*, Nottingham, UK: GEP Leverhulme Centre, University of Nottingham.

Phizacklea, A. (2000), 'The politics of belonging: sex work, domestic work – transnational household strategies', in S. Westwood and A. Phizacklea (eds) (2000), *Transnationalism and the Politics of Belonging*, London, UK: Routledge.

Piracha, M.E and R. Vickerman (2002), 'Immigration, mobility and EU enlargement', *University of Kent Studies in Economics No. 02/09*, Kent, UK: Department of Economics, University of Kent.

Puustinen-Hopper, K. (2005), *Mobile Minds: Survey of Foreign PhD Students and Researchers in Finland*, Helsinki, Finland: Academy of Finland.

Raghuram, P. (2004), 'The difference that skills make: gender, family migration strategies and regulated labour markets', *Journal of Ethnic and Migration*, **30** (2), 303–21.

Rangelova, R. and K. Vladimirova (2004), 'Migration from Central and Eastern Europe: the case of Bulgaria', *South-East Europe Review*, **3**, 7–30.

Regets, M.C. (2003), 'Impact of skilled migration on receiving countries', *SciDevNet Policy Brief*, May. Available at: http://www.scidev.net/en/policy-briefs/impact-of-skilled-migration-on-receiving-countries-html. Accessed: 19 April 2008.

Reichert, S. and C. Tauch (2003), *Trends III: Progress towards the European Higher Education Area*, Brussels: European University Association.

Reichert, S. and C. Tauch (2005), *Trends IV: European Universities Implementing Bologna*, Brussels: European University Association.

Roberts, G. (2002), *SET for Success: The Report of Sir Gareth Roberts' Review – The Supply of People with Science, Technology, Engineering and Mathematics Skills*, London: HM Treasury.

Roseneil, S. (2006), 'On not living with a partner: unpicking coupledom and cohabitation', *Sociological Research Online*, **11** (3). Available at: http://www.socresonline.org.uk/11/3/roseneil.html. Accessed: 19 April 2008.

Rothwell, N. (2002), *Who Wants to be a Scientist? Choosing Science as a Career*, Cambridge, UK: Cambridge University Press.

Rusconi, A. and H. Solga (2002), *Auswertung der Befragungd Deutscher Hochschulen zur 'Verflechtung von beruflichen Karrieren in Akademikerpartnerschaften'*, Berlin: Die Junge Akademie.

Salt, J. (1997), 'International movements of the highly skilled', *OECD Occasional Paper No. 3*, Paris, France: International Migration Unit, OECD. Available at: www.oecd.org/dataoecd/24/32/2383909.pdf. Accessed: 19 April 2008.

Salt, J. and R. Ford (1993), 'Skilled international migration in Europe: the shape of things to come?', in R. King (ed.), *Mass Migrations in Europe: The Legacy and the Future*, London: Belhaven Press, pp. 293–309.

Saxenian, A.L. (1999), 'Silicon valley's new immigrant entrepreneurs', *CCIS Working Paper 15*, California, USA: Center for Comparative Immigration Studies. Available at: http://www.ccis-ucsd.org/PUBLICATIONS/wrkg15.PDF. Accessed: 30 April 2008.

Schiermeier, Q. and P. Smaglik (2005), 'Homeward bound European Union', *Nature*, **433** (27 January), 440–41. Available at: http://www.nature.com/nature/journal/v433/n7024/full/nj7024-440a.html. Accessed: 24 April 2008.

Scott, S. (2006), 'The social morphology of skilled migration: the case of the British middle class in Paris', *Journal of Ethnic and Migration Studies*, **32** (7), 1105–29.

Séguin, B., P.A. Singer and A.S. Daar (2006a), 'Scientific diasporas', *Science*, **312** (5780), 16 June, 1602–603. Available at: www.sciencemag.org/cgi/content/full/312/5780/1602?ijkey=gYiJqpj1awq5.&keytype=ref&siteid=sci. Accessed: 28 April 2008.

Séguin, B., L. State, P.A Singer and A.S. Daar (2006b), 'Scientific diasporas as an option for brain drain: re-circulating knowledge for development', *International Journal of Biotechnology*, **8** (1–2) 78–90.

Slantcheva, S. (2003), 'The Bulgarian academic profession in transition', *Higher Education*, **45** (4), 425–54.

Slowinski, J. (1998), 'SOCRATES invades Central Europe', *Education Policy Analysis Archives*, **6** (9). Available at: http://epaa.asu.edu/epaa/v6n9.html. Accessed: 22 April 2008.

Smeby, J-C. and J. Trondal (2005), 'Globalization or Europeanization? International contact among university staff', *Higher Education*, **49** (4), 449–66.

Smith, D.P. (2004), 'An "untied" research agenda for family migration: loosening the "shackles" of the past', *Journal of Ethnic and Migration Studies*, **30** (2), 263–82.

Smith, M.P. and A. Favell (eds) (2006), *The Human Face of Global Mobility: International High Skilled Migrants in Europe, North America and the Asia Pacific*, New Brunswick, NJ: Transaction Press.

Social Rights Bulgaria (2007), 'Bulgaria's population in for long-term drop and ageing, Social Policy Ministry says Sofia, March 27 2007(BTA)'. Available at: http://www.socialniprava.info/article1779.html. Accessed: 21 April 2008.

Spitze, G. (1984), 'The effect of family migration on wives' employment: how long does it last?', *Social Science Quarterly*, **65** (1), 21–36.

Sretenova, N. (2003), 'Scientific mobility and "brain drain" issues in the higher education sector in Bulgaria', *CSLPE Research Report No.2*, Leeds, UK: University of Leeds.

Sretenova, N. (2004), 'Scientific mobility and the brain drain issue: the Bulgarian case', unpublished report prepared for MOBEX2 team.

Stark, O. (2004), 'Rethinking the brain drain,' *World Development*, **32** (1), 15–22.

Statistisches Bundesamt (2006a), *Bildung und Kultur Personal an Hochschulen 2005: Fachserie 11/Reihe 4.4*, Wiesbaden: Statistisches Bundesamt.

Statistisches Bundesamt (2006b), *Prüfungen an Hochschulen 2005: Fachserie 11/Reihe 4.2*, Wiesbaden: Statistisches Bundesamt.

Stevens, P.A. (2005), 'The job satisfaction of English academics and their intentions to quit academe', National Institute of Economic and Social Research, Discussion paper no. 262.

Suter, B. and M. Jandl (2006), *Comparative Study on Policies towards Foreign Graduates: Study on Admission and Retention Policies towards Foreign Students in Industrialised Countries*, Vienna: International Centre for Migration Policy Development.

THES (2006), 'No return on the overseas route', leader article, *Times Higher Education Supplement*, 11 August.

Thewlis, M. (2003), *Recruitment and Retention of Staff in UK Higher Education*, London: UCEA.

Tomiuc, E. (2003), 'East: brain drain – southern regions bear the brunt (part 2)', *Radio Free Europe and Radio Liberty*, 3 December. Available at: www.rferl.org/features/2002/12/03122002191936.asp. Accessed: 19 April 2008.

Van de Sande, D., H.L. Ackers and B. Gill (2005), *Impact Assessment of the Marie Curie Fellowships Under the 4th and 5th Framework Programmes of Research and Technological Development of the EU (1994–2002): Final Report*, Brussels: European Commission.

Velev, K. (2002), 'Young scientists in Bulgarian universities and the brain drain problem', paper to the Attracting Young Scientists: Strategies against Brain Drain – International Conference in Higher Education Management, Bulgarian Ministry of Education and Science, Sofia, 18–20 October.

Verwiebe, R. and K. Eder (2006), 'The positioning of transnationally mobile Europeans in the German labour market', *European Societies*, **8** (1), 141–67.

Vizi, E.S. (1993), 'Reversing the brain drain from Eastern European countries: the "push" and "pull" factors', *Technology in Society*, **15** (1), 101–9.

von Ruschkowski, E. (2003), 'Raising awareness', *Science Careers*, 7 March 2003. Available at: http://sciencecareers.sciencemag.org/career_development/previous_issues/articles/2240/raising_awareness. Accessed: 24 April 2008.

Wallace, C. (2002), 'Opening and closing borders: migration and mobility in East-Central Europe', *Journal of Ethnic and Migration Studies*, **28** (4), 603–25.

Wilén, H. (2005), 'Increasing numbers of foreign students in the EU, decreasing job-to-job mobility of HRST', *Statistics in Focus: Science and Technology*, 1/2005, Luxembourg: Eurostat.

Wilén, H. (2006), 'Ageing workforce – how old are Europe's human resources in science and technology', *Statistics in Focus, Science and Technology*, **11**, Brussels: Eurostat.

Williams, A. (2006), 'Lost in translation? International migration, learning and knowledge', *Progress in Human Geography*, **30** (5), 588–607.

Williams, A.M. and V. Baláž (2005), 'What human capital, which migrants? Returned skilled migration to Slovakia from the UK', *International Migration Review*, **39** (2), 439–68.

Williams, A.M., V. Baláž and C. Wallace (2004), 'International labour mobility and uneven regional development in Europe', *European Urban and Regional Studies*, **11** (1), 27–46.

Williams, F. (2004), *Rethinking Families*, Calouste Gulbenkian Foundation: London.

Wilson, R. (1999), 'The frustrating career of the "trailing spouse"', *The Chronicle of Higher Education*, **45** (28),12–13.

Witte, J. (2006), *Change of Degrees and Degrees of Change: Comparing Adaptations of European Higher Education Systems in the Context of the Bologna Process*, Enschede, Netherlands: CHEPS.

Wood, F. (2004) (ed.), *'Beyond Brain Drain': Mobility, Competitiveness and Scientific Excellence*, Australia: Centre for Higher Education Management and Policy.

Index

academic sector, lack of support for mobility 4–5
Ackers, H.L. 2, 5–10, 12, 14–16, 20–21, 23, 26, 62, 69, 73, 86, 88, 90–91, 93–5, 99, 103, 110, 112, 114–16, 118, 122, 124–5, 127, 151, 158–60, 166–7, 172–3, 176–7, 179, 185, 191, 246
Adams, J. 88
age discrimination 204–5
air travel costs 13
Alexander von Humboldt Foundation 83–4
Altbach, P. 162
Amin, A. 150
anchored moves, and migration decisions 66–8
Appleyard, R. 4, 12
'Assessing the impact of the Roberts' Review Enhanced Stipends and Salaries on Postgraduate and Postdoctoral Positions' (Research Councils UK) 158, 249
Aston, L. 39, 81, 163
Avveduto, S. 133

Bagatelas, W. 222
Bailey, A.J. 90, 122
Baláž, V. 2, 5, 9–10, 24–5, 34, 41, 56, 106, 142, 187
Balter, M. 18, 65
BAS (Bulgarian Academy of Science) 71, 136–7, 143, 219–20
Bekhradnia, B. 158, 161, 163, 168, 171–2, 184, 200, 208
beneficial brain drain effect *see* sending countries' migration impact, increased incentive to study
bi-national partnering 100–102
Bidar case 80–81
Biggin, S. 13
Blair, A. 176

Blake, M.K. 122
Bobeva, D. 31, 197, 206
Bonney, N. 103
boomerang movers 43, 45
Boswell, C. 40
bounded careers 64
Boyd, M. 90, 129, 134
Boyle, P. 90
brain circulation, definitions 3
brain drain
    BBC report 203
    definitions 2–3
    high rates of, definitions 30
    intersectoral moves 205–10
    see also internal brain drain
brain escape 228
brain freeze 110, 199, 233
brain gain effect 193
    see also sending countries' migration impact, loss of investment, circulationist paradigm
brain overflow 199
brain stagnation 18, 102, 110, 213, 216, 233
brain waste/de-skilling 17–18, 102–10, 199
    see also external brain waste; internal brain waste
Brewster, C. 63
British Academy 84
British Council 84
Brown, M. 149
Bryson, C. 166
Buchinger, B. 167
Bulgaria
    characteristics of positions 66–70
    data problems 30, 222
    demographic consequences 34–7
    diaspora links 146
    employment in science research 31
    likelihood of tertiary education 163

expectation of mobility 6–7, 60–61, 64, 231
external brain waste 17

Fajnzylber, P. 226
Falagas, M.E. 76
family connections 130–31
Favell, A. 1
feminization of academic labour markets, and quality 190–91
feminization of migration 38
Ferro, A. 41, 123–4, 136, 150, 157, 162
Findlay, A.M. 18, 44
flying academics/professors 20, 210
footloose movers 66
Ford, R. 13
free agent labour migration 64
Fryderyk 63, 190, 245
Future of Higher Education, The (UK White Paper) 161

Gächter, A. 30–31, 34, 41, 202, 206, 224, 227
Gaillard, A.M. 23
Gamlen, A. 25, 30, 56, 114, 133, 151, 216, 223, 226, 229
Gent, S. 213
geography of respondents moves 43–5
Georgieva, P. 37, 70, 136–7, 197, 199, 202, 205, 210, 220, 223
German Academic Exchange Service (DAAD) 83
Germany
 fellowship schemes 83
 linking international recruitment and excellence 161–2
 as migration target 44
 quality of human capital 180
 reliance on foreign staff 160
 retention 162, 174–5
 and shuttle migration 50
 tuition fees 79–80
Ghodsee, K. 34, 228–9
Gill, B. 2–3, 17, 66, 158, 160, 163, 176, 185
Glitz, A. 181
Gödl, D. 167
Godwin, M. 193, 197
Gorzelak, G.J. 76, 198, 202, 208, 228
Gotzfried, A. 31, 223

grandparents, use for childcare 117
Gschwandtner, U. 167
Guth, J. 185

habilitation 127, 204
Hadler, M. 59
Harris, E. 20
Hasluck, C. 166
Hatakenaka, S. 163, 176, 237
Haug, S. 13–14, 16, 30, 34, 38, 92, 102, 112, 114, 129, 188, 199, 206, 222
Hellemans, A. 18
Hilgendorf, S. 162
Hryniewicz, J. 32, 200
HSM (highly skilled migration)
 assessing quality of flows 9–12
 as investment 18–19, 213–17
 literature 3–4
 migration vs mobility 12–16
 motivations for moving 4–9

Iglicka, K. 29, 35, 38, 40
IMPAFEL (impact assessment of the Marie Curie Fellowship Scheme) 10, 61–2, 73, 92–3, 95, 173, 248–9
individual fellowships, and migration decisions 82–5
internal brain drain 18, 200
 see also sending countries' migration impact, intersectoral moves
internal brain waste 18
internationalization
 and excellence 160–63
 impact domestic supply chains 175–6
 sustainability 171–5
investment loss
 sending countries' migration impact 193–5
 see also HSM (highly skilled migration), as investment
Iredale, R. 4–5, 12, 16, 103, 199
Italy
 appointments system 8
 motivations for leaving 17
 unmatched outflows 3

Jalowiecki, B. 32, 76, 198, 202, 208, 228
Jandl, M. 172–3, 213
Johnston, R. 130